SCHOLARS
AND THE
INDIAN EXPERIENCE

BIBLIOGRAPHICAL SERIES

The D'Arcy McNickle Center
for the History of the American Indian,
Newberry Library

The Center is funded by gifts and grants from:

The National Endowment for the Humanities
The Ford Foundation
The W. Clement and Jessie V. Stone Foundation
The Woods Charitable Fund, Inc.
Mr. Gaylord Donnelley
The Andrew W. Mellon Foundation
The Robert R. McCormick Charitable Trust
The John D. and Catherine T. McArthur Foundation
Bequest of Frances C. Allen
Sterling Morton Trust
D & R Fund
Atlantic Richfield Foundation
Hyman and Marjorie Weinberg Foundation
Illinois Humanities Council
Frances C. Allen Book Memorial

SCHOLARS
AND THE
INDIAN EXPERIENCE

Critical Reviews of Recent Writing in the Social Sciences

EDITED BY

W. R. SWAGERTY

Published for
The D'Arcy McNickle Center for the History of the American Indian, Newberry Library

INDIANA UNIVERSITY PRESS
BLOOMINGTON

Library of Congress Cataloging in Publication Data
Main entry under title:

Scholars and the Indian experience.

(Bibliographical series / the D'Arcy McNickle Center for the History of the American Indian, Newberry Library)
Includes index.
1. Indians of North America—Bibliography. I. Swagerty, William R. II. D'Arcy McNickle Center the History of the American Indian. III. Series: Bibliographical series (D'Arcy McNickle Center for the History of the American Indian)
Z1209.2.N67S36 1984 016.970004'97 83-49510 [E77]

ISBN 0-253-35095-6
ISBN 0-253-35096-4 (pbk.)
1 2 3 4 5 88 87 86 85 84

Contents

Acknowledgments

Since Its Founding in 1972, The Newberry Library Center for the History of the American Indian has become an academic training ground for dozens of Indian and non-Indian scholars focusing on Native American history. All of the contributors to *Scholars and the Indian Experience* have, at one time or another, been attached to one or more of the many programs emanating from the Center. Authors Dean R. Snow, Henry F. Dobyns, Russell Thornton and Peter Iverson each have contributed previous bibliographical essays in this series. Frederick E. Hoxie, J. Frederick Fausz, Richard White, Peter Iverson, Donald Fixico, W. R. Swagerty and Henry F. Dobyns each have received predoctoral or postdoctoral fellowships as scholars in residence at the Center since its inception. Jacqueline Peterson was attached to the Center as the late D'Arcy McNickle's first assistant director from 1972 through 1973. Peterson subsequently spent three years working under the direction of Helen Hornbeck Tanner on *The Atlas of Great Lakes Indian History,* soon to be published as a Newberry Library-University of Oklahoma Press cooperative effort. As director of "The Native American Historic Demography Project," based at The Newberry from 1980 through 1983, Henry F. Dobyns has recently completed the first of what promises to be several major monographs in a Newberry Library-University of Tennessee Press joint publication program.

Despite their associations with the Center, however, none of the contributors completed their essays for this volume at The Newberry. Still, without the assistance of the current library and Center staffs, the anthology would not have been possible. As editor, I am especially grateful to Francis Jennings, Director Emeritus, for suggesting that I undertake this volume of the Center's *Bibliographical Series;* to Herbert T. Hoover, Acting Director from 1981 through 1983, for supporting the idea and for making it become a reality; and, to David R. Miller, Associate Director, for devoting many unheralded hours to logistics and communications. His desk has been the anchor for all of us physically removed from Chicago.

I am also indebted to Marcia Sprules of the I. D. Weeks Library at the University of South Dakota for providing authors with computerized bibliographical assistance, and to the entire staff of U.C.L.A.'s American Indian Studies Center, especially librarian Velma Salabiye, for their assistance during 1983. Much of the bibliographical work, as well as preparation of my own essay in this volume, was facilitated by a postdoctoral fellowship at that distinguished center.

Funding for this project was made possible by a combination of resources from the National Endowment for the Humanities' generous support of the D'Arcy McNickle Center for the History of the American Indian and The Newberry Library Publications Fund. On behalf of all contributors to the volume, I extend special gratitude to Lawrence W. Towner, President, and Richard H. Brown, Academic Vice President, for their continued support of American Indian history at The Newberry.

William R. Swagerty
Moscow, Idaho

Introduction

FRANCIS JENNINGS
Director Emeritus

The D'Arcy McNickle Center for the History of the American Indian

IN THIS 30TH VOLUME OF The Newberry Library's bibliography series, it seems appropriate to recall our original statement of purpose.

"A massive literature exists for the history and culture of American Indians, but the quality of that literature is very uneven. At its best it compares well with the finest scholarship and most interesting reading to be found anywhere. At its worst it may take the form of malicious fabrication. Sometimes, well-intentioned writers give false impressions of reality either because of their own limitations of mind or because they lack adequate information. The consequence is a kind of chaos through which advanced scholars as well as new students must warily pick their way. It is, after all, a history of hundreds, if not thousands, of human communities spread over an entire continent and enduring through millenia of pre-Columbian years as well as the five centuries that Europeans have documented since 1492. That is not a small amount of history.

Often, however, historians have been so concerned with the affairs of European colonies or the United States that they have almost omitted Indians from their own history. Frontier history and the history of Indian-White relations frequently focus upon the intentions and desires of Euramericans, treating Native Americans as though they were merely natural parts of the landscape, like forests, or mountains, or wild animals—obstacles to 'progress' or 'civilization.' One of the major purposes of the Newberry Library's Center for the History of the American Indian is to modify that narrow conception: to put Indians properly back into the central role in their own history and into the history of the United States of America as well—as participants in, rather than obstacles to, the creation of American society and culture.

The series of bibliographies, of which this book is one, is intended as a guide to reliable sources and studies in particular fields of the general literature. Some of these are devoted to culture areas; others treat selected individual tribes; and a third group speaks to significant contemporary and historical issues."

The series has been so well received that it seems to have fulfilled its purpose, although circumstances dictated a degree of selectivity that, as the editor, I have sometimes regretted. Now a turning point has been reached, and this volume appears in a new format. Instead of containing a single essay surveying the entire previous literature on a single subject, this volume contains a number of essays, each written by a specialist, reviewing the most recent literature in each field. The volume's table of contents clarifies our design. Some essays, such as Dean Snow's on "Native American Prehistory," and Henry F. Dobyns's on "Native American Population Collapse and Recovery," update previous volumes on these subjects in the series. Others, such as the essays on "Native Americans and the Environment," by Richard White, and "The Indian and the Fur Trade," by Jacqueline Peterson (with John Anfinson) explore fields omitted from earlier volumes. And a third group—among them J. Frederick Fausz's on "Anglo-Indian Relations," and Peter Iverson's on "Indian Tribal Histories"—collapse subjects previously reviewed in several area volumes.

The great outpouring of studies in recent years has made this desirable. Professor Francis Paul Prucha has compiled a bibliography of works in *Indian-White Relations in the United States* published from 1975 through 1980 that itemizes 3,400 titles without comment. Our series has a much larger number to select from, including anthropological studies and tribal histories in Canada as well as the United States. Sheer quantity of new material dictates supplementation of the critical essays and lists in the series' earlier volumes.

FRANCIS JENNINGS
Chilmark, Massachusetts

SCHOLARS
AND THE
INDIAN EXPERIENCE

Native American Prehistory: Some Recent Contributions

DEAN R. SNOW

State University of New York, Albany

THIS ESSAY IS DESIGNED TO supplement my *Native American Prehistory: A Critical Bibliography* [54]. I completed that work early in 1978, and my intention here is to discuss recent trends in the discipline and important sources that have been published in the few years since I submitted the original manuscript. In some cases, nothing has emerged to replace the works I recommended in the 1979 book, and in these cases I will repeat some earlier recommendations and assume the reader's knowledge of the rest. Whatever my specific recommendations, however, they are with the understanding that I am advising people with developing interests in North American prehistory, not professional archaeologists or advanced students of archaeology. I avoid reference to technical works generally and to most article-length works apart from those available in volumes of collected readings.

My 1979 book distinguished between topical works in archaeology and general or regional works dealing with prehistory. Some reviewers thought this might confuse readers, while others thought the distinction useful. Events of the last four years have reinforced the distinction, and I have no choice but to retain it. The discipline is evolving such that fewer and fewer young archaeologists identify themselves with specific regions or cultures, and this is reflected in their published works. Local, regional, and continental prehistories are still begin written, but increasingly they are works that are explicitly different in character from topical works in archaeology. It is a distinction that the Library of Congress has long recognized;

readers will find archaeology books shelved in the "CC" section, prehistory books shelved under "GN" or "E." For example, Arthur Keene's *Prehistoric Foraging in a Temperate Forest: A Linear Programming Model* [30] is above all else an application of linear programming techniques to archaeological data. The emphasis is on theory and method, not the fact that the data are relevant to our understanding of Michigan prehistory. Indeed, discussion of the archaeological data base in the Saginaw Valley occupies only twenty-three pages, about ten percent of the book. This emphasis on archaeology as a discipline rather than the archaeological production of prehistory characterizes most of the volumes in the "Studies in Archaeology" series of which Keene's book is a part. Some, like Keene's work, are too technically oriented to be recommended in a bibliography of works on prehistory. Others in the same series, such as Bruce D. Smith's *Mississippian Settlement Patterns* [53] are more regional in character, and can be read as prehistory by students having sufficient background. I have included such works partly in the hope that they will convince readers that there is more to archaeology than prehistory.

General Works on Archaeology

There are several introductory texts covering the discipline of archaeology. These have not changed much since 1978, and my recommendations then still apply. Brian M. Fagan's *Archaeology: A Brief Introduction* [18] has been published in a second edition, this time a small paperback version. It is directed at beginning college-level students, and is particularly useful in more general courses requiring a book on archaeology that can be managed in two or three weeks.

Two workbooks in archaeology have emerged recently, perhaps in response to the development of laboratory discussion sections connected with college-level courses in archaeology. Thomas C. Patterson's *The Theory and Practice of Archaeology: A Workbook* [47] presents the student with real and imaginary archaeological data for interpretation, a technique that permits practice in analysis that would otherwise not be available. *The Archaeology Workbook* [11] by Steve Daniels and Nicholas David does the same thing, but is entirely imaginary and less ambitious in its scope. Patterson's book contains references that are lacking in its competitor, and will be taken more seriously by students.

William Rathje and Michael Schiffer's new text *Introducing Archaeology* [49] discusses archaeology in a traditional topical manner, but attempts to break new ground by discussing prehistoric potsherds and discarded hamburger wrappers as similar data. The analogy is novel, but will appeal more to seasoned professionals than introductory students. The latter are drawn to archaeology because it is a window to the exotic and the mysterious; it takes time to come to think seriously of beer cans as archaeological data.

James Deetz's *Invitation to Archaeology* [12] remains popular with beginners at the high school level. David H. Thomas [61] and Irving Rouse [52] offer introductions at a somewhat more advanced level, the latter stressing archaeology as a means to discover prehistory. Thomas stresses archaeology as science dealing with topical problems. Frank Hole and Robert F. Heizer [28] no longer offer two volumes of different lengths, but the shorter volume still in print is suitable for college level introductory courses. Fagan [17] and S. J. Knudson [32] also offer good introductory texts at this level.

Two recent books offer practical advice to beginning students and amateur archaeologists. Both are significant improvements over earlier books by other authors that too often presented archaeology as either a healthy sport anyone can undertake, or as digging for fun and profit. George Sullivan's [60] book introduces tools and techniques along with advice on how and where to get proper training. Joseleen Wilson's [71] book is a guide to sites and fieldwork opportunities. Both provide detailed state-by-state summaries of sites, legislation, suggested reading, and work opportunities.

People tempted by popular books that pretend to prove that American Indians were influenced by visitors from the Old World (or even from out of this world) have Robert Wauchope's [64] amusing book, now in paperback, debunking nonsense perpetrated in the name of archaeology. We are in a period of little activity in pseudo-archaeology at the moment, but interest in Celtic voyagers and ancient astronauts is cyclical, and the next invasion of popular paperbacks may be near. My own effort to put pseudo-archaeology in perspective is available in larger libraries [57] and Joseph Thorndike's paperback book on the subject [62] may be available there in its earlier hardback version as well.

Mesoamerican Background

Most North American archaeologists still consider Mesoamerica to be essential background. The chapter by Patrick Culbert [10] in Jesse Jenning's edited volume remains a good brief introduction to Mesoamerica. Muriel Weaver [65] and Richard Adams [1] both offer us excellent single-author introductory books on the same theme. However, Weaver has taken the lead by republishing her book in a second edition. The first edition dates to 1972. While the publisher has undergone a name change and the book has been reduced in size somewhat, it remains the same solid work. Susan Magee's *Mesoamerican Archaeology* [36] is a guide to publications and other sources that can be used by both beginners and experienced scholars. It is cross-disciplinary, up-to-date, and inexpensive. Advanced students will want to refer to Norman Hammond's *Mesoamerican Archaeology* [23], or *Ancient Mesoamerica* by Richard Blanton et al. [6]. The first is an edited volume of twenty-five papers by different authors, while the second is the effort of four co-authors to synthesize recent research.

Students interested in archaeoastronomy in North America can still do no better than Anthony Aveni's work. His *Native American Astronomy* [4] and his edited volume entitled *Archaeoastronomy in Pre-Columbian America* [3] are solid pieces to which he has more recently added *Skywatchers of Ancient Mexico* [5]. The last has received both awards and critical praise. E.C. Krupp's [33] *In Search of Ancient Astronomies* has been republished in inexpensive paperback form. Perhaps profitable pseudoscientific nonsense in this topic has passed its peak and no longer needs Krupp's sober criticism, but rumors as of this writing that we are about to see ancient astronauts hitting the newsstands again suggest that such is not the case.

General Works on North American Prehistory

There have been some new attempts at continental synthesis, and some new editions of earlier works. The Smithsonian Institution's new *Handbook of North American Indians* has grown to five volumes covering four regions, each of which is mentioned below in its proper place. The series will run to about twenty volumes, which will appear in no particular order. Their chapters on prehistory tend to be out of date as soon as they are published, but the *Handbook* volumes are very comprehensive, and perhaps the best bargain in books today.

Alice Kehoe's *North American Indians: A Comprehensive Account* [31] is unusual in that it includes Mexico. Even more unusual, it deals with both prehistory and ethnohistory, the latter bringing the reader well into twentieth century issues. It is a good choice for readers wishing to see some ethnographic flesh on archaeological bones, and will help many beginners appreciate more fully the connections between America's archaeological remains and contemporary Indian communities. Such an approach is particularly valuable in light of the fantastic claims for pre-Columbian migrations to the New World that plague archaeologists periodically. Kehoe gives little credence to these claims, and her clear linkage of the archaeological evidence with American Indian cultures will serve her readers well. Unfortunately, by choosing to discuss both ethnohistory and prehistory, and by choosing to include Mexico, Kehoe has had to be brief everywhere and for all periods. No doubt regional specialists grumble about her treatments of their areas. Still, at this scale and level, the book is unique and deserves reading.

Betty J. Meggers has revised her 1972 book on *Prehistoric America* [38]. It is still a brief summary of New World prehistory emphasizing the civilizations of Mexico and Peru. The sections on North America are brief and easy to read, but contain a few conclusions not shared by most professional archaeologists. For example, the Holly Oak pendant, considered a fake by most, is illustrated as a credible piece of Paleo-Indian evidence. My own *Archaeology of North America* [55] has been republished in paperback, but remains the same as the 1976 hardback edition in everything but price. Gordon Willey's [67] classic introduction to American prehistory is remarkably still in print, and remains a valuable synthesis.

Three edited volumes remain useful as beginning texts. Shirley Gorenstein's *North America* [22], Jesse D. Jenning's *Ancient Native Americans* [29], and *New World Archaeology* by Zubrow, Fritz and Fritz [72] are all useful compilations of articles by many authors. The last contains articles originally published in *Scientific American*, some of which are now badly out of date. However, the Freeman publishing house regularly repackages *Scientific American* articles in new combinations. Willey's *Pre-Columbian Archaeology* [68] is another collection from *Scientific American*, which has the advantage of incorporating articles published since 1974. After my careful effort to distinguish archaeology from prehistory, it is a bit embarrassing to admit that many of the best and most recent prehistories continue to carry "archaeology" in their titles. This is perhaps because publishers often insist upon titles that will sell, and "archaeology" is a proven seller.

Sarunas Milisauskas, et al. have compiled *A Selected Bibliography of North American Archaeological Sites* [41] , and have published it at minimal cost through Human Relations Area Files, Incorporated. The volume is simply a numbered series of bibliographic entries arranged by state and author. The pages are reduced photocopies of typescript with printing on one side only. Certainly many published references to specific sites were missed, and most states have inventories of known sites that exceed the total of this volume. Beginning students will find the sources difficult to locate and probably difficult to understand if they are lucky enough to find them. Professionals will discover little they do not already know. Thus the book is probably most useful to students who have moved through the beginning stages of reading for a given region and wish to seek out older and more difficult site reports.

Histories of disciplines can be self-conscious works that are more interesting to professionals than to lay readers. This is particularly the case with a scientific discipline, where disciplinary development is usually seen as deriving from the nature of the subject rather than from the accidents of history or the personalities of its students. More than many other disciplines, however, archaeology must be understood in terms of its own history. American archaeology has been much influenced by the context of changing attitudes towards American Indians. Just as important, cycles of popular interest have determined in part how the discipline has evolved, as have the personalities of archaeologists themselves. Willey and Sabloff [70] offer that sort of perspective in their co-authored volume, now in its second edition. Fitting [19] and Willey [69] have each assembled papers by various other authors, each of which is discussed separately in the sections that follow.

Paleo-Indians

The most notable recent additions to the literature on the subject of the earliest Americans have been the chapters summarizing the Paleo-Indian period in the volumes of the *Handbook of North American Indians* published to date. The subject is avoided in Alfonso Ortiz's *Southwest* volumes [45, 46] in the series on grounds that it belongs in volume three, still unpublished. Two chapters in Helm's *Subarctic* volume [27] touch on Paleo-Indian. One of these includes a cautious reference to the 27,000 year-old remains found at Old Crow in the Yukon Territory. Heizer's *California* volume [26] again defers Paleo-Indian to volume three of the series, while Trigger's *Northeast* volume [63] contains a good summary of Paleo-Indian in that region by Robert Funk.

The authors and editors of *Handbook* volume three have no easy task. There have been many claims of very old Paleo-Indian (or even earlier) remains for North America. Those of recent years have sometimes been made by respected scholars. Yet the evidence is often comprised of naturally fractured rocks mistaken as human artifacts, or authentic artifacts erroneously dated. The Calico Hills site in California is disputed by many archaeologists as an example of the first case. The very ancient dates obtained through analysis of amino acids in human skeletons from the same state are similarly disputed on technical grounds. Anyone trying to synthesize information in this sharply disputed area of archaeological interest is apt to be accused of prejudice and error by nearly everyone else.

At the moment the tide of opinion appears to be moving away from claims for very early human remains in North America. In case after case evidence fails to stand up under close examination. The 27,000 year old material from the Yukon is the oldest evidence acceptable to many archaeologists, and even this is viewed with skepticism. Despite the recent publication of a popular book purporting to show evidence for the New World origins of Homo Sapiens, there is no credible evidence for even an early migration of biologically modern humans to the New World. It is unlikely that the 27,000 year threshold will be pushed back very much, and possible that it will be revised to a more recent date as more research is completed.

Regional Works

There has been a recent trend away from the use of state and provincial boundaries in regional prehistories. Publications by state archaeological societies are of declining importance, and regional publications by museums, colleges, and universities tend to be smaller in scale and to use archaeologically meaningful boundaries. For the most part, newer regional works are technical publications for professionals and advanced students, not the sort of thing one recommends to beginning students. However, filling the gap between these technical volumes and the general works on prehistory discussed above are some new books written by professionals for nonprofessional audiences. Several volumes in the "New World Archaeological Record" series published by Academic Press fall into this class, as do the *Handbook of North American Indians* volumes already mentioned. Although the latter series deals with prehistory in only part of each volume, both series are built around carefully constructed regional boundaries.

The Eastern Woodlands

Trigger's *Northeast* volume [63] still offers the best general synthesis for that part of the Eastern Woodlands. It will eventually be complemented by a *Southeast* volume in the series. In the meantime, Smith's edited volume on *Mississippian Settlement Patterns* [53] summarizes much of what is current in this most significant tradition of Southeast prehistory. Smith's book is written for a professional audience, but is useful to anyone taking the time to prepare by first reading either more general introductory volumes, or regional chapters by James B. Stoltman [59] and Jon D. Muller [43].

William Morgan has compiled brief descriptions, line drawings, and a few aerial photographs of 82 sites in his survey of *Prehistoric Architecture in the Eastern United States* [42]. The book is a good introduction to these monumental sites, and can serve as a tour guide for those visiting them. Some of the line drawings and air photos are oblique views, but most of each are vertical views. This is important, for the reader will want to compare sites using the vertical drawings as maps. It is especially good that Morgan has drawn all such projections at the same scale with a superimposed 200 meter grid on each. This was no easy task, because he had to work with often incomplete source maps drawn at a variety of scales in both the English and metric systems. The line drawings generally contain less information than one might hope, probably because Morgan had to work with the lowest common denominators of his sources. Unfortunately, his efforts are marred by two problems. First, he attempts to convey an appreciation of his standard scale and 200 meter grid by illustrating a typical expressway cloverleaf, a 70,000 seat football stadium, and a flock of four Boeing 747 airplanes superimposed on it. Only the football stadium has been drawn at proper scale. A typical cloverleaf is two to three times larger than he shows it, and a Boeing 747 is only 70.5 meters long, not 100. The examples hinder rather than help those trying to get a feel for the sizes of prehistoric mounds and temple platforms. A second problem is Morgan's decision not to use a standard shading technique to show relief. He has made the right choice by showing relief in vertical views by shading rather than contour lines, but the direction of the light is not consistent. Usually the scene is lit from the lower right in these drawings, less often from below or from the lower left. Moreover, because he has not adopted the convention of lighting such scenes consistently from the upper left, readers expecting such shading will tend to see swimming pools where they are supposed to be seeing temple mounds. Despite the problems, however, Morgan's compilation is useful for most readers. He even provides properly scaled plans of the Mesoamerican sites of Teotihuacán and Monte Albán, as well as some of Old World sites such as Stonehenge, Giza, and Angkor Wat. With these the reader can compare the sites of the Eastern Woodlands with not only each other but with a suitable collection of sites from other parts of the world as well.

Florida has been especially fortunate recently, at least insofar as regional prehistory is concerned. Milanich and Fairbank's *Florida Archaeology* [39] is a regional prehistory in the "New World Archaeological Record" series published by Academic Press. There is also Milanich and Proctor's *Tacachale* [40], an edited set of essays by several authors that deal with the historic Indians of Florida and southeastern Georgia. The historic groups are often tied to prehistoric sequences, and the book is an excellent companion to *Florida Ar-*

chaeology. In addition to both of these, there is *Florida's Prehistoric Stone Technology* [48] by Barbara Purdy. This book deals with both stone tools in the context of Florida prehistory and an introduction to lithic technology as an archaeological topic. It is pitched at an introductory level, and succeeds in dealing with both topical archaeology and regional prehistory in an intelligent and readable manner.

My own *Archaeology of New England* [56] is an attempt to synthesize regional prehistory from an anthropological point of view for a nonprofessional audience. The boundaries extend beyond modern political New England to include parts of New Brunswick and New York. Haviland and Power's *The Original Vermonters* [25] deals with only a small portion of this region, but is quite useful for readers having particular interests in Vermont.

William A. Ritchie's *Archaeology of New York State* [50] has been republished by Harbor Hill Books. The book retains the old state boundaries and is virtually unchanged from the 1969 edition. Ronald Mason's *Great Lakes Archaeology* [37] is an excellent synthesis of the prehistory of the Great Lakes Drainage. It complements the region I cover in my New England book such that we split in two the material covered by Ritchie in his older synthesis.

The Great Plains

George Frison's [21] synthesis of the High Plains was the first in the Academic Press series on the "New World Archaeological Record." However, it is a bit more difficult than the volumes that followed it in the series, and should be read after introductory chapters by Frison [20] and Waldo Wedel [66]. Carl H. Chapman's first volume [7] on the archaeology of Missouri provided a basic introduction to prehistory up to 1000 B.C. His second volume [8] completes the set with coverage of the succeeding three millenia. The two volumes are a good summary for the eastern part of the Great Plains.

The Southwest

It is interesting to trace the accumulation of archaeological evidence and the shifts in archaeological goals through several syntheses of Southwestern prehistory. Students interested in pottery types, chronologies, and geographic distributions should stay with McGregor [35]. It has been republished in what is supposed to be a new edition, but it remains essentially the same as its 1965 predecessor, and does not supercede other more recent syntheses. The principal improvement of the 1982 edition is that it is now in a less expensive paperback form. Comparison with more recent syntheses reveals trends away from traditional goals and toward more complex research topics.

Both the history of archaeological research in the Southwest and southwestern prehistory itself are rich legacies that will continue to produce new volumes every year. However, both are most often approached at small scale these days. Temporary museum exhibits and their catalogues often stress the history of research, while articles and monographs tend to be technical reports for professionals. Arthur H. Rohn [51] and William D. Lipe [34] introduce the beginner to these subjects, but there are few up-to-date syntheses to bridge the gap from these brief chapters to the more advanced technical literature. Volume 9 in the *Handbook of North American Indians* series [45] contains chapters on Southwest prehistory which do so well in this regard that the book would probably remain the introduction of choice even if it had strong recent competition. Recent release of the companion Volume 10 [46], also on the Southwest, certainly makes the *Handbook* the basic reference for years to come.

The Far West

The *California* volume of the *Handbook of North American Indians* [26] was edited by Robert Heizer, who died in the year following its publication. The volume covers a region slightly smaller than the modern state. Eastern portions of California are relegated to other volumes. The prehistory chapters do much to make sense of a complex and confusing array of local sequences.

Readers can also refer to Melvin C. Aikens's chapter [2] combining California and the Desert West in a single discussion. The Jennings volume [29] also contains coverage of the prehistory of the Northwest Coast by Don E. Dumond [16], although in this case it is combined with Alaska. The latter combination is unusual but informative. Typically, Alaska is discussed with the rest of the Arctic because of the common thread of Eskimo prehistory and because of the history of archaeological research in the North which Sprague's essay exemplifies [58]. However, the Eskimo of southern Alaska contrast with those above the Arctic Circle and have much in common with the cultures of the Northwest Coast.

The Arctic and Subarctic

Dumond's excellent volume entitled *The Eskimos and Aleuts* [15] is comprehensive, well written, and recent. In addition to the Eskimos, Aleuts, and their relatively recent ancestors, the book discusses both Paleo-Indians in the Arctic and historic European explorations. Illustrations are numerous and informative. Readers wishing less detailed introductions can turn to Dumond's "Alaska and the Northwest Coast" [16] and Elmer Harp's "Pioneer Cultures of the Sub-Arctic and the Arctic" [24] in Jennings's *Ancient Native Americans*. *The Far North: 2000 Years of American Eskimo and Indian Art* by Henry B. Collins et al. [9] remains a good introduction for those most interested in archaeology as art history. Dumond's book is still the best scientific context for this exhibition catalogue.

Albert A. Dekin's *Arctic Archaeology: A Bibliography and History* [14] has more to do with archaeologists and what they do than with prehistory. Nonetheless, it is an interesting history of Arctic archaeology and contains an extensive bibliography for readers wishing to specialize. It should be especially useful when combined with regional prehistoric syntheses. As an historical treatment of regional archaeology it replaces Dekin's 1973 chapter on the Arctic in James Fitting's *The Development of North American Archaeology* [13], as well as some of the chapter on Canada by William C. Noble [44] in the same volume.

Helm's volume [27] on the Subarctic in the *Handbook of North American Indians* contains three chapters on prehistory. Each covers one part of this vast region, and pulls together what is known at this time. Some old ideas and archaeological constructs have been abandoned, and as is the case in other *Handbook* volumes, these chapters will stand as basic sources for several years to come.

For the future, those interested in the prehistory of North America should watch for additional volumes in the *Handbook of*

North American Indians series (Smithsonian Institution) and the "New World Archaeological Record" series (Academic Press). Many other publishers will produce local, regional, and continental prehistories as well, but these are less easily predicted. More importantly, however, readers must realize that the regions of North America are gradually becoming the laboratories of topical archaeological research rather than stages of culture history. As in any science, the paradigm has shifted with the times, and the evolution of the discipline itself may yet become as interesting as its subject matter.

ALPHABETICAL LIST

[1] Adams, Richard E. E. 1977. *Prehistoric Mesoamerica*. Boston: Little, Brown and Company.

[2] Aikens, C. Melvin. 1978. "The Far West." In *Ancient Native Americans*, ed. Jesse D. Jennings, pp. 131-81. See [29].

[3] Aveni, Anthony F., ed. 1975. *Archaeoastronomy in Pre-Columbian America*. Austin: University of Texas Press.

[4] ———. 1977. *Native American Astronomy*. Austin: University of Texas Press.

[5] ———. 1980. *Skywatchers of Ancient Mexico*. Austin: University of Texas Press.

[6] Blanton, Richard E., Stephen A. Kowalewski, Gary M. Feinman, and Jill Appel. 1982. *Ancient Mesoamerica: A Comparison of Change in Three Regions*. New York: Cambridge University Press.

[7] Chapman, Carl H. 1975. *The Archaeology of Missouri, I*. Columbia: University of Missouri Press.

[8] ———. 1980. *The Archaeology of Missouri, II*. Columbia: University of Missouri Press.

[9] Collins, Henry B., Frederica De Laguna, Edward Carpenter, and Peter Stone. 1977. *The Far North: 2000 Years of American Eskimo and Indian Art*. Bloomington: Indian University Press.

[10] Culbert, T. Patrick. 1978. "Mesoamerica." In *Ancient Native Americans*, ed. Jesse D. Jennings, pp. 403-53. See [29].

[11] Daniels, Steve, and Nicholas David. 1982. *The Archaeology Workbook*. Philadelphia: University of Pennsylvania Press.

[12] Deetz, James. 1967. *Invitation to Archaeology*. Garden City, N.Y.: Natural History Press.

[13] Dekin, Albert A., Jr. 1973. "The Arctic." In *The Development of North American Archaeology*. ed. James E. Fitting, pp. 15-48. See [19].

[14] ———. 1978. *Arctic Archaeology: A Bibliography and History*. New York: Garland.

[15] Dumond, Don E. 1977. *The Eskimos and Aleuts*. London: Thames and Hudson.

[16] ———. 1978. "Alaska and the Northwest Coast." In *Ancient Native Americans*, ed. Jesse D. Jennings, pp. 43-93. See [29].

[17] Fagan, Brian M. 1981. *In the Beginning: An Introduction to Archaeology*. Boston: Little, Brown and Company.

[18] ———. 1983. *Archaeology: A Brief Introduction*. Boston: Little, Brown and Company.

[19] Fitting, James E., ed. 1973. *The Development of North American Archaeology*. Garden City, N.Y.: Doubleday Anchor.

[20] Frison, George C. 1973. "The Plains." In *The Development of North American Archaeology,* ed. James E. Fitting, pp. 151-84. See [19].

[21] ———. 1978. *Prehistoric Hunters of the High Plains*. New York: Academic Press.

[22] Gorenstein, Shirley, ed. 1975. *North America*. New York: St. Martin's Press.

[23] Hammond, Norman. 1974. *Mesoamerican Archaeology: New Approaches*. Austin: University of Texas Press.

[24] Harp, Elmer, Jr. 1978. "Pioneer Cultures of the Sub-Arctic and the Arctic." In *Ancient Native Americans*, ed. Jesse D. Jennings, pp. 95-129. See [29].

[25] Haviland, William A., and Marjory W. Power. 1981. *The Original Vermonters: Native Inhabitants Past and Present*. Hanover, New Hampshire: University Press of New England.

[26] Heizer, Robert F., ed. 1978. *California*. Vol. 8 of *Handbook of North American Indians*, gen. ed. William C. Sturtevant. Washington: Smithsonian Institution.

[27] Helm, June, ed. 1981. *Subarctic*. Vol. 6 of *Handbook of North American Indians*, gen. ed. William C. Sturtevant. Washington: Smithsonian Institution.

[28] Hole, Frank, and Robert F. Heizer. 1977. *Prehistoric Archaeology: A Brief Introduction*. New York: Holt, Rinehart and Winston.

[29] Jennings, Jesse D., ed. 1978. *Ancient Native Americans*. San Francisco: Freeman.

[30] Keene, Arthur S. 1981. *Prehistoric Foraging in a Temperate Forest: A Linear Programming Model*. New York: Academic Press.

[31] Kehoe, Alice B. 1981. *North American Indians: A Comprehensive Account*. Englewood Cliffs, N. J.: Prentice-Hall.

[32] Knudson, S. J. 1978. *Culture in Retrospect: An Introduction to Archaeology*. Chicago: Rand McNally.

[33] Krupp, E. C., ed. 1979. *In Search of Ancient Astronomies*. New York: Doubleday.

[34] Lipe, William D. 1978. "The Southwest." In *Ancient Native Americans*, ed. Jesse D. Jennings, pp. 327-401. See [29].

[35] McGregor, John C. 1982. *Southwestern Archaeology*. Urbana: University of Illinois Press.

[36] Magee, Susan Fortson. 1981. *Mesoamerican Archaeology: A Guide to the Literature and Other Information Sources*. Austin: University of Texas Press.

[37] Mason, Ronald J. 1981. *Great Lakes Archaeology*. New York: Academic Press.

[38] Meggers, Betty J. 1979. *Prehistoric America*. Chicago: Aldine.

[39] Milanich, Jerald T., and Charles H. Fairbanks. 1980. *Florida Archaeology*. New York: Academic Press.

[40] Milanich, Jerald, and Samuel Proctor, eds. 1978. *Tacachale: Essays on the Indians of Florida and Southeastern Georgia During the Historic Period*. Gainesville: University Presses of Florida.

[41] Milisauskas, Sarunas, Frances Pickin, and Charles Clark. 1981. *A Selected Bibliography of North American Archaeological Sites*. New Haven: Human Relations Area Files.

[42] Morgan, William N. 1980. *Prehistoric Architecture in the Eastern United States*. Cambridge, Mass.: M. I. T. Press.

[43] Muller, Jon D. 1978. "The Southeast." In *Ancient Native Americans*, ed. Jesse D. Jennings, pp. 281-325. See [29].

[44] Noble, William C. 1973. "Canada." In *The Development of North American Archaeology*, ed. James E. Fitting, pp. 49-83. See [19].

[45] Ortiz, Alfonso, ed. 1979. *Southwest*. Vol. 9 of *Handbook of North American Indians*, gen. ed. William C. Sturtevant. Washington: Smithsonian Institution.

[46] ———. 1983. *Southwest*. Vol. 10 of *Handbook of North American Indians*, gen. ed. William C. Sturtevant. Washington: Smithsonian Institution.

[47] Patterson, Thomas C. 1983. *The Theory and Practice of Archaeology: A Workbook*. Englewood Cliffs, N. J.: Prentice-Hall.

[48] Purdy, Barbara A. 1981. *Florida's Prehistoric Stone Technology*. Gainesville: University Presses of Florida.

[49] Rathje, William L., and Michael B. Schiffer. 1982. *Introducing Archaeology*. San Diego: Harcourt, Brace, Jovanovich.

[50] Ritchie, William A. 1980. *The Archaeology of New York State*. Harrison, New York: Harbor Hill Books.

[51] Rohn, Arthur H. 1973. "The Southwest and Intermontane West." In *The Development of North American Archaeology*, ed. James E. Fitting, pp. 185-211. See [19].

[52] Rouse, Irving. 1972. *Introduction to Prehistory: A Systematic Approach*. New York: McGraw-Hill.

[53] Smith, Bruce D., ed. 1978. *Mississippian Settlement Patterns*. New York: Academic Press.

[54] Snow, Dean R. 1979. *Native American Prehistory: A Critical Bibliography*. Bloomington: Indian University Press for the Newberry Library.

[55] ———. 1980. *Archaeology of North America*. New York: Thames and Hudson.

[56] ———. 1980. *The Archaeology of New England*. New York: Academic Press.

[57] ———. 1981. "Martians and Vikings, Madoc and Runes. *American Heritage* 32(6): 102-108.

[58] Sprague, Roderick. 1973. "The Pacific Northwest." In *The Development of North American Archaeology*, ed. James E. Fitting, pp. 250-85. See [19].

[59] Stoltman, James B. 1973. "The Southeastern United States." In *The Development of North American Archaeology*, ed. James E. Fitting, pp. 116-50. See [19].

[60] Sullivan, George. 1980. *Discover Archaeology: An Introduction to the Tools and Techniques of Archaeological Fieldwork*. New York: Penguin Books.

[61] Thomas, David H. 1979. *Archaeology*. New York: Holt, Rinehart and Winston.

[62] Thorndike, Joseph J., Jr., ed. 1981. *Mysteries of the Past*. New York: Scribner.

[63] Trigger, Bruce G., ed. 1978. *Northeast*. Vol. 15 of *Handbook of North American Indians*, gen. ed. William C. Sturtevant. Washington: Smithsonian Institution.

[64] Wauchope, Robert. 1982. *Lost Tribes and Sunken Continents*. Chicago: University of Chicago Press.

[65] Weaver, Muriel Porter. 1981. *The Aztecs, Maya, and Their Predecessors: Archaeology of Mesoamerica*. New York: Academic Press.

[66] Wedel, Waldo R. 1978. "The Prehistoric Plains." In *Ancient Native Americans*, ed. Jesse D. Jennings, pp. 183-219. See [29].

[67] Willey, Gordon R. 1966. *An Introduction to American Archaeology, Volume 1: North and Middle America*. Englewood Cliffs, N. J.: Prentice-Hall.

[68] ———. 1980. *Pre-Columbian Archaeology: Readings from Scientific American*. San Francisco: Freeman.

[69] ———, ed. 1982. *Archaeological Researches in Retrospect*. Cambridge: Winthrop Publisher.

[70] Willey, Gordon R., and Jeremy A. Sabloff. 1980. *A History of American Archaeology*. New York: Thames and Hudson.

[71] Wilson, Joseleen. 1980. *The Passionate Amateur's Guide to Archaeology in the United States*. New York: Collier Books.

[72] Zubrow, Ezra B. W., Margaret C. Fritz, and John M. Fritz. 1974. *New World Archaeology: Theory and Cultural Transformations*. San Francisco: Freeman.

Native American Population Collapse and Recovery

HENRY F. DOBYNS

Native American Historical Demography Project
The Newberry Library

THIS ESSAY SUMMARIZES important reports dealing with Native American historic demography that have appeared since 1976 when the author [10, 11] evaluated previous research. The author's monograph in this series [10] characterized 217 works. The short supplement [11] analyzed 30 others. The present essay considers 67 publications appearing prior to 1982.

Theory

In retrospect, 1976 stands out as a watershed year in studies of Native American historic demography. Until 1976, scholars estimated pre-Columbian New World population numbers and traced their historic decline. Reconstructing historic epidemiology emerged more and more clearly as the key to explaining and describing Native American depopulation. Such research has attracted an increasing number of scholars, yet much remains to be accomplished. By 1976, however, pioneer students of Native American historic demography had outlined the post-1519 continental population collapse and described dense protohistoric populations. Then theorists began discussing major social, economic, and psychological concommitants of historic Native American population collapse.

The major methodological statement challenging historians to reinterpret past events taking into account diseases' fundamental importance is William McNeill's *Plagues and Peoples* [29]. McNeill supplemented that volume with a succinct paper discussing historical migration patterns [30]. This seminal article builds a general theory of political state formation utilizing knowledge of disease morbidity and mortality impacts on susceptible populations.

In "The Ecological Basis for Aztec Sacrifice," Michael Harner [18] challenged anthropologists, urging them to confront the socio-cultural implications of the 25,000,000 central Mexicans S. F. Cook and W. W. Borah estimated lived in A. D. 1519. Harner's thesis gained wide press notice. One critic claimed that Aztecs did not suffer from protein deficiency, although human flesh helped keep nobles loyal to the throne [46]. Another asserted that Mesoamerica had domesticable herbivores that could have provided meat, yet admitted the impossibility of proving the domesticability of species which were never domesticated [20].

Russell Thornton perceived "Demographic Antecedents of a Revitalization Movement" [61] as large-scale disease mortality relative to a group's size. Thus, he significantly expanded the range of cultural phenomena social scientists hypothesize respond to population changes. Analyzing quantitative reports by Quaker Indian agents responsible for seven Nebraska tribal populations in the 1870s, Clyde A. Milner [37] discovered a similar response to population trends. His correlations "seem to argue that the Indians must grow and prosper in order to accept white ways." On the other hand, declining population and poverty generated resistance.

At an even more general theoretical level, employing Gila River Pima population data, Cary W. Meister [33] indicted the three-stage demographic transition model which demographers long used when analyzing population changes since the eighteenth century. Meister identified losing irrigation water as a major reason the Gila River Pimas lost population during the late nineteenth century.

Calvin Martin [32] proposed a provocative theory about Native American response to epidemic disease mortality. He recognized that Cree aboriginal beliefs concerning supernatural relationships, animals and mankind led the latter to conserve the former. Martin then theorized that historic mortality changed matters. Deciding that the beaver and other animals caused their high mortality, Crees retaliated against fur-bearing animals.

Martin's thesis immediately prompted debate. Shepard Krech, III [26] edited a volume of essays criticizing Martin's ideas. In it, Bruce Trigger argued that Hurons associated disease with the creator, not animal spirits, or suspected sorcerers. Charles Bishop reasoned that because disease effects were not constant and were at times attributed to Frenchmen, Martin's mechanism is an inadequate general explanation for trade. Dean Snow pointed out that causation is complex, criticizing the hypothesis as overly simplistic. He also noted that Abenakis blamed their shamans for causing illness and never indulged in overkill. Krech cited Subarctic Kutchin as also enthusiastically trading while blaming shamans for sickness, disease and death. Lydia T. Black similarly marshalled evidence that Aleuts did not conceptualize sea otters they hunted as causing disease.

Charles Hudson conceded that Southeastern Indians did believe that animals, particularly deer, caused disease. They sharply diminished deer numbers by hunting them for export hides. On the other hand, Hudson perceived that European demand caused overhunting of deer in precisely the same way that slave demand caused zealous hunting of humans for sale. William Sturtevant doubted whether Martin's hypothesis applies even to the Ojibwa. He quoted descriptions of their cultural tradition as defining a taboo violation as likely to cause animal scarcity rather than human illness. Martin's response makes clear that ethnographic reports of Ojibwa culture, like the *Bible,* are sufficiently ambiguous and inconsistent to enable partisans to find statements supporting mutually exclusive positions. Snow expressed the scholarly hope that Martin will write more on this and related subjects, "For there is clearly much work to be done and too few scholars ready to do it."

Peopling the Continent

Prehistorians remain uncertain about how many people originally colonized the Americas and when they did so. K. R. Fladmark [15] argued that recent geological studies indicate that late Pleistocene montane and continental ice caps did not leave a habitable inland corridor open from Alaska to the Plains. Fladmark argued that a greatly lowered sea level exposed ice-free coastal lands which migrants could traverse. Concentrating on artifactual evidence, D. E. Dumond [13] concluded that descendants of earlier colonists developed late Pleistocene fluted projectile points for hunting large game animals. So human beings apparently entered the New World well before 30,000 years ago.

Proto-Historic Population Estimates

Sociologist Russell Thornton [60] noted that George Catlin's estimated tribal numbers have been ignored during the twentieth century. He compared Catlin's 247,110 total to James Mooney's 246,800 for the same 37 tribes. Thornton concluded that the similarity despite a time difference of 50 to 230 years "suggests considerable inaccuracy on the part of either Mooney or Catlin." Thornton regarded Catlin as highly credible.

Previewing essays that will appear in the Smithsonian Institution's *Handbook of North American Indians*, Douglas Ubelaker [65] concluded that they will approximately double James Mooney's estimate for pre-contact Native North American population.

Other scholars have analyzed particular ethnic groups. John A. Dickinson [9] noted that "The question of the pre-contact Huron population is not closed." During the past decade, Bruce Trigger and Conrad Heidenreich estimated from 18,000 to 20,000 Hurons lived early in the seventeenth century. Samuel de Champlain's 1616 estimate was 30,000. A missionary who visited some Huron towns in 1623-24 estimated 30,000 to 40,000 souls. Taking 1630s epidemic mortality into account, Dickinson estimated 10,000 in 1640, 20,000 in 1620, and 25,000 to 30,000 in 1600. Indeed the question is not closed, inasmuch as none of the earlier authors recognized that three different diseases afflicted Hurons in 1633-34, 1637 and 1639.

Several scholars estimating early sixteenth century Native American population sizes have identified specific depopulation dynamics besides disease. Virginia P. Miller [36] pointed out that trading furs to Europeans disrupted the Micmac seasonal round. Aboriginal Micmacs gathered, hunted, and processed meat and plant foods for winter consumption. In the sixteenth century they congregated on the coast, trading with ships' crews for dried foods and wine. Storing only hardtack, Micmacs fell victim to lung, chest and intestinal disorders. Miller estimated 35,000 to 70,000 pre-Columbian Micmacs rather than 3,500.

Discussing interethnic resource competition and population change, R. W. Stoffle and M. J. Evans [55] described Mormon-Kaibab Paiute competition for irrigation water, irrigable fields, nut-bearing pinyon trees and other vegetation. As Mormons colonized Paiute irrigable fields, the latter adapted both by more intensively exploiting wild food sources, and by converting to Mormonism and thus obtaining Church-supplied foodstuffs.

Scholars continued analyzing diverse kinds of evidence bearing on pre-conquest Mesoamerican population sizes. H. P. Pollard and S. Gorenstein [43] called attention to Lake Patzcuaro's fluctuating levels. They argued that its waters inundated the best quality horticultural land available during prehistoric times. They concluded, therefore, that Tarascan population was about half the size Cook and Borah calculated. They recognized that Tarascans exported fish and imported maize without following through the demographic implications of the ability to export animal protein and import vegetable carbohydrates.

Jerome Offner [39] found a few sixteenth century colonial records of maize obtained from tribute fields and decided that the area could not have subsisted a population as large as Cook and Borah estimated for 1519. This analysis is flawed. First, it is based on maize only, whereas Chiconautla on Lake Texcoco was probably reliant largely on *chinampa* food production, the highest yielding in the environment. Second, Offner failed to consider that colonial officials recorded what *they* obtained from the tribute fields, not what the payers actually produced. The skill with which Vicos serfs paying land rent cultivating potatoes diverted tubers to their own stomachs prompts me to calculate that sixteenth century production was at least twice what officials reported. Taking colonial reports at face value is naive and displays a serious lack of knowledge of colonial society and serf and peasant survival skills.

Offner noted that epidemic disease resulted in a low 1546 Coatepec yield. Yet, he included that low figure in his Coatepec average, thus making it 12.5 percent too low to apply to pre-conquest/pre-epidemic times. Such methodologically unsound and culturally uninformed analyses do not effectively refute the Cook-Borah central Mexican population estimates.

Historic Epidemiology

Karl H. Schlesier [49] challenged the Eurocentric economic determinism George T. Hunt expressed in his very influential *The Wars of the Iroquois* [21]. Denying that Iroquois attempted to become fur trade middlemen, Schlesier cited evidence that they refused such a role. "The four terrible horsemen of the apocalypse, Plague, Famine, War, Death, not European trinkets and the beaver, shaped the historical process in the northeast," Schlesier wrote. He considered disease the greatest killer of all. Darrell A. Posey [44] emphasized the insect vector role in bubonic plague and typhus among Southeastern Native Americans.

Analyzing data from six parishes in and near Durango, Mexico, Michael M. Swann [57] quantitatively described how smallpox in 1780 differentially affected Indians, Spaniards and Mestizos. He pointed out that later in the decade famine killed more people than the virus.

Awareness of the historic importance of epidemic disease is spreading into U. S. National Park Service research and interpretation for the public. Michael K. Trimble's [64] ethnohistorical analysis of the 1837 smallpox epidemic's impact on upper Missouri River tribes identifies near-famine, abundant rats, unsanitary conditions, dwelling humidity, cold temperatures, rain and smoke factors in the high mortality the virus caused.

Two publications describe an epidemic disease that nearly exterminated Native Americans still living on western Nantucket Island in 1763. Edouard A. Stackpole [51] reprinted 1797 and 1789 letters attributing the contagion to an Irish brig's crew. E. A. Little and Marie Sussek [27] reproduced the names of 222 of 358 Nantucket Indians who died.

Robert H. Jackson [22] compiled a more complete list than has previously been published of epidemic disease episodes depopulating Baja California. Estimating perhaps 60,000 Native Americans in 1697, Jackson traced their decline to 1,000 to 1,500 survivors in

1835. He listed twenty-four smallpox, measles, dysentery, typhus or typhoid epidemics from 1697 to 1808. A sample southern peninsular mission lost 84 percent of its 1705 population by 1730. Measles caused an average 27.7 percent population decline in nine missions in 1768-1771. Typhus killed an average of one–third of the people at four missions in 1771-1774. The 1780-1782 smallpox slew 28.9 percent of the Native Americans in ten missions. These are grim figures and among the most accurate available calculations of Native American mortality rates during eighteenth century epidemics.

Jackson [23] also analyzed how the 1781 smallpox pandemic affected missionized Baja California natives. A military expedition destined for upper California carried the virus to Loreto, a peninsular port, that spring. Seeing Christian converts fall ill, natives fled the missions and unknowable numbers perished in caves and canyons. This pandemic and an earlier 1774 epidemic reduced the peninsular Native American population by 28 percent according to Jackson's calculations.

Rapidly accumulating published evidence of historic Native American population collapse inevitably generates some defensive responses. Franciscan Francis F. Guest, for example, accused Sherburne F. Cook of having mistranslated a few Spanish words. Guest built on that narrow platform a lengthy argument that Spanish missionaries belonging to his order did not forcefully convert Native California peoples [17]. Guest conceded that Spanish troops rounded up and moved Central Valley and mountain natives to missions. His claim that such forced migration was not coercive defies both logic and common sense. Ironically, Guest wrote that "One must study Spanish documentation thoroughly and see Spanish history through Spanish eyes." Quite correct—and a Spaniard of the time would recognize that Guest cites laws and official policies evidencing permissive behavior that actually stated ideals having little bearing on real Spanish colonial behavior. Cook consistently recognized that Old World diseases, not colonial policies and practices, killed most Native Americans. Consequently, Guest's accusation that Cook "contributed generously to the development of the Black Legend" betrays a temporal confusion. European polemicists fully developed the Black Legend long before Sherburne F. Cook was born. His research actually indicted the Black Legend's devil theory of history.

Endemic Diseases, Famines and Warfare

Famine. Much has been written about Native American-European competition for land and other natural resources. Colonists consistently claimed that they used land more efficiently than did Native Americans. Using 1666 farm sales records, Peter A. Thomas [59] calculated that like populations of southern New England natives and English colonists required approximately the same cultivate acreage. Plowing and domestic livestock enabled Europeans to support only about 25 percent more people than natives.

Using early colonial documents, Ross Hassig [19] outlined the causes and consequences of a serious 1450-1454 famine that disrupted life in Nahuatl cities. In the 1452 and 1453 growing seasons, droughts followed crop-destroying 1450 and 1451 fall frosts, so many commoners died. Rulers allowed people to flee and seek food in lowland rain forest areas. Afterwards, Aztecs expanded their intensive *chinampa* fields that avoided both frost and drought. Disaster motivated technological change and expanded food production that fueled the immediate pre-conquest population growth.

Assembling varied anthropological data, Cook and Borah [6] calculated that medium-sized pre-conquest central Mexicans required an average 1,900 kilocalories daily. They found that most lower class people consumed food supplying fewer kilocalories. Native American population rapidly collapsed to three percent of the 1519 population a century later, opening environmental niches to Spaniards and their domestic livestock. Consequently, post-conquest Native American diet apparently improved.

Far away, mid-nineteenth century Northwest Coast tribesmen visiting Victoria, a growing city, neglected their summer fishery and drying fish for winter consumption, according to Barry M. Gough [16]. Consequences resembled those among earlier Atlantic coast Micmacs.

Warfare. Robert Jackson [24] downgraded intertribal warfare as a major depopulation determinant among Rancherian peoples. Between 1743 and 1766, Apache raiders killed only five of the 439 persons buried at Northern Piman Guevavi mission, or only 1.1 percent of total mortality. On the other hand, battle losses could reach the hundreds under different circumstances. Keith F. Otterbein [40] calculated that an Iroquois army killed 780 or more Hurons on 16-17 March, 1649, while suffering about 340 casualties. The conflict was exceptional; Otterbein labeled it one of the most important North American battles ever fought.

Richard White [67] very effectively incorporated information about disease mortality and its demographic effects into his analysis of Western Sioux expansion. White credited differential epidemic mortality among sedentary horticultural villagers and mobile, mounted Sioux with initial Sioux military superiority. He then described how numerically superior mounted Sioux conquered Mandan, Arikara, Omaha, Hidatsa, Crow and Pawnee hunting territories. By 1851, Sioux negotiated a treaty with the United States based on the same right of conquest the latter claimed.

Barry M. Gough [16] briefly related how British naval gunboats discouraged intertribal hostilities between Northwest Coast tribes in the 1860s.

Alcoholic Beverages. Non-Indian entrepreneurs traded abundant alcoholic beverages to Northwest Coast groups for furs and pelts, thus furthering their impoverishment. Royal Navy personnel attempted to suppress the liquor traffic during the mid-nineteenth century because it generated Indian prostitution and negative demographic impacts [16].

Population Collapse

Although it does not deal with Native North Americans, Noble David Cook's *Demographic Collapse: Indian Peru, 1520-1620* [3] constitutes a major methodological advance in historic demographic studies. It should strongly influence future North American analysis. Cook employed an "epidemic disease mortality model," quantifying population collapse during the first century's invasion of New World populations by Old World pathogens. Thus, Cook made explicit what several investigators have implicitly done.

William A. Starna [54] re-estimated Mohawk numbers prior to several lethal epidemics that significantly diminished them during the 1630s. Utilizing archaeological and historical data, Starna calculated pre-epidemic Mohawk population ranged from 8,258 to 10,268 and 10,323 to 12,835. The higher figures approximately equal frequently repeated estimates that *all* Iroquois numbered only 10,000 to 12,000 individuals. Starna pointed out an important error in William N. Fenton's [14] estimate of post-epidemic Mohawk numbers. Fenton ignored abundant eyewitness statements that two nuclear families shared each longhouse central hearth, so his 2,700 estimate was only half what it should have been.

Describing the final 40 years of Mescalero depopulation, the author [12] found that recovery began in 1913. Newly discovered documentation enabled S. F. Cook and Woodrow Borah [6] to date with increased assurance the beginning of central Mexican population recovery around 1620-1625. They calculated that the area then held only 730,000 Native Americans, stating: "The decline was distinctly greater than we had previously thought." Their essay added precision to their reconstruction of central Mexican historic population collapse, which is the best-documented case in the Americas.

Ingeborg Marshall [31] sketched previously unpublished cartographic evidence of the Newfoundland Beothuck's final years. Extinct in 1829, Beothuck apparently numbered about 350 in the 1760s, less than 200 by 1800. Colonists pre-empted their major hunting and fishing locations to starve the Beothucks. Settlers also literally hunted the Indians down.

Population Recovery

Concisely summarizing the twentieth century Native American population increase, Sam Stanley and R. K. Thomas [53] labeled the post-1910 trend an "explosion." The U. S. 1950 census reported 357,499 Indians; the 1970 census 792,730. These authors correctly predicted that the 1980 enumeration would be about 1,000,000. They emphasized that in 1970, 45 percent of the Indians enumerated lived in cities and towns. They blamed urbanization for native language loss and a "staggering" increase in crime and social problems. Yet, level of Indian formal education changed spectacularly between 1950 and 1970. This tightly-written essay is an excellent introduction to Native American demographic and social reality.

In a wide-ranging summary of California Native American demography, S. F. Cook [5] concluded that California Indians have "effectively recovered from the traumatic demographic experience of the nineteenth century." Non-California Indian immigration increased the 1970 census count to 91,018, but Cook calculated that only half California's urban Native Americans were born out-of-state. He sketched a decline from 310,000 about 1769 to 20,000 between 1880 and 1900, and recovery to over 36,000 by 1950 and nearly 40,000 by 1960.

Cherokee population in the Southeast reported in 1809, 1826, 1828 and an 1835 census steadily increased despite emigration to Arkansas and Texas, a Creek war, famine and disease mortality, as W. G. McLoughlin and W. H. Conser [28] found.

Larry Blackwood [1] analyzed rising fertility trends between 1950 and 1962, followed by steady decline to 1978 among Alaskan Natives. Diminished breast-feeding contributed to the earlier trend, and Indian Health Service family planning services to the later. In a similar study, A. Romaniuk [47] found that Canadian fertility increased during early stages of "modernization." Changing from a semi-nomadic to sedentary life, and giving birth in medical institutions plus a massive shift from breast to bottle feeding seem responsible. Romaniuk noted that in contrast to the United States pattern, nearly 90 percent of persons of Indian origin enumerated by the 1971 Canadian census lived on reserves.

The New American Race. Native American marital unions with Europeans produced by the 1820s a considerable Upper Great Lakes region Métis population. Town and village dwellers, Métis were economic middlemen, language interpreters and cultural brokers, according to Jacqueline Peterson [42]. Helen H. Tanner [58] artfully described a 1792 multi-ethnic frontier trading town where some of the "New American Race" was created. Shawnee, Delaware and Miami towns were near an Ohio trading town containing European adults and children: English, Scots and French—some intermarried with Native Americans—and Mohawks.

The same process occurred on the Gulf Coast. Darrell A. Posey [45] outlined the history of a tri-racial Afro-American, Euroamerican and Native American Louisiana community.

William R. Swagerty [56] analyzed 312 Rocky Mountain trapper/trader marriages, finding that 39 percent first married an Indian woman. Over half those who remarried took Indian wives; 41 percent of third wives were Indians; 58 percent of a dozen fourth wives were Plains Indian women.

Using refractory colonial enumerations and other records, Alicia V. Tjarks [62] ably and quantitatively described late eighteenth century Texas frontier society. Rapidly amalgamating Indians, it tended toward a free and heterogeneous condition with significant upward mobility and presaged the later break with the old social order. Stanley and Thomas [53] identified much later intertribal marriages as a major cause of diminished use of Native American languages, English being the common tongue of spouses from different groups.

Demographic Case Studies

The United States Congress and Bureau of Indian Affairs have occasionally established legal criteria limiting individual and group eligibility to receive federal services. These criteria sometimes pose demographic questions, such as whether enough persons possess the minimum legally required Indian genes required to qualify as tribal officials. William E. Unrau [66], an historian who has carried out much public history, reported the Kaw case.

Enumerations

Professional demographers typically trust enumeration reports, although they concede imperfections. A Census Bureau demographer calculated that the 1970 national enumeration undercounted Native Americans seven percent, judging from birth and death statistics for the preceding 20-year period. One reason was that the Bureau's short form provided spaces to list only eight persons and the long (20 percent sample) for only seven, whereas Native American households frequently are larger. Jeffrey S. Passel [41] inferred that 67,000 persons changed their self-identification between 1960 and 1970, resulting in more adult Native Americans being counted in 1970 than predicted.

Historic demographers who take the trouble to examine the accuracy of Native American population enumerations typically warn that enumerators undercount minorities. Native American under-enumeration is not only an historic phenomenon; the 1970 United States census continued the custom. In a methodologically elegant and very important analysis, Cary W. Meister [34] demonstrated how the Bureau of the Census American Indian subject report inaccurately reported population characteristics of four reservations. This report was based on the 20 percent sample. Meister compared its figures to the complete count available on computer tapes. He found the 20 percent sample fell 3.7 percent short of the complete national Indian count. The sample underreported Gila River Reservation population by 2.5 percent and Ft. McDowell by 22.4 percent. It overreported Salt River by one percent and Ak Chin by 33.8 percent! The 20 percent sample seriously skewed sex ratios —83.1 at Ft. McDowell contrasted with the complete count's 120.2. Meister concluded that "no better example exists of the misleading nature of the 20 percent sample data for small reservations." Clearly even United States census reports of Native American numbers are not entirely accurate.

Harry A. Kersey [25] described how in the year 1900, surveyor J. O. Fries and bilingual guide A. A. Hendry counted 339 south Florida Seminoles. Five letters of Fries leave little doubt that they experienced difficulty locating Seminoles scattered widely throughout the Everglades, eliciting names for unnamed children and ages from people who did not count years.

New World scholars are beginning to utilize church records of rites of passage such as European historic demographers have productively exploited. S. F. Cook [4] analyzed California Franciscan mission registers. He and Borah [6] re-examined registers from eight California missions as "sources of vital statistics." They pointed out the difficulty raised when 549 of 2,846 persons baptized at one mission disappear from its records. They nonetheless counted gentiles baptized, their ages at baptism and death, years converts survived baptism, and baptisms and deaths of mission natives born. The latter analysis disclosed that child mortality was high although erratic throughout the mission period — 360 to 660 deaths per 1,000 births. They calculated the proportion of converts married before and after conversion; widows and widowers marrying previously unmarried converts, interethnic and interracial marital unions.

In a less complex analysis, Jackson [24] found that Northern

Piman mission population dropped from 4,088 in 1761 to 2,742 in 1766. Epidemic smallpox in 1764 and an unknown 1766 contagion caused most of the 37 percent decline. Jackson calculated an 80 percent depopulation during the 80-year Jesuit mission in Upper Pimeria, 1687-1767.

Several scholars have made progress locating and analyzing Spanish colonial civil enumerations. Tjarks [63] re-estimated New Mexico's Native American and colonist population during the latter half of the eighteenth century using mainly civil enumerations. In 1746-1748, Native Americans numbering 6,793 formed 58.6 percent of the provincial population. By 1790, 5,873 Indians comprised but 34.5 percent and by 1810 they were only 30.8 percent of the population. Donald C. Cutter [8] translated a newly-discovered 1765 statistical report on New Mexico. It showed 10,524 Native Americans in 2,703 families among 20,104 total population, or 52.3 percent of the total. (Autonomous Hopis were not counted.)

As already mentioned, U. S. Bureau of Indian Affairs and Census Bureau Native American counts typically are defective. Analyzing reports of Pima and Maricopa numbers, Cary W. Meister [35] found that the 1970 census did not report as much as 65 percent of Salt River Reservation's actual population.

Even a sketchy enumeration can, on the other hand, correct erroneous stereotypes. McLoughlin and Conser [28] pointed out that an 1835 Cherokee census shows that federal officials "persistently underestimated the total number of Cherokees in the East" as about 10,000, when over 16,500 existed. Federal officials claimed 50 percent mixed bloods; the enumeration found less than 23 percent. While removal advocates claimed that most Cherokees hunted and preferred emigrating where game abounded, the census found that virtually none relied on game alone.

Government officials have systematically enumerated Native Americans for purposes other than counting them, including fiscal control over annuity payments and land allotments. John H. Moore [38] demonstrated how such data yield quantitative information about pre-reservation supra-familial social and political organization. Analyzing Cheyenne data, Moore found that allotted land locations reflected a matrilocal residence pattern among Sand Creek massacre survivors persisting thirty years later.

Secondary Curriculum Supplements

My original essay in this series suggested several works as suitable secondary school readings. Alfred W. Crosby's *The Columbian Exchange* [7] has not been superceded by any better book-length introduction to biological and cultural changes following 1492. Since 1976, only very few brief, accurate and readable accounts of local demographic events have appeared that enable a good teacher to supplement standard curriculum materials.

Appropriate for Alaskan schools is Winson L. Sarafin's [48] description of Aleut population decline. Mississippi teachers might use Samuel Stanley's [52] summary of the final Natchez demise. South Dakota and other students could beneficially consult Joseph V. Siry's [50] finely composed Mandan history. West coast teachers may find William E. Coffer's [2] short comparison of racism toward California's Native Americans, Mexican-Americans, Chinese, Japanese and Blacks better for their purposes than longer, more scholarly discussions.

ALPHABETICAL LIST

[1] Blackwood, Larry. 1981. "Alaska Native Fertility Trends, 1950-1978." *Demography* 18: 173-79.

[2] Coffer, William E. 1977. "Genocide Among the California Indians, with a Comparative Study of Other Minorities." *Indian Historian* 10: 8-15.

[3] Cook, Noble David. 1981. *Demographic Collapse: Indian Peru, 1520-1620*. Cambridge: Cambridge University Press.

[4] Cook, Sherburne F. 1976. *The Conflict Between the California Indian and White Civilization*. Berkeley: University of California Press.

[5] ———. 1978. "Historical Demography." In *California*, ed. Robert F. Heizer, Vol 8 of *Handbook of North American Indians,* gen. ed. William C. Sturtevant, pp. 91-98. Washington: Smithsonian Institution.

[6] Cook, Sherburne F., and Woodrow Borah. 1979. *Essays in Population History: Mexico and California. Volume III*. Berkeley: University of California Press.

[7] Crosby, Alfred W. Jr. 1972. *The Columbian Exchange: Biological and Cultural Consequences of 1492*. Westport: Greenwood.

[8] Cutter, Donald C., trans. and ed. 1975. "An Anonymous Statistical Report on New Mexico in 1765." *New Mexico Historical Review* 50: 347-52.

[9] Dickinson, John A. 1980. "The Pre-contact Huron Population: A Re-appraisal." *Ontario History* 72: 173-79.

[10] Dobyns, Henry F. 1976. *Native American Historical Demogrphy: A Critical Bibliography*. Bloomington: Indiana University Press for The Newberry Library.

[11] ———. 1976. "Brief Perspective on a Scholarly Transformation: Widowing the 'Virgin' Land." *Ethnohistory* 23: 95-104.

[12] ———. 1977. "The Decline of the Mescalero Apache Indian Population from 1873 to 1913." In *Essays in Honor of Morris Edward Opler*, ed. Gerry C. Williams and Carolyn Pool, pp. 61-69. University of Oklahoma Papers in Anthropology 18.

[13] Dumond, Don E. 1980. "The Archaeology of Alaska and the Peopling of America." *Science* 209: 984-91.

[14] Fenton, William N. 1940. "Problems Arising from the Historic Northeastern Position of the Iroquois." In *Essays in Historical Anthropology of North America*, pp. 159-252. Smithsonian Institution, Miscellaneous Collections 100. Washington: Smithsonian Institution.

[15] Fladmark, K. R., 1979. "Routes: Alternate Migration Corridors for Early Man in North America." *American Antiquity* 44: 55-69.

[16] Gough, Barry M. 1978. "Send a Gunboat: Checking Slavery and Controlling Liquor Traffic among Coast Indians of British Columbia in the 1860s." *Pacific Northwest Quarterly* 69: 159-68.

[17] Guest, Francis F. 1979. "An Examination of the Thesis of S. F. Cook on the Forced Conversion of Indians in the California Missions." *Southern California Quarterly* 61: 1-78.

[18] Harner, Michael. 1977. "The Ecological Basis for Aztec Sacrifice." *American Ethnologist* 4: 117-35.

[19] Hassig, Ross. 1981. "'The Famine of One Rabbit': Ecological Causes and Social Consequences of a Pre-Columbian Calamity." *Journal of Anthropological Research* 37: 172-82.

[20] Hunn, Eugene. 1982. "Did the Aztecs Lack Potential Animal Domesticates?" *American Ethnologist* 9: 578-79.

[21] Hunt, George T. 1940. *The Wars of the Iroquois: A Study in Intertribal Relations*. Madison: University of Wisconsin Press.

[22] Jackson, Robert H. 1981. "Epidemic Disease and Indian Depopulation in the Baja California Missions, 1697-1834." *Southern California Quarterly* 63: 308-46.

[23] ———. 1981. "The 1781-1782 Smallpox Epidemic in Baja California. *Journal of California and the Great Basin Anthropology* 3: 138-43.

[24] ———. 1981. "The Last Jesuit Censuses of the Pimeria Alta Missions, 1761 and 1766." *The Kiva* 46: 243-72.

[25] Kersey, Harry A., Jr. 1981. "Florida Seminoles and the Census of 1900." *Florida Historical Quarterly* 60: 145-60.

[26] Krech, Shepard, III, ed. 1981. *Indians, Animals, and the Fur Trade: A Critique of Keepers of the Game*. Athens: University of Georgia Press.

[27] Little, Elizabeth A., and Marie Sussek. 1979. *Nantucket Indians Who Died of the Sickness: 1-8 mo-1763 to 2 mo-1764*. Nantucket: Nantucket Historical Association, Archaeology Department.

[28] McLoughlin, William G., and Walter H. Conser, Jr. 1977. "The Cherokees in Transition: A Statistical Analysis of the Federal Cherokee Census of 1835." *Journal of American History* 64: 678-703.

[29] McNeill, William H. 1976. *Plagues and Peoples*. Garden City: Anchor Doubleday.

[30] ———. 1979. "Historical Patterns of Migration." *Current Anthropology* 20: 95-98.

[31] Marshall, Ingeborg. 1977. "An Unpublished Map Made by John Cartwright Between 1768 and 1773 Showing Beothuck Indian Settlements and Artifacts and Allowing a New Population Estimate." *Ethnohistory* 24: 223-49.

[32] Martin, Calvin L. 1978. *Keepers of the Game: Indian-Animal Relationships and the Fur Trade*. Berkeley: University of California Press.

[33] Meister, Cary W. 1976. "Demographic Consequences of Euro-American Contact on Selected American Indian Populations and Their Relationship to the Demographic Transition." *Ethnohistory* 23: 161-72.

[34] ———. 1978. "The Misleading Nature of Data in the Bureau of the Census Subject Report on 1970 American Indian Population." *Indian Historian* 11: 12-19.

[35] ———. 1980. "Methods for Evaluating the Accuracy of Ethnohistorical Demographic Data on North American Indians: A Brief Assessment." *Ethnohistory* 27: 153-68.

[36] Miller, Virginia P. 1976. "Aboriginal Micmac Population: A Review of the Evidence." *Ethnohistory* 23: 117-27.

[37] Milner, Clyde A., II. 1981. "Off the White Road: Seven Nebraska Indian Societies in the 1870s—A Statistical Analysis of Assimilation, Population, and Prosperity. *Western Historical Quarterly* 12: 37-52.

[38] Moore, John H. 1980. "Aboriginal Indian Residence Patterns Preserved in Censuses and Allotments." *Science* 207: 201-03.

[39] Offner, Jerome A. 1980. "Archival Reports of Poor Crop Yields in the Early Postconquest Texcocan Heartland and Their Implications for Studies of Aztec Period Population." *American Antiquity* 45: 848-56.

[40] Otterbein, Keith F. 1979. "Huron vs. Iroquois: A Case Study in Inter-Tribal Warfare." *Ethnohistory* 26: 141-52.

[41] Passel, Jeffrey S. 1976. "Provisional Evaluation of the 1970 Census Count of American Indians." *Demography* 13: 397-409.

[42] Peterson, Jacqueline. 1978. "Prelude to Red River: A Social Portrait of the Great Lakes Metis." *Ethnohistory* 25: 41-68.

[43] Pollard, Helen P., and Shirley Gorenstein. 1980. "Agrarian Potential, Population, and the Tarascan State." *Science* 209: 274-77.

[44] Posey, Darrell A. 1976. "Entomological Considerations in Southeastern Aboriginal Demography." *Ethnohistory* 23: 147-60.

[45] ———. 1979. "Origin, Development and Maintenance of a Louisiana Mixed-Blood Community: The Ethnohistory of the Freejacks of the First Ward Settlement." *Ethnohistory* 26: 177-92.

[46] Price, Barbara J. 1978. "Demystification, Enriddlement, and Aztec Cannibalism: A Materialist Rejoinder to Harner." *American Ethnologist* 5: 98-115.

[47] Romaniuk, A. 1981. "Increase in Natural Fertility During the Early Stages of Modernization: Canadian Indians Case Study." *Demography* 18: 157-72.

[48] Sarafin, Winston L. 1977. "Smallpox Strikes the Aleuts." *Alaska Journal* 7: 46-49.

[49] Schlesier, Karl H. 1976. "Epidemics and Indian Middlemen: Rethinking the Wars of the Iroquois, 1609-1653." *Ethnohistory* 23: 129-45.

[50] Siry, Joseph V. 1978. "When the River Flows Upstream: The Appearance, Adaptation and Extinction of the Nu-Mah-Kakee People." *Indian Historian* 11: 6-14.

[51] Stackpole, Edouard A. 1975. "The Fatal Indian Sickness of Nantucket that Decimated the Island Aboriginees." *Historic Nantucket* 23: 8-13.

[52] Stanley, Samuel. 1978. "The End of the Natchez Indians." *History Today* 28: 612-18.

[53] Stanley, Sam, and Robert K. Thomas. 1978. "Current Demographic and Social Trends among North American Indians." *Annals of the American Academy of Political and Social Science* 436: 111-20.

[54] Starna, William A. 1980. "Mohawk Iroquois Populations: A Revision." *Ethnohistory* 27: 371-82.

[55] Stoffle, Richard W., and Michael J. Evans. 1976. "Resource Competition and Population Change: A Kaibab Paiute Ethnohistorical Case." *Ethnohistory* 23: 173-97.

[56] Swagerty, William R. 1980. "Marriage and Settlement Patterns of Rocky Mountain Trappers and Traders." *Western Historical Quarterly* 11: 159-80.

[57] Swann, Michael M. 1980. "The Demographic Impact of Disease and Famine in Late Colonial Northern Mexico." *Geoscience and Man* 21 (March 17): 97-109.

[58] Tanner, Helen H. 1978. "The Glaize in 1792: A Composite Indian Community," *Ethnohistory* 25: 15-40.

[59] Thomas, Peter A. 1976. "Contrastive Subsistence Strategies and

Land Use as Factors for Understanding Indian-White Relations in New England." *Ethnohistory* 23: 1-18.

[60] Thornton, Russell. 1978. "Implications of Catlin's American Indian Population Estimates for Revision of Mooney's Estimate." *American Journal of Physical Anthropology* 49: 11-13.

[61] ———. 1981. "Demographic Antecedents of a Revitalization Movement: Population Change, Population Size, and the 1890 Ghost Dance." *American Sociological Review* 46: 88-96.

[62] Tjarks, Alicia V. 1974. "Comparative Demographic Analysis of Texas, 1777-1793." *Southwestern Historical Quarterly* 77: 291-338.

[63] ———. 1978. "Demographic, Ethnic and Occupational Structure of New Mexico, 1790." *The Americas* 35: 45-88.

[64] Trimble, Michael K. 1979. *An Ethnohistorical Interpretation of the Spread of Smallpox in the Northern Plains Utilizing Concepts of Disease Ecology*. Columbia: University of Missouri Department of Anthropology for the National Park Service.

[65] Ubelaker, Douglas H. 1976. "Prehistoric New World Population Size: Historical Review and Current Appraisal of North American Estimates." *American Journal of Physical Anthropology* 45: 661-66.

[66] Unrau, William E. 1976. "Removal, Death, and Legal Reincarnation of the Kaw People." *Indian Historian* 9: 2-9.

[67] White, Richard. 1978. "The Winning of the West: The Expansion of the Western Sioux in the 18th and 19th Centuries." *Journal of American History* 65: 319-43.

Spanish-Indian Relations, 1513-1821

W. R. SWAGERTY

University of Idaho

SINCE THE DEATH OF Herbert Eugene Bolton in 1953, scholars focusing on the "Spanish Borderlands" have added much to our understanding of the region, its peoples, institutions and dynamics. No student of the geographical area comprising the present Mexican states of Sonora, Sinaloa, Durango, Chihauhau, Coahuila, Tamaulipas, Baja California, and Nuevo León; and, the North American states of California, Arizona, Utah, New Mexico, Colorado, Texas, Louisiana, Mississippi, Alabama, Georgia and Florida has come close to equaling Bolton's lifetime accomplishments in publication. Nor has a better set of criteria for defining the region and subject area been offered by historians. Yet, the volume of literature and, more importantly, the refined nature of recent studies suggest that the study of the Borderlands has, in very recent years, progressed to a more sophisticated, interdisciplinary plateau.

What has made this possible in the context of the study of Spanish-Indian relations can be explained as the result of three simultaneous trends. First, there are now fourth generation Borderlands historians who, while carrying forward the Bolton tradition, have filled in many gaps left untouched by the old masters. Secondly, many of these same scholars, their mentors and their students have built bridges between anthropology and history, utilizing ethnohistorical techniques in the writing of the "new Indian history," as well as in reassessing more traditional topics in Latin American and North American History. Finally, many anthropologists have engineered their own bridges or have met historians in mid-passage by recognizing the value of documentary research. Today there is no single means by which to characterize the "Borderlands scholar." Instead, we have a diverse cadre of individuals representing many disciplines, many backgrounds and age-groups. Together they have contributed to a noticeable maturation of the field. The following bibliographical essay is designed to introduce the reader to what this author considers to be the most important publications since 1969.

That beginning point is arbitrary, but logical and convenient. Under the guest editorship of Oakah L. Jones, Jr., a thematic issue of *Journal of the West* was released in 1969. Editor Jones provided a classic Boltonian explanation of the Borderlands as well as a "Selected Reading List" of some one hundred and sixty monographs, edited works and articles on all aspects of Spain in North American and what today is northern Mexico [105]. The issue contained nine additional articles, many of which are now considered seminal works on such topics as the presidio (Faulk [62], Christiansen [29], Moorhead [141]) and colonial settlement and village patterns (Simmons [192]). In addition to citing twenty-one works by Bolton, Jones included Edward H. Spicer's *Cycles of Conquest: The Impact of Spain, Mexico and the United States on the Indians of the Southwest, 1533-1960* (1962). Few other anthropologists made Jones's list, but it was clear by 1969 that historians had much to learn from Spicer, whose work remains the best ethnohistorical treatment of the western half of the Borderlands.

Another publication, entitled *Attitudes of Colonial Powers toward the American Indian*, edited by Howard Peckham and Charles Gibson, was released in 1969. Designed to provide comparative analysis of colonial powers' treatment of various Native American groups in the Americas, the anthology contained two articles of special interest to the student of Indian-White relations. Lewis Hanke provided a sensitive "personal view" of why Spain labored so diligently at resolving the juridical-ecclesiastical debate over what decades before he had described as "the Spanish struggle for justice in the conquest of America" [82], while Edward Spicer wrote yet another masterwork titled "Political Incorporation and Cultural Change in New Spain: A Study in Spanish-Indian Relations" [201]. In academic background and in method of scholarly inquiry, Hanke and Spicer shared little; yet, both were interested in Spain's impact on Native American societies. Both were humanists seeking the truth through scientific methods; both had much to gain from each other's discipline; and, both have made outstanding contributions in the field of their mutual interest—Spanish-Indian relations.

This same concern for broader approaches to understanding the Spaniard, the Indian and the mixing of the two prompted the Weatherhead Foundation in the summer of 1969 to plan a scholarly conference on "Plural Societies in the Southwest" for the fall of 1970. The resulting published collection of papers [204] contains articles which are now classics that have retained their currency, largely as a result of the theoretical parameters defined and exemplified by the late Edward Spicer.

Spicer led the charge of growing phalanxes of scholars interested in interdisciplinary work in American Indian studies in general, Borderlands studies in particular. A healthy outgrowth of the direction Spicer pointed toward has been the attention given to processes of acculturation between indigenous and non-native historical societies. Essays selected by Deward E. Walker, Jr. for *The Emergent Native Americans* [227] provide a case in point. Here one finds several key articles focusing on cultures of the Borderlands, but, more importantly, the processes involved in culture contact situations are analyzed—primarily by anthropologists. This trend has continued, although many traditional historians have not subscribed to the use of models, theories or non-diachronic source materials. In some cases, suspicions of new methods may have been well-founded, but overall our understanding of the region and its peoples—of yesteryear and today—has been greatly enhanced by applications of the newer methodologies.

Older approaches have not lost their validity or their importance, as evidenced by efforts made to synthesize previous generations' scholarship, thus laying a foundation for new foci, new techniques. The most important of these syntheses by a traditional historian is John F. Bannon's *The Spanish Borderlands Frontier, 1513-1821* [11], published in 1970. Bannon essentially provides a highly readable and authoritative update of Borderlands studies, focusing on institutions first outlined by Bolton and his generation. The reader learns little about Indian cultures or their own special histories in Bannon's work, but one does have (as was the author's primary goal) a firm understanding of the chronological development of Spain's occupation of the Borderlands and of the most important institutions she introduced into the region.

A companion volume in the "Histories of the American Frontier" series on *The Southern Colonial Frontier, 1607-1763* by W. Stitt Robinson [175] provides a basic overview of Spain's tenuous hold on the eastern half of the Borderlands from English colonization at Jamestown through Spanish loss of territory in 1763. Robinson's focus on European powers' rivalry and expansion in the Southeast often neglects the critical role of Indian polities in diplomatic and military struggles. A similar criticism must be made of J. Leitch Wright, Jr.'s *Anglo-Spanish Rivalry in North America* [233], a weakness Wright overcame in his more recent *The Only Land They Knew: The Tragic Story of the Indians of the Old South* [234]. The latter is one of the more important books under consideration here and, while not purely ethnohistorical, serves respectively with Charles Hudson, *The Southeastern Indians* [100] as the best recent overviews of Indian politics and Indian cultures in the Southeast. These two volumes are, in many respects, ideal counterparts to Elizabeth A. H. John's *Storms Brewed in Other Men's Worlds: The Confrontation of Indians, Spanish and French in the Southwest, 1540-1795* [103] and the aforementioned *Cycles of Conquest* by Spicer. John has updated and expanded Bolton's pioneering studies of Louisiana, Texas and New Mexico and, to her credit, one finds much more analytical discussion of Indian reaction to Spanish-French rivalry than in previous studies.

Of greater importance for understanding Spain's first advances in sixteenth century North America than any of the above surveys are Carl O. Sauer, *Sixteenth Century North America* [182] and David B. Quinn, *North America from Earliest Discovery to First Settlements* [167]. Both Sauer and Quinn attempted to treat the Indian side of contact situations with fairness. And, in large part, both succeeded. Sauer's analysis of the biological, physical and human landscapes of North America are unparalleled, while Quinn remains the unrivaled expert on European voyages of discovery and colonization in the sixteenth and early seventeenth centuries. Sauer's *Seventeenth Century North America* [183], published after his death in 1975, is also useful as an overview. It lacks the polish of his sixteenth century volume, but is nevertheless a little known gem of recent release. Sauer sprinkled his narrative with numerous ethnographic sketches of seventeenth century Indian life, much of the source material derived from Spanish and French accounts in the Borderlands region. Those seeking documentary sources will also find Quinn's edited work, *New American World* [168] of great value. Some Spanish documents, heretofore unavailable in translation, are included for the first time along with the standard sources on exploration and colonization attempts by various European powers on North American shores to 1612.

Sauer's lifetime investigations revealed the importance of biological exchanges between Europeans and Indians of cultigens, wild plants, fauna, and diseases. Moreover, Sauer was especially successful in identifying subsistence-demographic patterns and Indian cultural identities in the western half of the Borderlands. Several of these key themes, previously discussed by Henry F. Dobyns [47] and updated in this anthology, are the focus of Alfred W. Crosby's *The Columbian Exchange* [39]. This pathbreaking exploration into the catastrophic effects of Old World pathogens upon non-immunized native peoples in the Caribbean and Meso-America has forced all students of Spanish-Indian relations to reexamine the various conquests of native peoples. Current studies by Dobyns [50] go beyond Crosby in explaining the epidemiological history of native groups residing in sixteenth century North America.

One fascinating area of Borderlands studies that has increasingly drawn curious scholars into interdisciplinary studies is the connection between Meso-America and North America in prehistoric and protohistoric times. The implications of exchanges of ideas, material culture, biological baggage (such as disease, foodstuffs and additions to genetic pools), language, and possibly pre-European contact information about the invasion of the hemisphere by Spaniards are extremely important for piecing together pre- and post-contact tribal histories. For several decades, a few scholars have championed the significance of trans-American contacts and exchanges, but, until recently, their ideas remained on the periphery of mainstream schools of thought. Basil C. Hedrick, J. Charles Kelley, Carroll L. Riley and Charles C. Di Peso stand out as individuals who reopened doors of inquiry for the protohistoric Southwest. Three collections of essays edited by Kelley, Hedrick and Riley [85, 86, 174] as well as an important monograph by Riley on *Sixteenth*

Century Trade in the Greater Southwest [173] are indicative of this progressive approach to early Borderlands history.

Discussion of what constitutes "the Greater Southwest" is ongoing. Pailes and Whitecotton have provided a theoretical "exploratory model" based upon theories of frontier relationships [156], while Di Peso (in particular) has attempted to demonstrate the enormous importance and range of trade spheres (and hence biological and cultural zones) from his archaeological findings at Casas Grandes [46]. Spinoffs from interest in the late prehistoric and protohistoric Southwest are increasing in number and sophistication. Studies by Upham [219], Zubrow [237], Wilcox and Masse [230], Schroeder [185, 187] and others are examples here. This area is certainly fertile for further work. Unfortunately, for the Southeast, little energy has been devoted to rethinking trans-Gulf contacts, although the ideas of Gordon R. Willey, James B. Griffin and others have not died. Southeastern universities have poured resources and talent into projects focusing on historic archaeology, the fruits of which have already changed many notions of European-Indian interaction. These same institutions have also sponsored a resurgent interest in Mississippian cultures. Future publications may well provide interpretive counterparts to extant literature on the Southwest.

Sixteenth through eighteenth century Spanish expeditions continue to be studied and reevaluated by scholars. Few new documents have surfaced, but there is now a general consensus among ethnohistorians that these are the researcher's most important tools in reconstructing protohistoric societies. In addition to Quinn [167] and Sauer's overviews [182], important specific studies have been produced by the following: Robert R. Miller on Cortes's unsuccessful attempt to colonize Baja California in 1535 [140]; Paul Hoffman on Pedro de Salazar's slave-raiding expedition to Florida in 1515 [91] and Florida's fluctuating importance in Spanish policy-making from 1535-1585 [92]; José B. Hernández on contradictory images of Florida and its native inhabitants in the sixteenth century [90]; Barbara A. Purdy on "Weapons, Strategies, and Tactics of the Europeans and the Indians in 16th and 17th Century Florida" [166]; Brain, Toth and Rodríguez-Buckingham on "Ethnohistoric Archaeology and the Desoto Entrada" [19]; John J. TePaske on "Spanish Indian Policy and the Struggle for Empire in the Southeast, 1513-1776" [215]; Chester B. DePratter and Marvin Smith on the Juan Pardo expeditions of 1566-1568 [45]; W. R. Swagerty on Indian responses to European incursions in the Borderlands, 1513-1600 [210]; Steven Baker [8], Stanley South [200] and Charles Hudson [99] on Spanish contacts with Carolina Indians; James Covington [38], Eugene Lyon [128], Kathleen Deagan [43], and Jerald Milanich [137] on Timucuan-Spanish relations in early Florida; Lewis H. Larson, Jr. [122] and Grant D. Jones [104] on Spanish relations among the Guales of the Georgia coast; Smith and Gottlob [199] and Hally [81] on Spanish-Indian relationships in the Southeast through the eyes of archaeologists; Clifford M. Lewis [124] and Stephen Reilly [170] on Spanish-Calusa relations; Carroll Riley [172] on Meso-American Indians who accompanied expeditionaries in the Southwest and "Early Spanish-Indian Communication" [171]; Edward Dozier [54, 55], Marc Simmons [194] and Albert Schroeder [186] on Pueblo-Spanish relations; Edward Castillo [25] on "The Impact of Euro-American Exploration and Settlement" in California; and, Ralph Vigil [224] on the literature of "Exploration and Conquest" in the Borderlands.

In addition, Hedrick and Riley have translated and edited *Documents Ancillary to the Vaca Journey* [87] and Gerald Theisen has made available additional sources on this same expedition [216]. Rodack has performed the parallel task for Adolph F. Bandelier's *The Discovery of New Mexico by the Franciscan Monk, Friar Marcos de Niza in 1539* [176], as has Charles Bennett for French sixteenth century voyages to Florida [123]. Gertrude Muir has published a useful "selective checklist" on the bibliography of Spanish entradas into the Southwest, 1528-1610 [145]. For the Northwest Coast, an area often ignored by Borderlands scholars, but certainly one historically important in Spain's visions of her North American empire, Christon I. Archer has contributed two important articles on "The Making of Spanish Indian Policy on the Northwest Coast" [4] and "Spanish Exploration and Settlement of the Northwest Coast in the Eighteenth Century." [5]. Derek Pethick's *First Approaches to the Northwest Coast* [157] includes brief discussion of all Spanish voyages to the region before 1792, but lacks the analysis of these found in Warren L. Cook's impressive study, *Flood Tide of Empire* [33]. Iris H. W. Engstrand's *Spanish Scientists in the New World* [58] focuses on important scientific expeditions of the eighteenth century that acquainted Europeans with the diverse human, botanical and geological landscapes of the Pacific Coast from Mexico to present-day Canada. Engstrand has also translated and edited José Mariano Moziño's *Noticias de Nutka* [144], an important source on Indian life in the Nootka Sound area at 1792.

Several publications focusing upon European images of Indians and the intellectual perception of Native American societies have appeared since 1969. The most important of these for Iberian images are J. H. Elliott, *The Old World and the New, 1492-1650* [57], Hugh Honour, *The New Golden Land* [97], and Fredi Chiappelli, editor, *First Images of America* [28]. Essays in the Chiappelli volumes are especially germane for Spanish images of sixteenth and seventeenth century Native American societies.

Another area of intellectual history concerning Spanish-Indian relations focuses on the debate over Spanish sincerity in granting and preserving Indian rights. Benjamin Keen, in "The Black Legend Revisited: Assumptions and Realities" [108] reopened the issue in 1969. After reviewing the historiography concerning Bartolomé de las Casas's works and the evolution of the "Black" (anti-Spanish) and "White" (apologetic and pro-Spanish) legends, Keen concluded that the Black Legend is substantially accurate, but that both "legends" should be discarded. Keen's position was restated and a general defense of Las Casas was maintained by various authors who contributed to *Bartolomé de Las Casas in History: Toward an Understanding of the Man and His Work*, edited by Keen and Juan Friede [65]. Despite Keen's desire to bury the debate, his two publications met fierce resistance. In 1971, Philip Wayne Powell retraced the Black Legend in his *Tree of Hate* [163]. A student of Bolton, Powell was mainly concerned with hispanophobic attitudes historically and contemporarily affecting relations between the United States and the Hispanic world. This is a superb analysis of the propagandistic nature of Black Legendists and Anglocentrism in North American history.

Charles Gibson also saw currency in keeping the debate alive as evident in his edited work, *The Black Legend: Anti-Spanish Attitudes in the Old World and the New* [72]. Here the reader is given excerpts from some of the more important contributors to both legends. Unlike Gibson, Lewis Hanke would have preferred to have let the debate die. In "A Modest Proposal for a Moratorium on Grand Generalizations: Some Thoughts on the Black Legend" [83], Hanke attacked Keen for using twentieth century criteria to judge a complex problem dating from colonial times. He also chastized Keen for not providing case-specific examples from archival sources, using William B. Taylor's study of colonial land tenure patterns in Mexico [213] as evidence to refute Keen's assertion that Indians were not protected because they lost their land base. In defense, Keen responded point by point, stood his ground and used Charles Gibson's classic work, *The Aztecs Under Spanish Rule* (1964), as well as other then-current (1971) studies for supportive evidence [109]. Since 1971, little has been added to what many consider a dated and moot discussion.

Not dated is the continued effort to analyze effects of specific Spanish institutions on American Indian cultures and communities, as well as the legacy of Spanish institutions after Spain lost her northern territories. The latter is far less complex than the former, and has been nicely presented by such scholars as Donald Worcester [231] and Silvio Zavala [236]. Worcester singles out material culture, legal and political systems, linguistic and demographic patterns to illustrate the continuance of Spanish traditions in the United States, while Zavala compares Latin American (and Borderlands) frontiers with those in the United States. His conclusion: there are many similarities, but certain hallmarks of Indo-Spanish relations (especially miscegenation and the hybridization of a Creole society) are radically different from the Anglo-American experience formulated by Frederick J. Turner and his successors. Both of these essays have been reprinted in David J. Weber's excellent anthology, *New Spain's Far Northern Frontier* [228].

The question of "Borders and Frontiers" is the subject of Paul Kutsche's very recent historiographical appraisal [119]. Kutsche traces the literature on theories of frontiers and offers suggestions for improving our research in Borderlands studies. In "A Changing Culture Region" [148], Richard L. Nostrand explains the changing definitions across time of "The Spanish Borderlands" and how the region has been perceived by Spaniards, Mexicans, Anglos and Chicanos. He concludes that the Borderlands is best viewed as a zone of cultural transition where cultural, as well as biological fusion (especially in the context of Anglo-Latin convergence), underscores the fundamental significance of the region. Ralph H. Vigil shares the perspective that the richness of the Borderlands heritage is the product of Spanish and Mexican period institutions as well as of more modern developments [221]. His 1983 review of the literature on "Colonial Institutions" [223] provides a brief, but important guide to topical subjects, while his earlier appraisal of "The New Borderlands History: A Critique" [222] urges students of Mexican-American and Chicano history to rediscover the Spanish colonial legacy in order to better understand events since 1821.

The direct and indirect effects of Spanish colonial institutions upon Indians of the region has continued to generate exciting academic duels, although, as Henry F. Dobyns has cogently argued in "The Study of Spanish Colonial Institutions" [49], few scholars have used analytical models to test hypotheses and theories. That, despite the merging interests of historians, anthropologists and geographers. Deficiencies abound in the extant case studies of Spanish institutions, as Dobyns rightly points out, but some subject areas have matured appreciably. One of these is our understanding of Indian labor and land tenure after the Spanish conquest.

Building upon studies published in the 1950s and 1960s, James Lockhart opened a productive forum for discussion in 1969 with his "Encomienda and Hacienda: The Evolution of the Great Estate in the Spanish Indies" [125]. Lockhart singled out the city, the great estate, and the Indian village as the three principal elements in colonial Latin American history. The relationship between the establishment and growth of colonial cities and the concurrent growth of landed estates dependent upon Indian labor was fundamental, according to Lockhart. From the sixteenth century *encomiendas*, or grants to the tribute of conquered Indians, to the establishment of large estates, usually described as *haciendas*, Lockhart found continuity in the Indian labor systems. In theory, rights to encomienda entitled the *encomendero* to exact the tribute of individual Indians or groups of Indians living in particular geographical zones. The right to encomienda did not involve the right to Indian lands, but, in practice, landed estates formed within zones of native tributaries. The key to this progression was the institution of *repartimiento* whereby Indian towns (or leaders) were required to provide labor as well as tribute to Spanish grantees. Thus, encomienda, then repartimiento, then formation of haciendas and other land-based estates came to imply not only expropriation of Indian labor, but lands as well throughout Mexico and parts of the northern frontier. Indians theoretically protected by the Crown were thereby victimized by this process of dispossession of lands and erosion of sovereignty, becoming debt peons in late colonial times.

Lockhart's revisionist ideas were mildly challenged by Robert Keith [110] who saw discontinuities rather than similarities between the development of encomiendas and haciendas. To Keith, encomiendas required the survival of indigenous populations without radical change whereas the hacienda system depended on a labor force which had been largely removed from its traditional social (and often physical) environment and permanently settled on lands belonging to holders of Spanish estates. In Keith's analysis, the link between the two came in the institution of the *corregimiento* by which appointed officials rather than private citizens were given the right to administer Indian populations and to demand of them tribute (encomiendas) and/or labor (repartimiento). Abuses of the system by *corregiadores* was widespread and Indian land was absorbed in the process.

Magnus Mörner [143] takes this one step further, noting that the traditional view of a necessary link between the growth of haciendas and debt peonage on the part of native workers must be rejected. According to Mörner, Indians did lose much of their land base and their social organization with the growth of large estates, but this was mainly the result of a change in residence patterns. The dualistic patterns of Spanish towns separated from Indian villages (common in the sixteenth and early seventeenth centuries) became blurred by the eighteenth century. By then, the majority of rural Indians had formed remnant population clusters around Spanish cities and haciendas. Erwin P. Grieshaber agrees with this basic conclusion in his essay, "Hacienda-Indian Community Relations and Indian Acculturation" [77], but prefers to qualify the effect on native populations. He finds demographic and environmental factors critical in assessing the rate at which Indians lost their lands as well as their social and cultural systems. Where native towns were close to Spanish markets and communication centers, culture, population, and native economies (including the economic base—land) were lost rapidly. Even in densely populated native areas, as long as Spanish estates were not producing for world markets (and most were not until the nineteenth century), Indian social units changed but retained many native cultural traditions and lifeways. Remoteness from Spanish population clusters and a subsistence base that could not be readily transformed into Spanish agricultural enterprises served to insure cultural continuity, especially among such groups as the Mayos and the Yaquis of northern New Spain. Thus, despite the presence of encomenderos, hacendados, missionaries, miners and settlers, Indians of the Borderlands had much better chances of surviving as tribal units than their neighbors to the south, most of whom suffered cultural, social and demographic collapse, the survivors becoming assimilated in the melting pot as *mestizos*. The road to assimilation meant the transformation of independent Indian communities into semi-feudal peasant communities, the subject of Pedro Carrasco's "La transformación de la cultura indígena durante la colonia" [24].

All of these authors agree on the central point that both European and native land/labor systems were blended together in New Spain. There was much experimentation to find the best formula for attaining Spanish goals on the one hand and retaining an effective labor force among native groups on the other. Early efforts at congregating Indians into planned towns are discussed by Peter Gerhard [69] who has also published two essential reference works entitled *Introduction to the Historical Geography of New Spain* [68] and *The North Frontier of New Spain* [70]. Within these detailed historical atlas-encyclopedias, all the major European institutions introduced into New Spain and the Borderlands are mapped, charted, defined and specified for each geographic, ecclesiastical, juridical and political area. Furthermore, Gerhard provides demographic profiles and catalogues every major documented epidemic, refining our knowledge of the epidemiological effect of Spanish-Indian confrontation.

Indian labor in Spanish mining areas has not received much attention. Several recent studies, especially those of Peter Bakewell [9, 10] on Zacatecas indicate that unlike central Mexico, where repartimiento (forced rotational labor) was drawn from nucleated Indian villages near mining centers, in the north, Indian workers were of two types: slaves captured as prisoners of "just wars" in campaigns against unconquered tribes; and, *naborías* or free contractual laborers. Forced labor in mines ceased to be an important element throughout Mexico by around 1650 and wage-labor was always more common. Tarascans, Tlaxcalans and Texcocans (among others) migrated to mining centers and were generally more cooperative than antagonistic toward their Spanish employers. A few moved up the socio-economic ladder in mining as skilled machinists, carpenters and crew chiefs joining, as David A. Brading has found, a "labor aristocracy" alongside mestizos and mulattos by the eighteenth century [17]. Numbers of Indians in mining were always small in proportion to total native population. In another work, Brading makes clear that Indians ranked only above Blacks on the ethnic hierarchy in late colonial times [18]. Furthermore, as Evelyn Hu-DeHart discovered in her study, *Missionaries, Miners and Indians* [98], many Indian miners (including her principal subject, the Yaquis) worked only seasonally or for very brief periods of time in order to acquire such European items as horses, weapons and clothing. We know far too little about the number of Indian workers in the mines of Chihuahua and Parral (in particular) to reach conclusions on the effects of this form of free, migrant labor.

We do know much about Indians and mestizos who served as soldiers in the employ of the Spaniards and about cooperative Indian colonies established in the Borderlands to help populate the remote frontier outposts. Philip Wayne Powell's biography of *Mexico's Miguel Caldera* [164] underscores the opportunities made available to acculturated mixed-bloods and cooperative Indian allies. Caldera rose to the rank of "capitán" in the Chichimeca Wars of the late sixteenth century and held the important government post of Chief Justice of the Chichimeca frontier after 1590. Powell's resurrection of Caldera as a mestizo role model also provides insight into Spanish efforts to colonize the sparsely-settled northern frontier with colonies of Tlaxcalan families, also the subject of more indepth studies by David B. Adams for Spanish Coahuila and Nuevo León [1] and Michael Swann for Nueva Vizcaya [211]. Use of native colonists (especially Tlaxcalans) was so successful that experiments in the Gran Chichimec were repeated in Texas, New Mexico, and, as Theodore Corbett has shown [34], Florida.

Transplantation of acculturated, cooperative Indians as well as hostile prisoners of war resulted in a small flow of natives from Spanish northern settlements to southern Hispaniziced zones. All the while, Spain advanced northward. Robert L. Gold's study of Indian immigrants in eighteenth century New Spain [73] illustrates this movement. Missionized Indians of Florida became settlers near modern Veracruz after the British takeover of Florida in 1763. Cuba became the major deportation center for "barbarian" Indians (especially Apaches) captured in the interior provinces in the late eighteenth and early nineteenth centuries. There, men, women and children were forced to work on public projects and many became virtual slaves of private individuals, despite Crown regulations against such, as Christon I. Archer has discovered [2]. In other parts of the Borderlands, captive Plains Indians were often Hispanicized while serving as domestic servants of their captors, ransomers or purchasers. Russell Magnaghi has carved out a special research area in the study of the Indian slave trade [132, 133], while other scholars, especially Frances Leon Swadesh, have unfolded the social and political history of these peoples' lives in colonial New Mexico [208]. *Genízaros*, Hispanicized Plains Indians, formed several important colonial communities such as Abiquiú, New Mexico, and are the subject of a brief overview by Fray Angelico Chávez [26] and a more indepth cultural study by Swadesh [209].

The study of the racial mixing of peoples in the Borderlands has benefitted from the concerns of and techniques employed in the "new social history." Isidoro Moreno Navarro has built upon the categories and definitions of racial castes of Magnus Mörner (among others) with his study *Los cuadros del mestizaje americano* [146]. An excellent overview of the church's role in promoting *mestizaje* is provided by Delfina López Sarrelangue [126]. No general study of race, class and social structure for the Borderlands has been published, but Oakah Jones's *Los Paisanos* [106] is a good synthesis of what is generally known for the region (ca. 1979).

Rigid racial barriers characterized many aspects of Spain's New World empire, but on the frontier these boundaries were often ignored, cast aside, or proved impossible to maintain. In her "Comparative Demographic Analysis of Texas" [217], Alicia V. Tjarks found that the medieval caste system typical of most of Spanish

America did not apply in Spanish Texas by the second half of the eighteenth century. Classes and social ranking did exist, but color and race were not the critical factors in that Borderlands community. Eighteenth century St. Augustine has also been described as a racial "melting pot" by Kathleen Deagan [42]. Unlike Texas, color boundaries were important in social and economic ranking, but geographic isolation seems to have undermined the "ideal" structure Spaniards wanted to maintain.

Combining the techniques of the archaeologist and the ethnohistorian, Deagan [44] and Fairbanks [61] have demonstrated the possibilities of better understanding Spanish-Indian interaction in microcosm through their fieldwork in colonial St. Augustine. Using census data, Theodore Corbett [35] has shown that there were always more men than women in Hispanic St. Augustine (a pattern typical of all of the Borderlands). In the period, 1658-1756, 64.1% of all males who married were immigrants to the capital city, whereas only 15.1% of their wives had been born outside Florida's major settlement. Metizaje was many a Spanish soldier's only option. Living, working and intermarrying among Spaniards may well have been an Indian woman's most attractive option following the destruction of the Florida missions and the increase in English slave raiding in the early eighteenth century, a point Fairbanks has made in his "From Missionary to Mestizo" [60]. It may also have been the most important process enabling coexistence of red, white, brown and black-skinned residents in many other Hispanic settlements.

In many Borderlands communities, institutions were streamlined, social distinctions were somewhat blurred and society was more fluid than in more densely settled (and institutionalized) Spanish population centers. However, as Robert Archibald has discovered in "Acculturation and Assimilation in Colonial New Mexico" [7], the object for all ethnic groups within the Hispanic communities was to achieve a "whitening" rather than a "darkening" of one's descendants. This was true for all groups: Spaniards, mestizos, coyotes (mestizo-Indian), mulattos, genízaros, and Hispanicized Indians. Stated otherwise, the most important factor throughout the Borderlands for acceptance into Hispanic society was to be counted as a *gente de razón*, or a person who lived and acted like a Spaniard, regardless of one's parentage, a perspective traced throughout Jones's survey of the entire region [106], and argued most pursuasively by Ralph Vigil [221].

Complexities and ambiguities abound in the abovementioned general perspectives. Where reliable censuses for quantifying ethnic and social stratification exist, scholars are beginning to test such generalizations. Lacking precise data for the early history of New Mexico, Marc Simmons [194] has noted that some miscegenation between Spaniards, the various racial castes, and Pueblo Indians did occur from the beginning of Spanish settlement, but this was not the norm and led to awkward situations whereby the offspring of such unions were absorbed by either Pueblo or Hispanic society, depending on the circumstances of the birth. Biculturalism was not condoned or promoted.

Our best knowledge of New Mexico comes from Alicia Tjark's study of the "Demographic, Ethnic and Occupational Structure of New Mexico, 1790" [218]. Finding Gerhard's [70] population for New Mexico to be inflated, Tjarks reached several important conclusions about the 31,000 souls listed in the 1790 census. From the Reconquest (1692) to the end of the eighteenth century, the islands of Spanish influence had experienced very slow demographic growth; all the while the Indian population declined through miscegenation, decrease in native birth rates, and a very high mortality rate—primarily the result of disease. From 1598 on, New Mexico was a colony of small nuclear families (average size of 4 at 1790) whose leading "Spanish" families successfully maintained a predominance of endogamic marriages among families of the same caste from the Reconquest until around the middle of the eighteenth century. By the end of the century, the process of ethnic hybridization was proceeding in high gear and the increase in exogamic or interracial marriages contributed to the creation of a more homogeneous population. About half the population at 1790 was "Spanish," but these were largely descendants not of pure Spaniards who originally settled the province, but of the post-Reconquest Spanish-American families, most of whom had already intermarried before entering (or reentering) the Rio Grande communities. In short, ethnic fusion was imported by the pioneering Spanish-American settlers, was rejected within white boundaries, but developed anyway at a very slow pace. Unlike many presidial-mission frontiers (such as Florida and Texas), few unmarried males migrated to New Mexico; few Blacks or mulattos were present, genízaros did not form a large enough group to change the caste structure appreciably, and the population identified as mestizo never increased fast enough to challenge the dominant Spanish-American corporate network of the interrelated families. These patterns of social, cultural and ethnic boundaries in colonial New Mexico have also been analyzed by Judith Brostoff Sauceda in her study, "From the Inner Circle: The Relationship of the Space Occupied, Past and Present, by Southwest American Indian Women to the Southwest Indo-Hispanic Women" [181].

The settlement of Alta California was quite different, as Manuel Servín has argued in "California's Hispanic Heritage: A View into the Spanish Myth" [189]. Mexican mixed-bloods and Indians from Baja California comprised the majority of "Spanish" colonists, but, according to Servín, these people were discriminated against by Spanish officials and Franciscan priests. Mestizos and other Hispanicized castes resented the *Españoles* who controlled the colony. They did not aspire to become like "Spaniards," a thesis many scholars, especially Ralph Vigil [221], have difficulty accepting, in part because these very people were soldiers as well as colonists and there was much vertical mobility among the military personnel assigned frontier duty.

Many Indians served in the various military organizations created by Spanish officials throughout the Borderlands. Several good works on the presidio and the armies of New Spain have been published in recent years. Philip Powell has explained the sixteenth-century "Genesis of the Frontier Presidio in North America" [165] while Max L. Moorhead's *The Presidio: Bastion of the Spanish Borderlands* [142] is the most comprehensive study of the institution. Here and in a previous article [141], Moorhead outlined four types of soldiers who served New Spain until 1778, when major changes were made. Of the four, we know the most about the *soldado de cuera* or the standard common soldier of the northern frontier presidios and a lesser amount about the militias, Indian auxiliary armies and Indian allies. Inspection reports for sixteen presidios between 1773 and 1781 indicate that around one-half of the men at arms were "Caucasians," 37% were mixed-bloods, and 13.3% were Indians who served mainly as scouts. All were poorly paid, poorly armed, and far from effective in policing the frontier from stationary fortresses, a point Odie Faulk has made in "The Presidio: Fortress or Farce?" [62]. Whether or not the presidio was as important as the mission in Spain's prolonged struggle to hold her northern territories (as Leon G. Campbell has contended for Alta California [21]), the institution definitely served in conjunction with missions to make proselytizing possible and to create a semblance of imperial presence, the central Bolton thesis Bannon [11], in particular, continues to promote.

Indians fought or rounded up fellow Indians throughout the Borderlands as employees and allies of Spanish troops as Dunlay [56], Christiansen [29], Kessell [113], Archer [3], Jones [106], and Moorhead [142] have shown. Many of these Indian warriors were not necessarily desired or trusted, as Archer makes clear [3]; nor were they promoted, if California serves as a model (Langellier and Peterson [121]). But they were considered essential in New Mexico during and after the Reconquest (Kessell [114], Sánchez [178]); in the Mississippi Valley during the eighteenth century (Green [74], Ewers [59], White [229], Holmes [96]); in the Pimería Alta (Dobyns [48], Kessell [113]); and, throughout the Southwest during the protracted Apache, Navajo, Comanche and Ute wars (Worcester [232], McNitt [131], O'Neil [151], and Lange [120]). A full-length study of the various Indian allies in the armies of New Spain and the Borderlands is yet to be written.

The mission, that institution which impressed Herbert Bolton as the complement and equal of the presidio in providing a "civilizing" influence on the frontier and in giving Spain legitimate symbols of her presence in the remote stretches of her borderlands, has been the subject of intensive investigation in recent years. Most of these studies, as John F. Bannon points out in reviewing literature of the period, 1917-1979 [12], have not challenged Bolton's original thoughts on the importance of the institution. They have greatly reduced the previous generations' overviews to meaningful particular case studies. Bannon's essay and his own overview in his widely-read text [11] are testaments of the continued adherence to the belief by many scholars that the mission was the most benevolent and humane institution to enter the Borderlands, especially when compared with civil and military affairs. That it may have been, but the ultimate effect upon native populations was often disastrous, as has become increasingly clear in the case of the missions of Alta California. Studies by Cook [31], Heizer and Almquist [88], Borah [15], Castillo [25], Forbes [63], Garr [67], Phillips [158], and Sizelove [198] emphasize the brutality and human suffering that resulted from congregating diverse native Californians into twenty-one Hispanic missions between 1769 and 1821.

Cook's demographic studies [32] provide the best evidence of native cultural and demographic decline. Moreover, Cook was never convinced that California Indians were willing converts and residents at disease-ridden, overcrowded and often repressive mission complexes. His research led to the conclusion that especially after 1790, when missionaries endorsed the forced relocation of Indians from their villages into mission-fortresses, victims of such policies resorted to apostasy, fugitivism and physical resistance. George H. Phillips's *Chiefs and Challengers: Indian Resistance and Cooperation in Southern California* [159] corroborates Cook's thesis that most Indians whose lands were chosen for mission sites cooperated with Spanish authorities until the 1790s. As long as baptism, conversion and residency at missions were voluntary, Indian leaders took advantage of the Spanish presence by cementing economic and military ties, allowing those who desired to hear the Christian word. When policies changed and it became apparent that living at the missions was anathema to cultural and physical survival, native leaders fostered and led resistance movements.

In a lengthy rebuttal to Cook's thesis, Francis F. Guest has recently challenged indictments of his order (Franciscans) for mistreatment of California mission Indians [80]. Guest provides numerous examples where conversion was not forced on neophytes, but does not address the question of whether or not Christianity and its accompanying processes of deculturation destroyed rather than improved the lives of California natives. That question is often purposefully overlooked or avoided by apologists of the mission experience, a point Daniel S. Matson and Bernard L. Fontana have recently made in their excellent introduction to *Friar Bringas Reports to the King: Methods of Indoctrination on the Frontier of New Spain, 1796-1797* [135]. Rather than view the missionary as a self-sacrificing humanitarian, Matson and Fontana suggest that he was the ultimate aggressor in the context of what he sought to change. In their words, "Simply to 'spread news of great joy' [as Friar Bringas and all missionaries held as their goal] is one matter; to invade the most sacred inner precincts of another man's being, and thereby to defile him, is something else again. It seems to us there can be no greater form of violence than this" (brackets mine).

Close examination of indoctrination methods sheds light on the enormous task Catholic missionaries undertook in the Borderlands and the wide gulf between Native American and Judeo-Christian ethics and religion. The *Bringas Report* is a superb microstudy of eighteenth-century Franciscan methods used to bridge the cultural gap and change Indian lifestyles and belief systems. Early Franciscan efforts to radically alter the social structure, norms and values of Florida Indians have been explained by Milanich and Sturtevant [138], both of whom are anthropologists well-equipped to analyze the impact of such Catholic practices as the confessional. Amy Bushnell [20] has analyzed Spanish efforts to stop Indian *pelota* or ball playing, which Franciscans viewed as lewd and excessive as well as dangerous to Spanish control (the games were often quite physical). Hu-DeHart [98] and, more importantly, Spicer [203] both provide historical and ethnohistorical explanations for the mission experience of the Yaquis, while Sheridan and Naylor [191] have bettered our understanding of why the Tarahumaras rebelled against Spanish authority in the mid-seventeenth century in their *Rarámuri*. Sheridan has also analyzed how the Seris resisted both missionaries and Spanish military actions against them from 1729 to 1750 [190] and Roberto Salmón has written a comparative analysis of all Indian revolts in New Spain from 1680 to 1786 [177]. Pradeau and Rasmussen have translated, clarified and annotated Jesuit Juan Nentvig's well-known *Rudo Ensayo: A Description of Sonora and Arizona in 1764* [147]. This personal chronicle highlights both the frustrations missionaries underwent in trying to change native religion and lifestyle (in this case Pimas, Seris and Opatas) and the persistent ability of those tribes not decimated by disease and warfare to retain their cultural systems, all the while accommodating some outsiders and their belief systems, a theme also found in Dobyns's study of colonial Tucson for the Pimas and Papagos [48].

This continuity of persistent cultural systems, first set forth by

Edward Spicer [202] is best explored in his cumulative cultural history of the Yaquis [203] and in other tribally-focused anthropological/ethnohistorical works such as N. Ross Crumrine's book on the Mayo of Sonora [40]. Many contributors to the tribal ethnographies published in Alfonso Ortiz's *Handbook of North American Indians* volumes on the Southwest [153, 154] weave their articles on frameworks exploring cultural continuity as well as change across time.

The Pueblos are usually cited as the best example of persistent cultural systems wherein native religion and Catholicism were successfully compartmentalized into separate, but mutually tolerable spheres. Works by Spicer [201], Dozier [53, 55], Schroeder [186], Sando [179], Ortiz [153], and others support this. However, successful division of belief systems became realistic only after Spanish authorities and priests were made to understand through armed rebellion that native shamen could not be suppressed in the interest of the Christian mission. Resistance coalesced in the Great Pueblo Revolt of 1680. The recent tricentennial of that most successful native revolt in all of colonial North American history and contemporary interest in the history of Indian resistance movements in general have led to several new publications on the Revolt.

All of these substantiate France V. Scholes's contention in the 1930s that much conlict between Pueblos and Spaniards was the result of deep rift between Spanish civil and ecclesiastical authorities as well as between those two Hispanic groups and individual pueblos. These recent publications also build upon the work of Charles W. Hackett and C. C. Shelby, who first systematically analyzed the Revolt in 1942. Most important among the new literature are Henry W. Bowden's "Spanish Missions, Cultural Conflict and the Pueblo Revolt of 1680" [16], Joe S. Sando's "The Pueblo Revolt" article in Ortiz's *Southwest* [180], and articles by Simmons [195], Ortiz [152], Chávez [27], and Kessell [116] in a thematic issue of *El Palacio* on "The Pueblo People." Van H. Garner [66] and Jane C. Sánchez [178] have also contributed articles that clarify the interregnum between the Revolt of 1680 and the Reconquest of the 1690s. Once John L. Kessell has completed translation and editing of the papers of Diego de Vargas, governor and recolonizer of New Mexico, 1691-1704, we should know much more about the Revolt's aftermath.

Kessell's important *Kiva, Cross and Crown* [114] focuses on the history of Pecos Pueblo but contains themes for understanding all of New Mexican Spanish-Indian relations from 1540 to 1840. That work underscores the complexities of assigning causal factors to specific events in Borderlands history and shows that intergroup factionalism as well as a preference for autonomy characterized the Pueblos except during the collective revolt of 1680, participation in trading nexi throughout the Southwest, and in military alliances with Spaniards against common enemies—Plains Indian raiders.

Other important works on the missions include the following. For Florida: Robert A. Matter's "Missions in the Defense of Spanish Florida, 1566-1710" [136], a summary of his dissertation that focuses on the church-state feud typical not only of New Mexican history; Lana J. Loucks's doctoral thesis on political and economic interaction between Spaniards and Indians in Florida's mission communities [127]; Lewis H. Larson on Spanish missionary efforts among the Guales [122], which led to several Indian revolts in the late sixteenth century; and, James Covington on the Apalachee missions from 1704 to 1763 [37].

For New Mexico, in addition to works previously mentioned: Adams and Chávez's 1956 translation of *The Missions of New Mexico, 1776; A Description by Fray Francisco Atanasio Dominguez, with Other Contemporary Documents* [52] has been reissued and merits citation because of its unrivaled importance as a comprehensive document on all aspects of eighteenth-century Spanish-Pueblo relations. Kessell has produced the useful sequel in his work, *The Missions of New Mexico Since 1776* [115], a lavishly illustrated reference work; and, Simmons has contributed a translation of *Father Juan Agustín de Morfi's Account of Disorders in New Mexico, 1778* [197] as well as interpretive overviews on mission history in his "History of Pueblo-Spanish Relations" [194] and in his prize-winning *Albuquerque: A Narrative History* [196].

For Sonora and Arizona, Schmutz has produced "Jesuit Missionary Methods in Northwestern New Spain" [184]; McCarty [129], Griffen [78], and Polzer [160, 162] have added to our knowledge of Franciscan and Jesuit beginnings and methods; Voss has explained how "Societal Competition in Northwest New Spain" between settlers, soldiers, miners and priests led to widespread resentment of Jesuits [225]; Matson has translated and edited the useful "Letters of

Friar Pedro Font, 1776-1777" [134]; and, Kessell has produced two important narrative histories, one focusing on the troubled final years of the Jesuits at their "mission of sorrows," or Guevavi, 1691-1767 [111] and the much more ambitious sequel (after Franciscans took over) in *Friars, Soldiers and Reformers: Hispanic Arizona and the Sonora Mission Frontier, 1767-1856* [113]. Kessell's skills, patience and thoroughness in archival research as well as his humanizing, biographical approach to writing institutional histories, demonstrate the possibilities yet remaining for original contributions in micro- and macro-narrative studies. A central theme in his writing is the conflict between friars and bureaucrats with Indians caught in between, the subject of two separate articles for this region [112, 117].

For Texas, few studies have built upon Carlos Castañeda's *Our Catholic Heritage in Texas, 1519-1936* (1936-58) and Robert Weddle's monographs published in the 1960s on specific missions. Mardith Keithly Schuetz's dissertation, "The Indians of the San Antonio Missions, 1718-1821" [188] revises previous ideas that native population among Coahuiltecans, Karankawans and Tonkawans (all indigenous to Texas), steadily declined to insignificant numbers from first contact in the 1530s to the end of the Spanish era. Her study shows that at Mission San Antonio de Valero, waning native population stabilized and was on the increase by late colonial times, becoming by then, "as important to the make-up and development of San Antonio and southern Texas as any other ethnic group." Gary B. Starnes's *The San Gabriel Missions, 1746-1756* [205] is difficult to obtain but worth the effort despite his one-decade focus. Elizabeth John's overview [103] places importance on the missions in the context of Franco-Spanish rivalry, while Gilbert Cruz's dissertation traces municipalities in Texas from 1610-1810, with many observations on mission patterns [41].

Great interest has been taken in Indian land and water rights since the United States Indian Claims Commission began hearings in the 1940's. This topic is central to understanding Spanish-Indian relations in all areas of the Borderlands where colonies were planted among what Spaniards considered "civilized" or sedentary peoples. William B. Taylor has shown in his "Land and Water Rights in the Viceroyalty of New Spain" [214] that Indians within colonized regions were expected to provide tribute and/or labor, but they were also given protective guarantees for their lands and their usage of water to irrigate those lands. Prior use and residency were paramount in Indians' abilities throughout New Spain to obtain royal or viceregal protection of their homes, their land base and their livelihoods. Despite these guarantees, due to economic and political decisions, as well as demographic decline, many native towns lost land (without which their "rights" meant little). Landed estates developed; Spanish settlers squatted on Indian lands; and, in some cases, Spanish officials closed their eyes to abuses and illegalities.

Our present knowledge of how this general process in New Spain affected Borderlands communities is best for those areas where Indians' residency continued *in situ* after the Mexican and/or United States takeover in the nineteenth century. For New Mexico in particular, the literature is vast and has accelerated at a pace difficult to follow. Works by Jones [106] on Spanish settlement practices throughout the Borderlands and Simmons [192] specifically on New Mexico are beginning points for understanding Spanish-Indian co-occupation and co-utilization of lands and water. Richard Greenleaf's "Land and Water in Mexico and New Mexico, 1700-1821" [75] is an excellent comparative study of the legal and theoretical evolution of Pueblo land and water rights. Roxanne Dunbar Ortiz's *Roots of Resistance* [155] is the best overview of Pueblo land tenure under Spanish law and leads to the conclusion that what rights Indians were given in Spain and Mexico City did not always protect them on the frontier. Alvar W. Carlson's study of late eighteenth-century Spanish towns also indicates that illegal Spanish trespass on Indian lands was all too common among the northern Rio Grande Pueblos [22, 23]. Much of the disparity between theory and practice in Indian land rights was the result of policies designed to punish the Pueblos for their revolt of 1680, a point Myra Ellen Jenkins has made in the context of "Spanish Land Grants in the Tewa Area" [102]. Indians retained village sites and croplands, but their sizes were reduced along the fertile riverbanks desired by the Spanish colonists. Moreover, as other land grant studies have shown [149], many grants to Spaniards overlapped previous grants to Pueblos.

Also overlapping were ideas about water usage and water rights. Pueblos had excellent irrigation techniques at the time of Spanish colonization so Spaniards borrowed these in constructing their own mother ditches and canals. Simmons [193], Ford [64], and Vlasich [226] have written on this. Experimentation with various systems of communal and private management led Spaniards to improvise common laws for maintenance and usage of ditches. Again, they learned from the Pueblos, and in turn gave their Indian neighbors such ideas as the elected *mayordomo* or ditch boss. In general, relations were compatible on the question of water, but altercations over Spanish stock fouling Indian water and eating native croplands were not uncommon. Nevertheless, Pueblos were better off in Spanish New Mexico than they would be under the "protection" of the United States, as Alvin R. Sunseri's study reveals [207].

Few specific studies provide comparative data for other Borderlands regions, but works by Heizer and Almquist [88], Hutchinson [101], and Cook [31] support Sunseri's conclusions for California Indians under post-Spanish regimes. Elsewhere, we now know from C. Richard Arena's study of "Land Settlement Policies and Practices in Spanish Louisiana" [6] that Christian Indians could legally hold land on a basis of equality with white settlers, but non-Christians (while protected legally by Spanish law) could alienate or transfer lands only with the governor's consent. This contrasts sharply with the southern Indian experience after 1783. The ethnic fluidity and economic reliance upon native trade by colonial Frenchmen and Spaniards in Louisiana changed demonstrably as the region changed flags across the eighteenth century, a pattern Daniel Usner has unfolded [220]. Clearly, southern Indians had more rights before American takeover, a theme that surfaces vividly in J. Leitch Wright's survey [234].

One facet of Spanish-Indian relations that indicates pragmatism on the parts of Spaniards in recognizing degrees of Indian sovereignty is treaty-making. For years, as Charles Gibson has pointed out [71], most historians have overlooked this. And for good reason. Treaties *per se* were not common in Spanish America, but they were concluded in the interest of expediency with eighteenth century tribal polities in both the Southwest and the Southeast. We have long known that such leaders as Juan Bautista de Anza resorted to pacification by purchase and by cementing military alliances with Comanches, Utes, Navajos and Jicarilla Apaches against other bands of

Apaches. The work of Frank Reeve [169], Frank McNitt [131], and J. Lee Correll [36] on the Navajos; Worcester [232] and Delores Gunnerson [79] on the Apaches; O'Neil [151] and Swadesh [208] on the Utes; and, Magnaghi [132] on the Comanches has provided new pieces to the old puzzles of Spanish relations with non-Puebloan peoples.

In the Southeast, treaties having a non-Hispanic look were formalized in several large congresses between native leaders and Spanish officials in the same period (1780s and 1790s) while treaties were being made in the Southwest. Holmes [94, 95], Kinnaird [118], Ewers [59], Zahendra [235], Tanner [212], and Green [74] have published on the history of treaty-making with Creeks, Choctaws, Chickasaws and other major southeastern tribes. Designed as diplomatic and military alliances to protect Spain against foreign powers (especially the English and Americans), these agreements guaranteed to tribes Spanish intervention against other white invasions of Indian lands, sovereignty over their villages and subsistence lands, and favorable trading relationships with Spanish subjects. Through treaties, Spain's last years in the eastern Borderlands were made more secure and her diplomacy with tribes improved markedly.

For most of the centuries of contact between Spaniards and Indians in the Borderlands, relations—socially, politically, economically and militarily—were strained and not as flexible as discussion of the abovementioned themes of accommodation might indicate. By the end of her North American tenure, Spain had managed to alienate, displace, dispossess and, however unintentionally, depopulate Native American polities and cultures in all parts of the Borderlands. However rigid social, cultural and ethnic boundaries had been throughout the three centuries of contact, at 1821, both the Iberian and mestizo invaders, as well as most tribes who managed to maintain population bases and viable degrees of sovereignty, had learned to accept each others' presence, often to mutual advantage. New strategies for survival and cultural maintenance would accompany Indians' responses to the Mexican and American periods thereafter.

Studies such as those cited in this essay demonstrate that we have moved away from thinking about both "Spaniards" and "Indians" as generic peoples respectively. Our improved bibliographical inventory of comparative and interdisciplinary scholarship, as well as continued publication of traditional histories, is evidence that Borderlands studies have moved well beyond the horizons seen by Bolton's generation. No longer can the serious scholar afford to focus exclusively on the Spaniard *or* the Indian whose lands he invaded and occupied. One without the other is but half the story; and, many full stories remain to be told.

Recent research tools designed to supplement older guides include the following: Henry P. Beers, *Spanish and Mexican Records of the American Southwest: A Bibliographic Guide to Archives and Manuscript Sources* [14]; Richard E. Greenleaf and Michael C. Meyer, editors, *Research in Mexican History: Topics, Methodology, Sources, and a Practical Guide to Field Research* [76]; Thomas C. Barnes, Thomas H. Naylor and Charles W. Polzer, preparers, *Northern New Spain: A Research Guide* [13], designed to acquaint the user with the "Documentary Relations of the Southwest" Project [161] of the Arizona State Museum; three bibliographical essays by O'Neill, Hébert and Gardiner included in John Francis McDermott, editor, *The Spanish in the Mississippi Valley, 1762-1804* [130]; Michael M. Harris, compiler, *Florida History: A Bibliography* [84]; William S. Coker and Jack D. L. Holmes, "Sources for the History of the Spanish Borderlands" [30]; Holmes, "Interpretations and Trends in the Study of the Spanish Borderlands: The Old Southwest" [93]; an excellent bibliographical essay, circa 1970 by John F. Bannon in his *The Spanish Borderlands Frontier* [11]; essays and the most comprehensive interdisciplinary bibliography published to date on the western Borderlands and northern Mexico in Stoddard, Nostrand and West, editors, *Borderlands Sourcebook* [206]; bibliographies accompanying volumes eight through ten, *California* [89] and *Southwest* [153, 154] of the *Handbook of North American Indians*; and, previous volumes relating to the region in the Center for the History of the American Indian Bibliographical Series, especially Dobyns [47], Dobyns and Euler [51], and O'Donnell [150].

Many other aspects of Spanish-Indian relations are found in the growing list of tribal histories, the subject of Peter Iverson's essay in this anthology; in the "Indian Tribal Series," edited by Dobyns and Euler; and, in the *American Indian Ethnohistory Series* from the United States Indian Claims Commission Proceedings and Hearings, edited by David Agee Horr.

ALPHABETICAL LIST

[1] Adams, David Bergen. 1971. "The Tlaxcalan Colonies of Spanish Coahuila and Nuevo León: An Aspect of the Settlement of Northern Mexico." Ph.D. dissertation, University of Texas at Austin. Ann Arbor: University Microfilms.

[2] Archer, Christon I. 1973. "The Deportation of the Barbarian Indians from the Internal Provinces of New Spain, 1789-1810." *The Americas* (Academy of American Franciscan History) 29:376-85.

[3] ———. 1974. "Pardos, Indians, and the Army of New Spain: Inter-Relationships and Conflicts, 1780-1810." *Journal of Latin American Studies* (Great Britain) 6:231-55.

[4] ———. 1977. "The Making of Spanish Indian Policy on the Northwest Coast." *New Mexico Historical Review* 52:45-69.

[5] ———. 1978. "Spanish Exploration and Settlement of the Northwest Coast in the Eighteenth Century." *Sound Heritage* (Canada) 7:32-53.

[6] Arena, C. Richard. 1974. "Land Settlement Policies and Practices in Spanish Louisiana." In John Francis McDermott, ed., *The Spanish in the Mississippi Valley, 1762-1804*, pp. 51-60. Urbana: University of Illinois Press.

[7] Archibald, Robert. 1978. "Acculturation and Assimilation in Colonial New Mexico." *New Mexico Historical Review* 53:205-18.

[8] Baker, Steven G. 1974. "Cofitachique: Fair Province of Carolina: History and Archaeology of the Carolina Indians." M. A. thesis, University of South Carolina. Ann Arbor: University Microfilms.

[9] Bakewell, Peter J. 1972. *Silver Mining and Society in Colonial Mexico, Zacatecas, 1546-1700*. Cambridge, Eng.: Cambridge University Press.

[10] ———. 1976. "Zacatecas: An Economic and Social Outline of a Silver Mining District, 1547-1700." In *Provinces of Early Mexico: Variants of Spanish American Regional Evolution*, ed. Ida Altman and James Lockhart, pp. 199-229. Los Angeles: UCLA Latin American Center.

[11] Bannon, John Francis. 1970. *The Spanish Borderlands Frontier, 1513-1821*. New York: Holt, Rinehart and Winston. Reissued, Albuquerque: University of New Mexico Press, 1974.

[12] ———. 1979. "The Mission as a Frontier Institution: Sixty Years of Interest and Research." *Western Historical Quarterly* 10:303-22.

[13] Barnes, Thomas C., Thomas H. Naylor, and Charles W. Polzer. 1981. *Northern New Spain: A Research Guide*. Tucson: University of Arizona Press.

[14] Beers, Henry P. 1979. *Spanish and Mexican Records of the American Southwest: A Bibliographic Guide to Archives and Manuscript Sources*. Tucson: University of Arizona Press.

[15] Borah, Woodrow. 1970. "The California Mission." In Charles Wollenberg, ed., *Ethnic Conflict in California History*, pp. 1-22. Los Angeles: Tinnon Brown, Inc.

[16] Bowden, Henry Warner. 1975. "Spanish Missions, Cultural Conflict and the Pueblo Revolt of 1680." *Church History* 44:217-28.

[17] Brading, David A. 1971. *Miners and Merchants in Bourbon Mexico, 1763-1810*. Cambridge, Eng.: Cambridge University Press.

[18] ———. 1973. "Government and Elite in Late Colonial Mexico." *Hispanic American Historical Review* 53:389-414.

[19] Brain, Jeffrey P., Alan Toth, and Antonio Rodríguez-Buckingham. 1974. "Ethnohistoric Archaeology and the Desoto Entrada into the Lower Mississippi Valley." In *The Conference on Historic Site Archaeology Papers* 7(1972):232-89. Columbia: Institute of Archaeology and Anthropology, University of South Carolina.

[20] Bushnell, Amy. 1978. "'That Demonic Game': The Campaign to Stop Indian Pelota Playing in Spanish Florida, 1675-1684." *The Americas* (Academy of American Franciscan History) 35:1-19.

[21] Campbell, Leon G. 1977. "The Spanish Presidio in Alta California during the Mission Period, 1769-1784." *Journal of the West* 16:63-77.

[22] Carlson, Alvar W. 1975. "Spanish-American Acquisition of Cropland Within the Northern Pueblo Indian Grants, New Mexico." *Ethnohistory* 22:95-110.

[23] ———. 1979. "El Rancho and Vadito: Spanish Settlements on Indian Land Grants." *El Palacio* 85:28-39.

[24] Carrasco, Pedro. 1975. "La transformación de la cultura indígena durante la colonia." *Historia Mexicana* 25:175-203.

[25] Castillo, Edward D. 1978. "The Impact of Euro-American Exploration and Settlement." In *California*, ed. Robert F. Heizer, Vol. 8 of *Handbook of North American Indians*, gen. ed. William C. Sturtevant, pp. 99-127. Washington: Smithsonian Institution.

[26] Chávez, Fray Angelico. 1979. "Genizaros." In *Southwest*, ed. Alfonso Ortiz, Vol. 9 of *Handbook of North American Indians*, gen. ed. William C. Sturtevant, pp. 198-200. Washington: Smithsonian Institution.

[27] Chávez, Thomas E. 1980-1981. "But Were They All Natives?" *El Palacio* 86(4):32.

[28] Chiappelli, Fredi, ed. 1978. *First Images of America: The Impact of the New World on the Old*. 2 vols. Berkeley and Los Angeles: University of California Press.

[29] Christiansen, Paige W. 1969. "The Presidio and the Borderlands: A Case Study." *Journal of the West* 8:29-37. Reprinted in *The Spanish Borderlands–A First Reader*, ed. Oakah L. Jones, Jr., pp. 78-86. See [107].

[30] Coker, William S., and Jack D. L. Holmes. 1971. "Sources for the History of the Spanish Borderlands." *Florida Historical Quarterly* 69:380-93.

[31] Cook, Sherburne F. 1976. *The Population of the California Indians, 1769-1970*. Berkeley: University of California Press.

[32] ———. 1978. "Historical Demography." In *California*, ed. Robert F. Heizer, Vol. 8 of *Handbook of North American Indians*, gen. ed. William C. Sturtevant, pp. 91-98. Washington: Smithsonian Institution.

[33] Cook, Warren L. 1973. *Flood Tide of Empire: Spain and the Pacific Northwest, 1543-1819*. New Haven: Yale University Press.

[34] Corbett, Theodore G. 1974. "Migration to a Spanish Imperial Frontier in the Seventeenth and Eighteenth Centuries: St. Augustine." *Hispanic American Historical Review* 54:414-30.

[35] ———. 1976. "Population Structure in Hispanic St. Augustine, 1629-1763." *Florida Historical Quarterly* 54:263-84.

[36] Correll, J. Lee, ed. 1976. *Through White Men's Eyes: A Contribution to Navajo History; A Chronological Record of the Navajo People from Earliest Times to the Treaty of June 1, 1868*. Window Rock, Arizona: Navajo Times Publishing Co.

[37] Covington, James W. 1972. "Apalachee Indians, 1704-1763." *Florida Historical Quarterly* 50:366-84.

[38] ———. 1975. "Relations between the Eastern Timucuan Indians and the French and Spanish, 1564-1567." In *Four Centuries of Southern Indians*, ed. Charles Hudson, pp. 11-27. Athens: University of Georgia Press.

[39] Crosby, Alfred W., Jr. 1972. *The Columbian Exchange: Biological and Cultural Consequences of 1492*. Westport, Conn.: Greenwood Press.

[40] Crumrine, N. Ross. 1977. *The Mayo Indians of Sonora: A People Who Refuse to Die*. Tucson: University of Arizona Press.

[41] Cruz, Gilbert Ralph. 1974. "Spanish Town Patterns in the Borderlands: Municipal Origins in Texas and the Southwest, 1610-1810." Ph.D. dissertation, Saint Louis University. Ann Arbor: University Microfilms.

[42] Deagan, Kathleen. 1973. "Mestizaje in Colonial St. Augustine." *Ethnohistory* 20:55-65.

[43] ———. 1978. "Cultures in Transition: Fusion and Assimilation among the Eastern Timucua." In *Tacachale: Essays on the Indians of Florida and Southeastern Georgia during the Historic Period*, ed. J. T. Milanich and S. Proctor, pp. 89-119. See [139].

[44] ———. 1980. "Archaeology in the Ancient City: Past, Present and Future." In *Spanish Colonial Frontier Research*, comp. and ed. Henry F. Dobyns, pp. 47-54. Spanish Borderlands Research No. 1. Albuquerque: Center for Anthropological Studies.

[45] DePratter, Chester B., and Marvin T. Smith. 1980. "Sixteenth Century European Trade in the Southeastern United States: Evidence from the Juan Pardo Expeditions (1566-1568)." In *Spanish Colonial Frontier Research*, comp. and ed. Henry F. Dobyns, pp. 67-77.

Spanish Borderlands Research No. 1. Albuquerque: Center for Anthropological Studies.

[46] Di Peso, Charles C., et al. 1974. *Casas Grandes, A Fallen Trading Center of the Gran Chichimeca*. 8 vols. Flagstaff, Arizona: Northland Press for the Amerind Foundation.

[47] Dobyns, Henry F. 1976. *Native American Historical Demography: A Critical Bibliography*. Bloomington: Indiana University Press for The Newberry Library.

[48] ———. 1976. *Spanish Colonial Tucson: A Demographic History*. Tucson: University of Arizona Press.

[49] ———. 1980. "The Study of Spanish Colonial Frontier Institutions." In *Spanish Colonial Frontier Research*, comp. and ed. Henry F. Dobyns, pp. 5-26. Spanish Borderlands Research No. 1. Albuquerque: Center for Anthropological Studies.

[50] ———. 1983. *Their Number Become Thinned: Essays on Native American Population Dynamics in Eastern North America*. Knoxville: University of Tennessee Press.

[51] Dobyns, Henry F., and Robert C. Euler. 1980. *Indians of the Southwest: A Critical Bibliography*. Bloomington: Indiana University Press for The Newberry Library.

[52] Dominguez, Francisco A. [1956] 1975. *The Missions of New Mexico, 1776; a Description by Fray Francisco Atanasio Dominguez, with Other Contemporary Documents*, trans. Eleanor B. Adams and Fray Angélico Chávez. Albuquerque: University of New Mexico Press. Reprinted, 1975.

[53] Dozier, Edward P. 1970. *The Pueblo Indians of North America*. New York: Holt, Rinehart and Winston.

[54] ———. 1971. "The American Southwest." In Eleanor Burke Leacock and Nancy Oestreich Lurie, eds., *North American Indians in Historical Perspective*, pp. 228-56. New York: Random House.

[55] ———. 1972. "Pueblo Indian Response to Culture Contact." In *Studies in Linguistics in Honor of George L. Trager*, ed. M. Estellie Smith, pp. 457-67. The Hague: Mouton.

[56] Dunlay, Thomas William. 1981. "Indian Allies in the Armies of New Spain and the United States: A Comparative Study." *New Mexico Historical Review* 56:239-60.

[57] Elliott, J. H. 1970. *The Old World and the New, 1492-1650*. London: Cambridge University Press.

[58] Engstrand, Iris H. W. 1981. *Spanish Scientists in the New World: The Eighteenth Century Expeditions*. Seattle and London: University of Washington Press.

[59] Ewers, John C. 1974. "Symbols of Chiefly Authority in Spanish Louisiana." In John Francis McDermott, ed., *The Spanish in The Mississippi Valley, 1762-1804*, pp. 272-86. Urbana: University of Illinois Press.

[60] Fairbanks, Charles H. 1976. "From Missionary to Mestizo: Chang-

ing Culture of Eighteenth Century St. Augustine." In *Eighteenth Century Florida and the Caribbean*, ed. Samuel Proctor, pp. 88-99. Gainesville: University Presses of Florida.

[61] ———. 1980. "Archaeology and Ethnohistory in Colonial St. Augustine." In *Spanish Colonial Frontier Research*, comp. and ed. Henry F. Dobyns, pp. 41-46. Spanish Borderlands Research No. 1. Albuquerque: Center for Anthropological Studies.

[62] Faulk, Odie B. 1969. "The Presidio: Fortress or Farce?" *Journal of the West* 8:22-28. Reprinted in *The Spanish Borderlands–A First Reader*, ed. Oakah L. Jones, Jr., pp. 70-77. See [107]. Reprinted in *New Spain's Far Northern Frontier*, ed. David J. Weber, pp. 67-76. See [228].

[63] Forbes, Jack D. 1971. "The Native American Experience in California History." *California Historical Quarterly* 50:234-42.

[64] Ford, Richard I. 1977. "The Technology of Irrigation in a New Mexico Pueblo." In *Material Culture*, ed. Heather Lechtman and Robert Merrill. Seattle: University of Washington Press.

[65] Friede, Juan, and Benjamin Keen, eds. 1971. *Bartolomé de Las Casas in History: Toward an Understanding of the Man and His Work*. DeKalb: Northern Illinois University Press.

[66] Garner, Van H. 1979. "The Dynamics of Change: New Mexico 1680 to 1690." *Journal of the West* 18:4-13.

[67] Garr, Daniel. 1972. "Planning, Politics and Plunder: The Missions and Indian Pueblos of Hispanic California." *Southern California Quarterly* 54:291-312.

[68] Gerhard, Peter H. 1972. *Introduction to the Historical Geography of New Spain*. Cambridge, Eng.: Cambridge University Press.

[69] ———. 1977. "Congregaciones de indios en la Nueva España antes de 1570." *Historia Mexicana* 26:347-95.

[70] ———. 1982. *The North Frontier of New Spain*. Princeton: Princeton University Press.

[71] Gibson, Charles. 1978. "Conquest, Capitulation and Indian Treaties." *American Historical Review* 83:1-15.

[72] Gibson, Charles, ed. 1971. *The Black Legend: Anti-Spanish Attitudes in the Old World and the New*. New York: Alfred A. Knopf.

[73] Gold, Robert L. 1970. "Conflict in San Carlos: Indian Immigrants in Eighteenth Century New Spain." *Ethnohistory* 17:1-10.

[74] Green, Michael D. 1980. "Alexander McGillivray." In *American Indian Leaders: Studies in Diversity*, ed. R. David Edmunds, pp. 41-63. Lincoln: University of Nebraska Press.

[75] Greenleaf, Richard E. 1972. "Land and Water in New Mexico and Mexico, 1700-1821." *New Mexico Historical Review* 47:85-112.

[76] Greenleaf, Richard E., and Michael C. Meyer, eds. 1973. *Research in Mexican History: Topics, Methodology, Sources, and a Practical Guide to Field Research*. Lincoln: University of Nebraska Press.

[77] Grieshaber, Erwin P. 1979. "Hacienda-Indian Community Rela-

tions and Indian Acculturation: An Historiographical Essay" *Latin American Research Review* 14:107-28.

[78] Griffen, William B. 1979. *Indian Assimilation in the Franciscan Area of Nueva Vizcaya*. Anthropological Papers of the University of Arizona No. 33. Tucson: University of Arizona Press.

[79] Gunnerson, Delores A. 1974. *The Jicarilla Apaches: A Study in Survival*. DeKalb: Northern Illinois University Press.

[80] Guest, Francis F. 1979. "An Examination of the Thesis of S. F. Cook on the Forced Conversion of the Indians in the California Missions." *Southern California Quarterly* 61:1-77.

[81] Hally, David J. 1971. "The Archaeology of European-Indian Contact in the Southeast." In *Red, White, and Black: Symposium on Indians in the Old South*, ed. Charles M. Hudson, pp. 55-66. Southern Anthropological Society Proceedings 5. Athens: University of Georgia for the Southern Anthropological Society.

[82] Hanke, Lewis. 1969. "Indians and Spaniards in the New World: A Personal View." In *Attitudes of Colonial Powers toward the American Indian*, ed. Howard Peckham and Charles Gibson, pp. 1-18. Salt Lake City: University of Utah Press.

[83] ———. 1971. "A Modest Proposal for a Moratorium on Grand Generalizations: Some Thoughts on the Black Legend." *Hispanic American Historical Review* 51:112-27.

[84] Harris, Michael H., comp. 1972. *Florida History: A Bibliography*. Metuchen, N.J.: Scarecrow Press.

[85] Hedrick, Basil C., ed., with J. Charles Kelley and Carroll L. Riley. 1971. *The North Mexican Frontier: Readings in Archaeology, Ethnohistory and Ethnography*. Carbondale: Southern Illinois University Press.

[86] Hedrick, Basil C., J. Charles Kelley, and Carroll L. Riley, eds. 1974. *The Mesoamerican Southwest: Readings in Archaeology, Ethnohistory and Ethnology*. Carbondale and Edwardsville: Southern Illinois University Press.

[87] Hedrick, Basil C., and Carroll L. Riley, trans. and eds. 1976. *Documents Ancillary to the Vaca Journey*. University Museum Studies 5. Carbondale: University Museum and Art Galleries, Southern Illinois University.

[88] Heizer, Robert F., and Alan F. Almquist. 1971. *The Other Californians: Prejudice and Discrimination under Spain, Mexico and the United States to 1920*. Berkeley and Los Angeles: University of California Press.

[89] Heizer, Robert F., ed. 1978. *California*. Volume 8 of *Handbook of North American Indians*, gen. ed. William C. Sturtevant. Washington: Smithsonian Institution.

[90] Hernández, José B. 1976. "Opposing Views of La Florida: Álvar Núñez Cabeza de Vaca and El Inca Garcilaso de la Vega." *Florida Historical Quarterly* 55:170-80.

[91] Hoffman, Paul E. 1980. "A New Voyage of North American Discovery: Pedro de Salazar's Visit to the 'Island of Giants'." *Florida Historical Quarterly* 58:415-26.

[92] ———. 1980. *The Spanish Crown and the Defense of the Caribbean, 1535-1585*. Baton Rouge: Louisiana State University Press.

[93] Holmes, Jack D. L. 1971. "Interpretations and Trends in the Study of the Spanish Borderlands: The Old Southwest." *Southwestern Historical Quarterly* 74:461-77.

[94] ———. 1975. "Spanish Policy toward the Southern Indians in the 1790s." In *Four Centuries of Southern Indians*, ed. Charles Hudson, pp. 65-82. Athens: University of Georgia Press.

[95] ———. 1978. "Up the Tombigbee with the Spaniards: Juan de la Villebeuvre and the Treaty of Boucfouca (1793)." *Alabama Historical Quarterly* 40:51-61.

[96] ———. 1980. "Juan de la Villebeuvre and Spanish Indian Policy in West Florida, 1784-1797." *Florida Historical Quarterly* 58:387-99.

[97] Honour, Hugh. 1975. *The New Golden Land: European Images of American from the Discoveries to the Present Time*. New York: Pantheon Books.

[98] Hu-DeHart, Evelyn. 1981. *Missionaries, Miners and Indians: Spanish Contact with the Yaqui Nation of Northwestern New Spain, 1533-1820*. Tucson: University of Arizona Press.

[99] Hudson, Charles M. 1970. *The Catawba Nation*. University of Georgia Monographs 18. Athens: University of Georgia Press.

[100] ———. 1976. *The Southeastern Indians*. Knoxville: University of Tennessee Press.

[101] Hutchinson, C. Alan. 1969. "The California Frontier," from *Frontier Settlement in Mexican California: The Híjar-Padrés Colony and Its Origins*. New Haven: Yale University Press, pp. 393-99. Reprinted in *New Spain's Far Northern Frontier: Essays on Spain in the American West, 1540-1821*, ed. David J. Weber, pp. 171-77. Albuquerque: University of New Mexico Press, 1979.

[102] Jenkins, Myra Ellen. 1972. "Spanish Land Grants in the Tewa Area." *New Mexico Historical Review* 47:113-34.

[103] John, Elizabeth A. H. 1975. *Storms Brewed in Other Men's Worlds: The Confrontation of Indians, Spanish and French in the Southwest, 1540-1795*. College Station, Texas: Texas A & M University Press. Reprinted, Lincoln: University of Nebraska Press, 1981.

[104] Jones, Grant D. 1978. "The Ethnohistory of the Guale Coast through 1684." In David Hurst Thomas, et al., *The Anthropology of St. Catherines Island*, pp. 179-210. Anthropological Papers of the American Museum of Natural History 55, part 2.

[105] Jones, Oakah L., Jr. 1969. "The Spanish Borderlands— Introduction" and "A Selected Reading List." *Journal of the West* 8:1-6, 137-42.

[106] ———. 1979. *Los Paisanos: Spanish Settlers on the Northern Frontier of New Spain*. Norman: University of Oklahoma Press.

[107] ———, ed. 1974. *The Spanish Borderlands–A First Reader*. Los Angeles: Lorrin L. Morrison Publisher.

[108] Keen, Benjamin. 1969. "The Black Legend Revisited: Assumptions and Realities." *Hispanic American Historical Review* 49:703-19.

[109] ———. 1971. "The White Legend Revisited: A Reply to Professor Hanke's 'Modest Proposal'." *Hispanic American Historical Review* 51:336-55.

[110] Keith, Robert G. 1971. "Encomienda, Hacienda and Corregimiento in Spanish America: A Structural Analysis." *Hispanic American Historical Review* 51:431-46.

[111] Kessell, John L. 1970. *Mission of Sorrows: Jesuit Guevavi and the Pimas, 1691-1767*. Tucson: University of Arizona Press.

[112] ———. 1975. "Friars, Bureaucrats, and the Seris of Sonora." *New Mexico Historical Review* 50:73-95.

[113] ———. 1976. *Friars, Soldiers, and Reformers: Hispanic Arizona and the Sonora Mission Frontier, 1767-1856*. Tucson: University of Arizona Press.

[114] ———. 1979. *Kiva, Cross and Crown: The Pecos Indians and New Mexico, 1540-1840*. Washington: Government Printing Office for the National Park Service.

[115] ———. 1980. *The Missions of New Mexico Since 1776*. Albuquerque: University of New Mexico Press.

[116] ———. 1980-1981. "Esteban Clemente: Precursor of the Revolt." *El Palacio* 86:16-17.

[117] ———., ed. 1972. "Anza Damns the Missions: A Spanish Soldier's Criticism of Indian Policy, 1772." *The Journal of Arizona History* 13:53-63.

[118] Kinnaird, Lawrence. 1979. "Spanish Treaties with Indian Tribes." *Western Historical Quarterly* 10:39-48.

[119] Kutsche, Paul. 1983. "Borders and Frontiers." In Ellwyn R. Stoddard, Richard L. Nostrand and Jonathan P. West, eds., *Borderlands Sourcebook: A Guide to the Literature on Northern Mexico and the American Southwest*, pp. 16-19. Norman: University of Oklahoma Press.

[120] Lange, Charles H. 1979. "Relations of the Southwest with the Plains and Great Basin." In *Southwest*, ed. Alfonso Ortiz, Vol. 9 of *Handbook of North American Indians*, gen. ed. William C. Sturtevant, pp. 201-05. Washington: Smithsonian Institution.

[121] Langellier, John Phillip, and Katherine Meyers Peterson. 1981. "Lances and Leather Jackets: Presidial Forces in Spanish Alta California, 1769-1821." *Journal of the West* 20:3-11.

[122] Larson, Lewis H. 1978. "Historic Guale Indians of the Georgia Coast and the Impact of the Spanish Mission Effort." In *Tacachale*, ed. J.T. Milanich and S. Proctor, pp. 120-49. See [139].

[123] Laudonnière, René Goulaine de. [1586] 1975 . *Three Voyages*. Trans-

lated with an introduction and notes by Charles E. Bennett. Gainesville: University Presses of Florida.
[124] Lewis, Clifford M. 1978. "The Calusa." In *Tacachale*, ed. J. T. Milanich and S. Proctor, pp. 19-49. See [139].
[125] Lockhart, James. 1969. "Encomienda and Hacienda: The Evolution of the Great Estate in the Spanish Indies." *Hispanic American Historical Review* 49:411-29.
[126] López Sarrelangue, Delfina. 1973. "Mestizaje y catolicismo en la Nueva España." *Historia Mexicana* 23:1-42.
[127] Loucks, Lana Jill. 1979. "Political and Economic Interactions between Spaniards and Indians: Archeological and Ethnohistorical Perspectives of the Mission System in Florida." Ph.D. dissertation, University of Florida. Ann Arbor: University Microfilms.
[128] Lyon, Eugene. 1976. *The Enterprise of Florida: Pedro Menéndez de Aviles and the Spanish Conquest, 1565-1568*. Gainesville: University Presses of Florida.
[129] McCarty, Kieran Robert. 1974. "Franciscan Beginnings on the Arizona-Sonora Desert, 1767-1770." Ph.D. dissertation, Catholic University of America, 1973. Ann Arbor: University Microfilms.
[130] McDermott, John Francis, ed. 1974. *The Spanish in the Mississippi Valley, 1762-1804*. Urbana: University of Illinois Press.
[131] McNitt, Frank. 1972. *Navajo Wars: Military Campaigns, Slave Raids, and Reprisals*. Albuquerque: University of Mexico Press.
[132] Magnaghi, Russell Mario. 1970. "The Indian Slave Trader: The Comanche, A Case Study." Ph.D. dissertation, Saint Louis University. Ann Arbor: University Microfilms.
[133] ———. 1975. "The Role of Indian Slavery in Colonial St. Louis." *Bulletin of the Missouri Historical Society* 31:264-72.
[134] Matson, Daniel S., trans. 1975. "Letters of Friar Pedro Pont, 1776-1777, Translation." *Ethnohistory* 22:263-93.
[135] Matson, Daniel S., trans., and Bernard L. Fontana, ed. 1977. *Friar Bringas Reports to the King: Methods of Indoctrination on the Frontier of New Spain, 1796-1797*. Tucson: University of Arizona Press.
[136] Matter, Robert A. 1975. "Missions in the Defense of Spanish Florida, 1566-1710." *Florida Historical Quarterly* 54:18-38.
[137] Milanich, Jerald T. 1978. "The Western Timucua: Patterns of Acculturation and Change." In *Tacachale*, ed. J. T. Milanich and S. Proctor, pp. 59-88. See [139].
[138] Milanich, Jerald T., and William C. Sturtevant, eds. 1972. *Francisco Pareja's 1613 Confessionario: A Documentary Source for Timucuan Ethnography*. Tallahassee: Florida Department of State, Division of Archives, History and Records Management.
[139] Milanich, Jerald T., and Samuel Proctor, eds. 1978. *Tacachale: Essays on the Indians of Florida and Southeastern Georgia during the Historic Period*. Gainesville: University Presses of Florida.

[140] Miller, Robert R. 1974. "Cortes and the First Attempt to Colonize California." *California Historical Quarterly* 53:4-16.
[141] Moorhead, Max L. 1969. "The Soldado de Cuera: Stalwart of the Spanish Borderlands." *Journal of the West* 8:38-55.
[142] ———. 1975. *The Presidio: Bastion of the Spanish Borderlands*. Norman: University of Oklahoma Press.
[143] Mörner, Magnus. 1973. "The Spanish American Hacienda: A Survey of Recent Research and Debate." *Hispanic American Historical Review* 53:183-216.
[144] Moziño, José Mariano. [1913] 1970. *Noticias de Nutka: An Account of Nootka Sound in 1792*, trans. and ed. Iris Higbie Wilson (Engstrand). Seattle: University of Washington Press.
[145] Muir, Gertrude H. 1977. "The Spanish Entrada into the Southwest, 1528-1610: A Selective Checklist." *American Book Collector* 23:17-24.
[146] Navarro, Isidoro Moreno. 1973. *Los cuadros del mestizaje americano. Estudio anthropológico del mestizaje*. Colección Chimalistac 34. Madrid: José Porrua Turanzas.
[147] Nentvig, Juan. [1863] 1980. *Rudo Ensayo, tentative de una prevencional descripción geográfica de la Provincia de Sonora*, ed. Buckingham Smith. Albany: Munsell. New edition, trans. Alberto F. Pradeau and Robert R. Rasmussen, issued as *Rudo Ensayo: A Description of Sonora and Arizona in 1764*. Tucson: University of Arizona Press, 1980.
[148] Nostrand, Richard L. 1983. "A Changing Culture Region." In Ellwyn R. Stoddard, Richard L. Nostrand and Jonathan P. West, eds., *Borderlands Sourcebook: A Guide to the Literature on Northern Mexico and the American Southwest*, pp. 6-15. Norman: University of Oklahoma Press.
[149] Oczon, Annabelle M. 1982. "Land Grants in New Mexico: A Selective Bibliography." *New Mexico Historical Review* 57:81-88.
[150] O'Donnell, James Howlett, III. 1982. *Southeastern Frontiers: Europeans, Africans, and American Indians, 1513-1840–A Critical Bibliography*. Bloomington: Indiana University Press for The Newberry Library.
[151] O'Neil, Floyd A. 1973. "A History of the Ute Indians of Utah until 1890." Ph.D. dissertation, University of Utah. Ann Arbor: University Microfilms.
[152] Ortiz, Alfonso. 1980-1981. "Popay's Leadership: A Pueblo Perspective." *El Palacio* 86:18-22.
[153] ———, ed. 1979. *Southwest*. Vol. 9 of *Handbook of North American Indians*, gen. ed. William C. Sturtevant. Washington: Smithsonian Institution.
[154] ———, ed. 1983. *Southwest*. Vol. 10 of *Handbook of North American Indians*, gen. ed. William C. Sturtevant. Washington: Smithsonian Institution.
[155] Ortiz, Roxanne Dunbar. 1980. *Roots of Resistance: Land Tenure in*

New Mexico, 1680-1980. Los Angeles: Chicano Studies Research Center and American Indian Studies Center, University of California at Los Angeles.

[156] Pailes, R. A., and Joseph W. Whitecotton. 1979. "The Greater Southwest and the Mesoamerican 'World' System: An Exploratory Model of Frontier Relationships." In *The Frontier: Comparative Studies, Volume Two*, ed. William W. Savage and Stephen I. Thompson, pp. 105-22. Norman: University of Oklahoma Press.

[157] Pethick, Derek. 1976. *First Approaches to the Northwest Coast*. Vancouver: Douglas and McIntyre.

[158] Phillips, George Harwood. 1974. "Indians and the Breakdown of the Spanish Mission System in California." *Ethnohistory* 21:291-301. Reprinted, with minor alterations in *New Spain's Far Northern Frontier*, ed. David J. Weber, pp. 257-69. See [228].

[159] ———. 1975. *Chiefs and Challengers: Indian Resistance and Cooperation in Southern California*. Berkeley: University of California Press.

[160] Polzer, Charles W. 1976. *Rules and Precepts of the Jesuit Missions of Northwestern New Spain*. Tucson: University of Arizona Press.

[161] ———. 1978. "The Documentary Relations of the Southwest." *Hispanic American Historical Review* 58:460-65.

[162] ———, ed. 1972. "The Franciscan Entrada into Sonora, 1645-1652: A Jesuit Chronicle." *Arizona and the West* 14:253-78.

[163] Powell, Philip Wayne. 1971. *Tree of Hate: Propaganda and Prejudices Affecting United States Relations with the Hispanic World*. New York: Basic Books.

[164] ———. 1977. *Mexico's Miguel Caldera: The Taming of America's First Frontier, 1548-1597*. Tucson: University of Arizona Press.

[165] ———. 1982. "Genesis of the Frontier Presidio in North America." *Western Historical Quarterly* 13:125-41.

[166] Purdy, Barbara A. 1977. "Weapons, Strategies and Tactics of the Europeans and the Indians in 16th and 17th Century Florida." *Florida Historical Quarterly* 56:259-76.

[167] Quinn, David Beers. 1977. *North America from Earliest Discovery to First Settlements: The Norse Voyages to 1612*. New York: Harper and Row.

[168] ———, ed. 1979. *New American World: A Documentary History of North America to 1612*. 5 vols. New York: Arno Press and Hector Bye.

[169] Reeve, Frank D. 1971. "Navaho Foreign Affairs, 1795-1846," ed. Eleanor B. Adams and John L. Kessell. *New Mexico Historical Review* 66:100-32, 233-51.

[170] Reilly, Stephen Edward. 1981. "A Marriage of Expedience: The Calusa Indians and Their Relations with Pedro Menendez de Aviles in Southwest Florida, 1566-1569." *Florida Historical Quarterly* 59:395-421.

[171] Riley, Carroll L. 1971. "Early Spanish-Indian Communication in the Greater Southwest." *New Mexico Historical Review* 66:284-313.

[172] ———. 1974. "Mesoamerican Indians in the Early Southwest." *Ethnohistory* 21:25-36.

[173] ———. 1976. *Sixteenth Century Trade in the Greater Southwest.* Mesoamerican Studies 10. Carbondale: University Museum and Art Galleries, Southern Illinois University.

[174] Riley, Carroll L., and Basil C. Hedrick, eds. 1978. *Across the Chichimec Sea: Papers in Honor of J. Charles Kelley*. Carbondale: Southern Illinois University Press.

[175] Robinson, W. Stitt, Jr. 1979. *The Southern Colonial Frontier, 1607-1763*. Albuquerque: University of New Mexico Press.

[176] Rodack, Madeleine Turrell, trans. and ed. 1981. *Adolph F. Bandelier's The Discovery of New Mexico by the Franciscan Monk, Friar Marcos de Niza in 1539*. Tucson: University of Arizona Press.

[177] Salmón, Roberto Mario. 1978. "Indian Revolts in Northern New Spain, 1680-1786—A Comparative Analysis." Ph.D. dissertation, University of New Mexico.

[178] Sánchez, Jane C. 1983. "Spanish-Indian Relations during the Otermín Administration, 1677-1683." *New Mexico Historical Review* 58:133-51.

[179] Sando, Joe. 1976. *The Pueblo Indians*. San Francisco: Indian Historian Press.

[180] ———. 1979. "The Pueblo Revolt." In *Southwest,* ed. Alfonso Ortiz, Vol. 9 of *Handbook of North American Indians*, gen. ed. William C. Sturtevant, pp. 194-197. Washington: Smithsonian Institution.

[181] Sauceda, Judith Brostoff. 1979. "From the Inner Circle: The Relationship of the Space Occupied, Past and Present, by Southwest American Indian Women to the Southwest Indo-Hispanic Women of Yesteryear and Today." Ph.D. diss., University of Colorado, Boulder. Ann Arbor: University Microfilms.

[182] Sauer, Carl Ortwin. 1971. *Sixteenth Century North America: The Land and the People as Seen by the First Europeans*. Berkeley: University of California Press.

[183] ———. 1980. *Seventeenth Century North America*. Berkeley: Turtle Island Press.

[184] Schmutz, Richard. 1969. "Jesuit Missionary Methods in Northwestern Mexico." *Journal of the West* 8:76-89.

[185] Schroeder, Albert H. 1979. "Shifting for Survival in the Spanish Southwest." In *New Spain's Far Northern Frontier: Essays on Spain in the American West, 1540-1821*, ed. David J. Weber. Albuquerque: University of New Mexico Press, pp. 237-55. Originally published in *New Mexico Historical Review* 43(1968): 291-310.

[186] ———. 1972. "Rio Grande Ethnohistory." In *New Perspectives on the Pueblos*, ed. Alfonso Ortiz, pp. 41-70. Albuquerque: University of New Mexico Press for the School of American Research.

[187] ———. 1979. "Pueblos Abandoned in Historic Times." In *Southwest*, ed. Alfonso Ortiz, Vol. 9 of *Handbook of North American Indians*, gen. ed. William C. Sturtevant, pp. 236-54. Washington: Smithsonian Institution.

[188] Schuetz, Mardith Keithly. 1980. "The Indians of the San Antonio Missions, 1718-1821." Ph.D. dissertation, University of Texas at Austin. Ann Arbor: University Microfilms.

[189] Servín, Manuel Patricio. 1973. "California's Hispanic Heritage: A View into the Spanish Myth." *Journal of San Diego History* 19:1-9. Reprinted in *New Spain's Far Northern Frontier: Essays on Spain in the American West, 1540-1821*, ed. David J. Weber, pp. 117-33. See [228].

[190] Sheridan, Thomas E. 1979. "Cross or Arrow? The Breakdown in Spanish-Seri Relations, 1729-1750." *Arizona and the West* 21:317-34.

[191] Sheridan, Thomas E., and Thomas H. Naylor, eds. 1979. *Rarámuri: A Tarahumara Colonial Chronicle, 1607-1791*. Flagstaff: Northland Press.

[192] Simmons, Marc. 1969. "Settlement Patterns and Village Plans in Colonial New Mexico." *Journal of the West* 8:7-21. Reprinted in *New Spain's Far Northern Frontier*, ed. David J. Weber, pp. 97-115. See [228].

[193] ———. 1972. "Spanish Irrigation Practices in New Mexico." *New Mexico Historical Review* 47:135-50.

[194] ———. 1979. "History of Pueblo-Spanish Relations to 1821." In *Southwest*, ed. Alfonso Ortiz, Vol. 9 of *Handbook of North American Indians*, gen. ed. William C. Sturtevant, pp. 178-93. Washington: Smithsonian Institution.

[195] ———. 1980-1981. "The Pueblo Revolt: Why Did It Happen?" *El Palacio* 86:11-15.

[196] ———. 1982. *Albuquerque: A Narrative History*. Albuquerque: University of New Mexico Press.

[197] ———, trans. and ed. 1977. *Father Juan Agustín de Morfi's Account of Disorders in New Mexico, 1778*. Isleta Pueblo, New Mexico: Rev. James T. Burke for the Historical Society of New Mexico.

[198] Sizelove, Linda. 1978. "Indian Adaptations to the Spanish Missions." *Pacific Historian* 22:393-402.

[199] Smith, Hale G., and Mark Gottlob. 1978. "Spanish-Indian Relationships: Synoptic History and Archaeological Evidence, 1500-1763." In *Tacachale*, ed. J. T. Milanich and S. Proctor, pp. 1-18. See [139].

[200] South, Stanley. 1980. *The Discovery of Santa Elena*. Research Manuscript Series 165. Columbia, S.C.: University of South Carolina Institute of Archeology and Anthropology.

[201] Spicer, Edward H. 1969. "Political Incorporation and Cultural Change in New Spain: A Study in Spanish-Indian Relations." In *Attitudes of Colonial Powers toward the American Indian*, ed. Howard Peckham and Charles Gibson, pp. 107-35. Salt Lake City: University of Utah Press.

[202] ———. 1971. "Persistent Cultural Systems." *Science* 174:795-800.

[203] ———. 1980. *The Yaquis: A Cultural History*. Tucson: University of Arizona Press.

[204] Spicer, Edward H., and Raymond H. Thompson, eds. 1972. *Plural Society in the Southwest*. New York: Interbook, Inc. for the Weatherhead Foundation.

[205] Starnes, Gary B. 1969. *The San Gabriel Missions, 1746-1756*. Madrid: Ministry of Foreign Affairs.

[206] Stoddard, Ellwyn R., Richard L. Nostrand, and Jonathan P. West, eds. 1983. *Borderlands Sourcebook: A Guide to the Literature on Northern Mexico and the American Southwest*. Norman: University of Oklahoma Press.

[207] Sunseri, Alvin R. 1973. "Agricultural Techniques in New Mexico at the Time of the Anglo-American Conquest." *Agricultural History* 47:329-37.

[208] Swadesh, Frances Leon. 1974. *Los Primeros Pobladores: Hispanic Americans of the Ute Frontier*. Notre Dame, Ind. and London: University of Notre Dame Press.

[209] ———. 1979. "Structure of Hispanic-Indian Relations in New Mexico." *Colorado College Studies* 15:53-61.

[210] Swagerty, William R. 1981. "Beyond Bimini: Indian Responses to European Incursions in the Spanish Borderlands, 1513-1600." Ph.D. dissertation, University of California at Santa Barbara. Ann Arbor: University Microfilms.

[211] Swann, Michael M. 1980. "Population and Settlement in Late Colonial Nueva Vizcaya: The Causes, Patterns and Consequences of Demographic Change in a Frontier Region." Ph.D. dissertation, Syracuse University. Ann Arbor: University Microfilms.

[212] Tanner, Helen Hornbeck. 1975. "Pipesmoke and Muskets: Florida Indian Intrigues of the Revolutionary Era." In *Eighteenth Century Florida and Its Borderlands*, ed. Samuel Proctor, pp. 13-39. Gainesville: University Presses of Florida.

[213] Taylor, William B. 1974. "Landed Society in New Spain: A View from the South." *Hispanic American Historical Review* 54:387-413.

[214] ———. 1975. "Land and Water Rights in the Viceroyalty of New Spain." *New Mexico Historical Review* 50:189-212.

[215] TePaske, John J. 1975. "Spanish-Indian Policy and the Struggle for Empire in the Southeast, 1513-1776." In *Contest for Empire, 1500-1775: Proceedings of an Indiana American Revolution Bicentennial Symposium*, ed. John B. Elliot, pp. 25-40. Indianapolis: Indiana Historical Society.

[216] Theisen, Gerald, ed. 1972. *The Narrative of Alvar Núñez Cabeza de Vaca*. Translated by Fanny Bandelier with an introduction by John Francis Bannon, illustrated by Michael McCurdy, with Oviedo's version of the lost Joint Report Presented to the Audiencia of Santo

Domingo, translated by Gerald Theisen. Barre, Mass.: Imprint Society.

[217] Tjarks, Alicia Vidaurreta. 1974. "Comparative Demographic Analysis of Texas, 1777-1793." *Southwestern Historical Quarterly* 77:291-338. Reprinted in *Essays on Spain in the American West, 1540-1821*, ed. David J. Weber, pp. 135-69. Albuquerque: University of New Mexico Press, 1979.

[218] ———. 1978. "Demographic, Ethnic and Occupational Structure of New Mexico, 1790." *The Americas* (Academy of American Franciscan History) 35:45-88.

[219] Upham, Steadman. 1982. *Politics and Power: An Economic and Political History of the Western Pueblo*. New York: Academic Press.

[220] Usner, Daniel H., Jr. 1981. "Frontier Exchange in the Lower Mississippi Valley: Race Relations and Economic Life in Colonial Louisiana, 1699-1783." Ph.D. diss., Duke University. Ann Arbor: University Microfilms.

[221] Vigil, Ralph H. 1973. "The Hispanic Heritage and the Borderlands." *Journal of San Diego History* 19:1-9.

[222] ———. 1973. "The New Borderlands History: A Critique." *New Mexico Historical Review* 48:189-208.

[223] ———. 1983. "Colonial Institutions." In Ellwyn R. Stoddard, Richard L. Nostrand and Jonathan P. West, eds., *Borderlands Sourcebook: A Guide to Literature on Northern Mexico and the American Southwest*, pp. 36-41. See [206].

[224] ———. 1983. "Exploration and Conquest." In Ellwyn R. Stoddard, Richard L. Nostrand and Jonathan P. West, eds., *Borderlands Sourcebook: A Guide to the Literature on Northern Mexico and the American Southwest*, pp. 31-35. See [206].

[225] Voss, Stuart F. 1981. "Societal Competition in Northwest New Spain." *The Americas* (Academy of American Franciscan History) 38:185-204.

[226] Vlasich, James A. 1980. "Pueblo Indian Agriculture, Irrigation and Water Rights." Ph.D. dissertation, University of Utah. Ann Arbor: University Microfilms.

[227] Walker, Deward E., Jr., ed. 1972. *The Emergent Native Americans: A Reader in Culture Contact*. Boston: Little, Brown and Co.

[228] Weber, David J., ed. 1979. *New Spain's Far Northern Frontier: Essays on Spain in the American West, 1540-1821*. Albuquerque: University of New Mexico Press.

[229] White, David H. 1975. "The Indian Policy of Juan Vicente Folch, Governor of Spanish Mobile, 1781-1792." *Alabama Review* 28:261-75.

[230] Wilcox, David R., and W. Bruce Masse, eds. 1981. *The Protohistoric Period in the North American Southwest, A.D. 1450-1700*. Arizona State University Anthropological Research Papers 24. Tempe: Arizona State University.

[231] Worcester, Donald E. 1976. "The Significance of the Spanish Borderlands to the United States." *Western Historical Quarterly* 7:5-18. Reprinted in *New Spain's Far Northern Frontier*, ed. David J. Weber, pp. 1-14. See [228].

[232] ———. 1979. *The Apaches: Eagles of the Southwest*. Norman: University of Oklahoma Press.

[233] Wright, J. Leitch, Jr. 1971. *Anglo-Spanish Rivalry in North America*. Athens: University of Georgia Press.

[234] ———. 1981. *The Only Land They Knew: The Tragic Story of the Indians in the Old South*. New York: Free Press.

[235] Zahendra, Peter. 1976. "Spanish West Florida, 1781-1821." Ph.D. dissertation, University of Michigan. Ann Arbor: University Microfilms.

[236] Zavala, Silvio. [1965] 1979. "The Frontiers of Hispanic America." In *The Frontier in Perspective*, ed. Walker D. Wyman and Clifton B. Kroeber, pp. 35-58. Madison: University of Wisconsin Press. Reprinted in *New Spain's Far Northern Frontier*, ed. David J. Weber, pp. 179-99. See [228].

[237] Zubrow, Ezra B. W. 1974. *Population, Contact and Climate in the New Mexican Pueblos*. University of Arizona Anthropological Papers 24. Tucson: University of Arizona Press.

Anglo-Indian Relations in Colonial North America

J. FREDERICK FAUSZ

St. Mary's College of Maryland

> [T]here is so much to think over that I do not know how to describe it, seeing things . . . that had never been heard of or seen before, not even dreamed about.
> —Bernal Díaz del Castillo, 1519

IN A FAMOUS 1622 SERMON, the Reverend John Donne wrote: "I am an adventurer; . . . for every man that prints, adventures." The following bibliographical "adventure" attempts to survey, through a representative sampling of "adventures" by other authors, one portion of a boundless and boundaryless field, which, in its own way, has proven to be as exciting and awe-inspiring as Díaz's first glimpse of the Aztec capital.

In recent years social scientists from a variety of disciplines have contributed to an impressive and growing literature on Indian-White relations in colonial North America, interpreting the contacts of scores of Amerindian and Euroamerican groups throughout the continent from the early sixteenth to the late eighteenth century. This bibliography treats "only" the Anglo-Indian portion of that larger whole, reviewing studies of contacts in the thirteen British seaboard colonies and contiguous territories from the late sixteenth century to 1775.

The bibliography that follows is a representative, not comprehensive, review of important books, articles, and dissertations published or completed between 1975 and 1982. Preference was given to works that deal with contact relations in an historical context; ethnographies, archaeological reports, historiographical essays, and narrow documentary collections are generally excluded. Because of space limitations, I have not included titles in the Newberry Library Center for the History of the American Indian Bibliographical Series, individual essays in the highly-recommended *Handbook of North American Indians*, Vol. 15: *Northeast* [56], edited by Bruce G. Trigger, or recent studies on topics that are specifically covered in other bibliographies in this volume.

Since 1975 a virtual revolution in scholarship has transformed and informed the interpretation of Anglo-Indian relations in colonial North America. Hundreds of works have focused on the events of that era and are from among the thousands of books, articles, and dissertations produced on all aspects of Native American History in the last decade. One reason for this recent "take-off" is that the field of Colonial American History in general has grown rapidly and innovatively since the 1940s. The historians' unflagging fascination with the origins and evolution of English colonial institutions and societies produced two mature "schools," or broad overviews, for interpreting the period. But while both the England-focused Imperial School and the America-focused Frontier School increased our knowledge of Whites in the colonial era, each approach ignored or distorted the considerable contributions of Native Americans, who had strongly influenced London policymakers and New World frontiersmen alike over the centuries.

The mere realization that distortions and deficiencies exist in historical interpretations is usually insufficient to bring about corrective revisions unless compelling catalysts, such as changes in social attitudes and/or methodological breakthroughs, are present to encourage and enable reassessments. In the late 1960s and early 1970s such catalysts or influences existed simultaneously. One important impulse for reevaluating the colonial period derived from search in the 1960s for social justice and ethnic pride at home and the waging of the Vietnam War abroad. Precisely when scholars were researching dissertations or books on North American colonization, the United States was fighting a fierce neo-colonial war against a culturally alien, nonwhite, native population. At least one scholar, Richard Drinnon, *Facing West: The Metaphysics of Indian-Hating and Empire-Building* [9], recently made the connection between the Puritan slaughter of the Pequots at Mystic in 1637 and the United States Army's mass murder of Vietnamese villagers at My Lai in 1968. Although Drinnon contended that the two episodes revealed the consistency of American racism over the centuries, his book more convincingly demonstrates how current events or generational attitudes directly influence the interests and interpretations of historians. As humanists curious about the wider world outside their studies, historians could not be oblivious to Vietnam, Wounded Knee II, the Civil Rights Movement, Kent State, the impassioned writings of Frantz Fanon and Albert Memmi, or countless other events of the last two decades.

The second catalyst came from the growth of the "new social history" within the historical profession itself. Evolving from the emphasis of the French *Annales* School on a holistic, interdisciplinary, processual approach to history, and from the methods of the Cambridge historical demographers in interpreting local history and family life in preindustrial England, the "new" social history was applied by American scholars to the study of New England towns beginning in the mid-1960s. New methodologies led to new questions asked about the past and vice versa, and the insights of other disciplines, notably anthropology, increased both the depth and breadth of historical thinking. Once historians discovered the keys to comprehending the once-impenetrable, irretrievable world of "inarticulate," "common" people in small societies, they were much better equipped to ask and answer the kinds of questions posed by poet Preston Newman:

> "The Indians in the movies say 'Ugh'!
>
> . . .
>
> I wonder what the Indians really did say? How did they act?
> What did they do with their hands?"

The methodology that coalesced disciplines and perspectives to make possible the reinvestigation and reevaluation of Anglo-Indian relations in colonial North America was ethnohistory. Ethnohistory brought together anthropologists, with their disciplinary commitment to preliterate, nonwestern, native peoples, and historians, with their traditional focus on literate European societies, for the cooperative, interdisciplinary investigation of cultural interaction and change between the colonizers and the colonized in North America. The complementary methods and insights of anthropology and history could now focus on the intertwined fortunes and futures of native and newcomer, with a commitment to analyze reciprocal acculturation in a chronological context and to emphasize the essential role that Amerindians played in the geopolitical and sociocultural development of this continent. As historian Lester Cappon observed a quarter century ago, anthropological and historical perspectives could indeed be "profitably . . . brought together to illuminate not merely the Indian in terms of white society or the Indian in terms of his own society, but each in his own terms *and* in terms of the other. The study of Indian-white relations must encompass both self-knowledge and knowledge of others."

The ethnohistorical approach to colonial Anglo-Indian relations reached maturity and achieved scholarly respectability among historians in the mid-1970s. Between 1974 and 1976, four major works were published that emphasized the new focus. In 1975 Francis Jennings published *The Invasion of America: Indians, Colonialism, and the Cant of Conquest* [18], a work so influential that its appearance marks the beginning point of this bibliography. Jennings became a sort of "Martin Luther" spreading the ethnohistorical faith among traditionally-trained historians, and his book served as his ninety-five theses. Jennings was in the best revisionist tradition a "myth-raker," and his masterful manifesto attacked the fallacious assumptions of the "cant of conquest" that had distorted Anglo-Indian relations since the seventeenth century. In *The Invasion of America* he denied that the continent was a sparsely-populated "virgin land" when the Europeans arrived but demonstrated how it soon became a "widowed land" following a demographic disaster of incalculable proportions. He showed how erroneous and pejorative was the "civilization vs. savagery" conception of contact relations, and throughout the book, he argued for restoring Native Americans to their rightful place as actors, protagonists, and major determinants in colonial North America.

The Invasion of America was neither a complete nor perfect example of ethnohistory, but it provoked other scholars to reevaluate their assumptions and to reinvestigate the events lightly touched upon by Jennings's broad brush strokes. Whether expanding upon the strengths of the book or correcting its flaws and omissions, ethnohistorians have in recent years concentrated their research on those topics—such as aboriginal cultures, demography and disease, European ideology, and Puritan-Indian relations—that Jennings first brought into the open.

With less vehemence but equal dedication, Gary B. Nash, in *Red, White, and Black: The Peoples of Early America* [30], and Wilcomb E. Washburn, in *The Indian in America* [61], also signalled the arrival of ethnohistory as an important new discipline. These were the first two broad overviews or "textbooks" to adopt interdisciplinary perspectives and revised assumptions about cultural interaction. Nash brought together the "new social history" of the Euroamericans and fresh insights on Native American and Afro-American cultures for his analysis of acculturation across the various ethnic frontiers in the colonial period. He included valuable perspectives on the long-ignored interaction between Indians and Africans and presented an arresting portrait of revolutionary America with a biologically and culturally hybrid population. Washburn's *Indian in America* was an ambitious synthesis of a complex subject; although he covered the topic almost to the present, six of twelve chapters were devoted to European-Indian relations in the colonial period. The book was notable for, among other things, its organization of contacts according to stages: the period of aboriginal development was followed by early relations with Euroamericans, in which Indians often maintained their equality; in time this was challenged and eroded by growing numbers of Whites, until, finally, Native Americans had only unequal and dependent status.

The fourth book to represent the revisionist trends in Colonial American History was Bruce G. Trigger's *Children of Aataentsic* [55], an impressive two-volume ethnohistory of the Hurons to 1660 that soon became a model for others to emulate. Trigger's research was multi-disciplinary; his perspective was the whole of northeastern North America; and his focus was Huron-centered, grounded in an extensive analysis of aboriginal culture and formulated to show how the Hurons dealt with Europeans and other Amerindians according to the strong dictates of their cultural traditions. Trigger's organizational scheme, not unlike Washburn's, illustrated evolving relationships—from the aboriginal to a period of "non-directed" European contact (1609-1634, when traditional Huron culture predominated), and ultimately to "directed" or "coercive" contact (1634-1660, when French policy and other factors hastened the disintegration of the Huron Nation). One of Trigger's most enduring and influential contributions to ethnohistorical research may be his emphasis on, and handling of, interest group interaction, which transcended cultural differences in the contact experiences in Huronia.

Trigger's skillful blending of many disciplines to present a holistic account of who the Hurons were and how they viewed their world helped inspire scholars to research thoroughly the cultural foundations of other Amerindian groups, in order to better comprehend how they accepted and integrated changes in their societies and promoted it in others. Since 1975 the premises, promises, and performances of ethnohistorians have resulted in an unusually rich new literature on Anglo-Indian relations in colonial North America. The prospects for the future are even brighter as scholars become ever more sophisticated in their use of archaeology, political, ecological, economic, and psychological anthropology, demography, historical geography, and linguistics to inform a curious present about the long-buried past.

Ethnohistorians are increasingly turning to archaeology and the earliest European descriptions of native life for a better understanding of Amerindian cultures in their aboriginal state. Recent trends in archaeology reveal that many Indian groups experienced a longterm *in situ* development before contact with Europeans and that their cultures were stable, but hardly static—the result of selective changes and frequent, though rarely disruptive, adaptations. A new emphasis on sixteenth-century European contacts indicates that many Amerindians had less time "to themselves" than was previously thought. North American coastal contacts in that century produced reciprocal explorations and constituted an important transition period between an aboriginal era entirely free of European influences ("prehistory") and the later, generally seventeenth-century, "historic" era of largescale European settlement (or "invasion").

The generally-acknowledged master of interpretation for these sixteenth-century English contacts is David Beers Quinn. His monumental, five-volume *New American World* [36] represents a lifetime of collecting, compiling, editing, and interpreting the crucial, but often-neglected, European accounts that reveal so much about the Amerindian "world we have lost." Admired for his multicultural, interdisciplinary, and continental focus, Quinn has established some exacting standards for ethnohistorians less familiar with European documents in this work and in his narrative overview of the same period, *North America from Earliest Discovery to First Settlements: The Norse Voyages to 1612* [35]. In his most recent *Sources for the Ethnography of Northeastern North America to 1611* [37], Quinn lends added support to the trend toward a more refined and realistic periodization to accommodate the contacts made between the "prehistoric" and "historic" eras.

While Quinn dealt with the raw materials of ethnohistorical research [36] and extracted important cultural details from a specific group of European reports [37], James Axtell has imaginatively selected, compiled, and organized seventeenth- and eighteenth-century accounts of native lifeways in *The Indian Peoples of Eastern America: A Documentary History of the Sexes* [2]. In portraying the social, sexual *rites de passage* for Amerindian men and women through the eyes of Europeans, Axtell, by his choice of documents and his insightful headnotes, reveals almost as much about the observers as the observed.

While one group of scholars studies European accounts for the information they contain on Amerindian cultures despite their obvious prejudices and distortions, other scholars use them precisely because of the biases they reveal. Historians of the latter variety research European ideas, images and stereotypes about the New World and its native peoples for a better understanding of European intellectual history and only incidentally the Indians themselves. Although an appreciation of European preconceptions and misconceptions certainly complements the study of contact relations, the "Indian as . . ." approach should never be confused with, or substituted for, ethnohistorical research on Native Americans within a realistic cultural and chronological context.

Robert F. Berkhofer, Jr., *The White Man's Indian: Images of the American Indian from Columbus to the Present* [3], illustrates how the portrayals of "The Indian" over the centuries were convenient refractions—not reflections—of reality, designed to give Europeans the kind of native they needed for specific plans and projects. By recognizing the ambiguous, ambivalent, mutable nature of European perceptions and projections and relating them to the expedient ends they served, Berkhofer remains scrupulously detached and avoids the conceptual confusion that seems to be an occupational hazard associated with this methodology.

Recent studies by Karen Ordahl Kupperman, *Settling with the Indians: The Meeting of English and Indian Cultures in America, 1580-1640* [23], and Bernard Sheehan, *Savagism and Civility: Indians and Englishmen in Colonial Virginia* [47], reveal the swamp in which authors can become mired if they fail to use Indians as guides through treacherous territory. Subtitles notwithstanding, only faceless, fleshless Indians are considered—or rendered—here. Indians and Englishmen do not actually see each other, as through a windowpane; rather, the English look into a kind of New World mirror to obtain a refracted image of themselves while trying in vain to view Indians through the opaque substance of their own preconceptions. Kupperman argues that neither the cultural nor racial characteristics of "Indians" were as important to the English as "the category" of social status, concluding, somewhat circuitously, that Indians were treated as people without rights because they were considered "powerless." Sheehan sees English prejudices as firmly rooted in their conceptions of "noble and ignoble savagery," which were largely unaltered by cultural contacts that contradicted their broad generalizations. Unfortunately the reader can rarely determine if the seventeenth-century English or the twentieth-century author had more trouble relating ideas to events and attitudes to actions because of rigid misconceptions that sapped the vitality and uniqueness from people on both sides of the colonial frontiers. Both Kupperman and Sheehan search futilely for consistency and coherence where none exists and assume a dichotomy between European biases and New World experiences when particular ideas and images of Indians usually contained generous portions of both. The flaws of these works confirm one of Sheehan's own observations: that for four centuries White commentators have "proved incapable . . . of transcending the limitations of their conventional way of interpreting alien [i.e., Native American] people" (p.x).

Yet another walk into the swamp was made by H. C. Porter, *The Inconstant Savage: England and the North American Indian, 1500-1660* [34]. The book is a lengthy, detailed compilation of English descriptions of and perspectives on Indians, mainly in Virginia. It succeeds more as a reference work of sources than as history, for the author refused to allow himself to be confused by contradictory images by omitting analysis and interpretation almost altogether. In contrast to Berkhofer's skillful treading in a tangled interpretive forest, Porter leads his readers into a large and fertile maize field filled with potentially good harvests but fails to give them the digging sticks so necessary to achieving that end.

Studies of Anglo-Indian relations within specific areas and time periods have in recent years proved to offer the soundest approach to ethnohistorical analysis. A disproportionate amount of this research has focused on seventeenth-century New England, enabling the land of the first thanksgiving and the "Puritan mind" to dominate ethnohistory much as it has done for more traditional early American studies since the nineteenth century. The reasons for this dominance are many. Some of our more misleading and persistent national myths originated with the Puritans, and revisionists cannot resist the desire to shock their readers with the slaughter of sacred cows. Secondly, New England is a researcher's paradise, with unmatched English colonial records and some prominent archaeological sites. Thirdly, colonial New England generated the most interest and excitement among the "new" social historians in the late 1960s and early 1970s. As historians came to know the English colonists more thoroughly and intimately than ever before, it seemed apparent by contrast that they knew proportionately less about the Indian villagers who predated and often preoccupied the Puritan townspeople. Fourthly, and more specifically, ethnohistorians had a recent and well-received example of older, flawed scholarship—Alden T. Vaughan's *New England Frontier: Puritans and Indians, 1620-1675* [58]—to use as a convenient foil and scapegoat for their revisionist interpretations.

When Vaughan's book originally appeared in 1965, his contention that the Puritans "followed a relatively humane, considerate, and just policy in their dealings with the Indians" (p. vii) was itself a corrective to earlier works that had castigated colonial New Englanders for their cruelty to the native population. But both the mood of the country and the priorities of scholarship changed rapidly in the 1970s, and Vaughan's book became the object of bitter invective and, more constructively, the starting point for informed reappraisal of Anglo-Indian relations in the Northeast. More than any other single work, *New England Frontier* exemplifies the trends of the last two decades. In 1965 Vaughan was content to let the Puritans tell a one-sided story and to portray the natives of New England as mere objects of, and antagonists to, colonization—the direct opposites of the "unified, visionary, disciplined, and dynamic" (p. 323) Englishmen who would "inevitably" sweep them away. However, owing to the critical assaults on his methods and conclusions, Vaughan, in the 1979 revised edition of *New England Frontier*, recommended an interdisciplinary, ethnohistorical approach as the most promising to interpret "culture contact from both sides of the frontier" (p. xliv).

The starting point for researching the Indian side of the frontier has recently been pushed back centuries or even millenia before contact. William A. Haviland and Marjory W. Power, working from the anthropological side of the ethnohistorical frontier, have written *The Original Vermonters* [16], an informed and informative historical ethnography of the Abenaki and their ancestors from 11,000 B.P. through the eighteenth century. The book corrects the erroneous assumptions held by many that Vermont was "uninhabited" before European settlement. The authors argue that, although the Abenaki adopted much of the colonizers' culture (outward conformity), they retained their core values and traditions (inward uniqueness). A less successful treatment of precontact Amerindian lifeways is Howard S. Russell, *Indian New England Before the Mayflower* [43], which is, however, quite informed on Native American subsistence and material culture.

While these works emphasize aboriginal traits with relatively little attention to later relations with Europeans, Neal Salisbury has achieved a remarkably balanced perspective on both pre- and postcontact periods in his *Manitou and Providence: Indians, Europeans, and the Making of New England, 1500-1643* [46], the most impressive ethnohistory yet written on colonial New England. Here and in a more limited fashion in "Squanto: Last of the Patuxets" [45], Salisbury analyzes the changes wrought by two waves of Europeans (non-settlers before 1620 and settlers after) on the stable and abundant aboriginal culture of southern New England. Although sixteenth-century contacts with small numbers of Europeans did not threaten the Indians' cultural hegemony, the virgin soil epidemics they precipitated severely disrupted native life and left them vulnerable to the subsequent arrival of thousands of uprooted, land-hungry Englishmen seeking the abundance and stability in the New World that they had been denied in the Old. With more detailed information on the sixteenth-century preconditions to seventeenth-century emigration and settlement, scholars are in a better position to argue that Europeans did not suddenly "invade" North America, but rather slowly infiltrated it through a subtle, longterm process of intrusion and visitation by mariners, fishermen, traders, farmers—and deadly microbes.

Salisbury's success in integrating archaeological, anthropological, and historical data in a holistic view of contact confirms the validity of interdisciplinary methodologies. Similar approaches were adopted by Lynn Ceci, "The Effect of European Contact and Trade on the Settlement Pattern of Indians in Coastal New York, 1524-1665" [7], and Peter Allen Thomas, "In the Maelstrom of Change: The Indian Trade and Cultural Process in the Middle Connecticut River Valley, 1635-1665" [54]. Ceci argued that maize horticulture and sedentary village patterns, usually consistent with precontact "Late Woodland" development among coastal Algonquians, occurred in New York only after 1524, the result of early trade relations with Europeans and the later establishment of "wampum factories." Thomas found that a sixteenth-century trade with Europeans in the interior of southern New England set in motion political and material changes in native life that resulted in significant dependence on the English in the next century.

As scholars reinvestigated seventeenth-century Anglo-Indian relations, in recent years, they began to appreciate the diverse and complex nature of those contacts. Edward McM. Larrabee, "Recurrent Themes and Sequences in North American Indian-European Culture Contact" [24], provides important comparative focus to the inherent differences in the value systems and land use patterns of indigenous and immigrant populations and shows how incompatibility and the mutual lack of understanding led to competition and conflict. Peter A. Thomas, "Contrastive Subsistence Strategies and

Land Use as Factors for Understanding Indian-White Relations in New England" [53], similarly explains how the two groups fell out over mutual misunderstandings regarding the exploitation of a finite, shared land base.

The subtlety and complexity of Anglo-Indian relationships is further revealed in works that treat English hostility toward the very people they were often dependent upon for food, trade, and military assistance. Richard R. Johnson, "The Search for a Usable Indian" [21], demonstrates how the Puritans and some Indian groups grew increasingly dependent upon each other in the late seventeenth and early eighteenth century as they faced common threats from the French and their native allies. The English also found it expedient to recruit Indian allies, but native cooperation in protecting the Puritans did not help promote peaceful coexistence. As the colonists grew increasingly envious, fearful, and disdainful of their allies the more militarily successful the "bloody-thirsty" warriors became. The English could disguise their hostility and prejudice for the sake of expediency, as Lyle Koehler suggests in "Red-White Power Relations and Justice in the Courts of Seventeenth-Century New England" [22]. Koehler found that the Puritans imposed discriminatory and frequently harsh legal judgments on their native neighbors, but only later in the seventeenth century after the English advantages assured them that Indian hostility would pose only minimal danger to the colony. The very different demands, attitudes, and demeanors of the French and English in their dealings with Indians is the subject of Kenneth M. Morrison's "People of the Dawn: The Abnaki and Their Relations with New England and New France, 1600-1727" [29]. He concluded that cultural self-interest guided the Abenaki in their relations with both groups and that the English proved to be far less convincing and appealing than the French.

Much recent research focuses upon the English attempts at directed or "coercive" culture change, specifically the Puritan efforts to "civilize" and Christianize Indians. Scholars now challenge the hagiography of the past, interpreting missionaries as "cultural revolutionaries" who urged conformity on Indians who had already suffered from the harsh effects of contact. Many case studies show that it was easier to alter the social and material aspects of Native American cultures than it was to effect a complete ideological conversion to Christianity.

James Axtell, in the essay, "The Invasion Within," contained in his *European and the Indian: Essays in the Ethnohistory of Colonial North America* [1], presented an excellent summary analysis of the goals of, and the obstacles to, European conversion efforts. He found that the northeastern Indians creatively adapted to missionary demands, changing behavior and beliefs selectively while resisting more complete acculturation. Gary B. Nash, in "Perspectives on the History of Seventeenth-Century Missionary Activity in Colonial America" [31], briefly compared Virginia and New England experiences and concluded that Christian conversion was viewed by both groups of Englishmen as an important political weapon for undermining the integrity of Indian cultures. Nash, along with Jennings, *Invasion of America* [18], and Neal Salisbury, "Red Puritans: The 'Praying Indians' of Massachusetts Bay and John Eliot" [44], argued that John Eliot and other "cultural revolutionaries" enjoyed the highest degree of their limited success in conversion activities among native groups already ravaged by the biological, social, and military consequences of the Puritan "invasion."

By focusing on different missionaries (the Thomas Mayhews, junior and senior), in a different location (Martha's Vineyard), and following different approaches to conversion, James P. Ronda, "Generations of Faith" [42], and William S. Simmons, "Conversion from Indian to Puritan" [49], emphasized how Christianity revitalized native lifeways in the late seventeenth century and how Indian converts shaped the foreign faith to fit their needs in a radically-altered New England world. The Mayhews successfully secured the voluntary conversion of Indian kin and neighbor groups on Martha's Vineyard and then gradually helped them adapt to other elements of English culture. After studying the methods of the Mayhews, Simmons concluded that "where the traditional culture was most intact, the transference of the dominant culture was most complete."

Ethnohistorians are giving more attention than ever before to English religious prejudices and Indian belief systems in an effort to understand why and how conversion succeeded or failed. In Simmons's "Cultural Bias in the New England Puritans' Perception of Indians" [51], English conceptions of good and evil, derived from Christian theology, are seen to have produced a distorted stereotype of Indians that prevented mutual respect and doomed most conversion efforts. Drinnon, *Facing West* [9], concurs, but states the argument in stronger terms; he contends that the Puritans were more interested in dispatching their militant, racist "Army of Christ" to kill their "devilish" native neighbors than to convert them.

Ronda, "'We Are Well As We Are'" [41], and Simmons, "Southern New England Shamanism" [48], demonstrate how valuable analyses of Indian spiritual beliefs and cultural traditions can be in comprehending native responses, both literal and figurative, to Christian missionaries. In *Keepers of the Game* [25], Calvin Martin illustrates how complex and baffling a Native American spiritual world view could be for seventeenth-century Europeans to comprehend.

With a recent emphasis on how the Christian message was received, perceived, and responded to by Indians of the Northeast, Ronda the historian and Simmons the anthropologist have both turned to colonial documents that reveal the intimate interactions between missionary and native neophytes. *John Eliot's Indian Dialogues*, edited by Henry W. Bowden and James Ronda [5], reveals both sides of the seventeenth–century conversion frontier and is an especially useful source for interpreting Amerindian resistance and response to Puritan proselytizing. *Old Light on Separate Ways: The Narrangansett Diary of Joseph Fish, 1765-1776*, edited by Simmons and Cheryl L. Simmons [52], illustrates a degree of clerical insensitivity and native skepticism similar to that experienced in the Eliot mission one hundred years before. Both of these books contain valuable ethnographic details on southern New England tribes.

Studies of eighteenth-century missionary activities are sparse compared to those for the seventeenth. Important exceptions are Henry Warner Bowden, *American Indians and Christian Missions* [4] (Chapter Five); and Simmons, "The Great Awakening and Indian Conversion" [50], in which he explained how the Narragansetts were finally convinced to come out of the "darkness" into the (New) Light of evangelical Christianity. In "Dr. Wheelock's Little Red School" [1], Axtell reveals why the famous eighteenth-century clergyman grew frustrated with his futile attempts at converting Indians and founded Dartmouth College for the education of English youths.

Since 1975 studies of missionary activities have generally been considered as one component in the larger analysis of acculturation, for ethnohistorians ultimately want to know how, and to what extent,

English colonists changed Native Americans and vice versa. In "The Scholastic Philosophy of the Wilderness," recently reprinted in *European and the Indian* [1], Axtell likened contact situations to schools, in which the indigenous inhabitants were consistently the abler "teachers" in helping the colonists adjust to a new and novel environment. The Indians proved to be affective, as well as effective, instructors, and in "The White Indians of Colonial America" [1], Axtell analyzed eighteenth-century English captivity experiences to show how congenial native values and an affectionate approach to acculturation convinced many Whites to abandon the meetinghouse for a new life in the longhouse. In the most thorough summaries to date, Axtell assessed acculturation in "The English Colonial Impact on Indian Culture" and "The Indian Impact on English Colonial Culture" [1]. He finds that, despite the disruption to native life caused by European disease, firearms, trade goods, alcohol, and Christianity, Indians of the Northeast selectively adapted and ultimately persisted, remaining true to their most basic cultural values. By implication, Indians did a much better job of enculturating their young, which accounts for their success in resisting acculturation and in effecting the transculturation of outsiders. By their presence and persistence, Indians helped shape a unique early American world of two centuries of contact and influenced Anglo-American ideas and ideals in ways that are only now being scrutinized by scholars.

In "Crossing the Cultural Divide: Indians and New Englanders, 1605-1763" [59], Alden T. Vaughan and Daniel K. Richter challenge Axtell's contention that few Indians became "civilized" Christians while many colonists accepted a one-way ticket across the cultural frontier. They argue that the English "were probably more successful than Indians in attracting social and religious converts," but ironically, "Indian culture incorporated strangers far more thoroughly and enthusiastically than did Puritan New England" (p. 25). Supported by a statistical analysis of both groups that crossed cultural boundaries, Vaughan and Richter conclude that, while acculturation was an "integral and irresistible" result of contact, the more complete and permanent experience of transculturation was not, given the cultural obstacles and biases that made for a "divide" in the first place. "In early New England, at least, very few Indians and even fewer colonists crossed the cultural divide. On both sides of that divide, however, almost everyone moved closer to the middle" (p. 90).

In contrast to the impressive amount of research on Anglo-Indian relations in New England, the last seven years have not seen a comparable scholarly interest in other areas of the Northeast. This is perhaps partially explained by the heavy emphasis placed on Iroquois studies by prominent scholars in the two decades prior to 1975. For an excellent summary of individual tribes from the northern Atlantic coast to the Great Lakes, the *Northeast* volume of the *Handbook of North American Indians* [56] is highly recommended.

In recent studies of the League Iroquois, Richard L. Haan and Francis Jennings have contributed to a better appreciation of that group's role in eighteenth-century Anglo-Indian diplomacy. Haan, in "The Covenant Chain: Iroquois Diplomacy on the Niagara Frontier, 1697-1730" [14], analyzes how the League tried to undermine French authority in the Great Lakes region by formulating an alliance with western tribes. This important "Covenant Chain," allying Delawares, Shawnees, and other Ohio Valley tribes to British colonies that recognized the Iroquois as diplomatic spokesmen and power brokers, was destined to disintegrate during the European contests for empire in North America. In "The Indians' Revolution" [19], Jennings reveals how the shattering of the Covenant Chain after 1750 permitted the American revolutionaries to extend their hegemony over Indians along the banks of the Ohio just when they were destroying Britain's hegemony over themselves along the shores of the Atlantic.

In recent years studies of Anglo-Indian relations in the southern English colonies have flourished, representing significant revisions and new visions along ethnohistorical lines. Essential to a full appreciation of the cultural complexity of the region is Charles Hudson, *The Southeastern Indians* [17]. While only the final chapter treats contact relations per se, Hudson's richly detailed ethnographic analysis of the major southern tribes is important for assessing Indian vulnerability and resiliency in their dealings with Whites.

Two historical overviews, W. Stitt Robinson's *The Southern Colonial Frontier, 1607-1763* [40] and J. Leitch Wright, Jr.'s *The Only Land They Knew* [62] help place Anglo-Indian relations in perspective. Robinson's book is a traditional narrative of (white-focused) frontier history, although the extent to which he considers the role of Native

Americans is welcome in a work of this genre. Wright's book is written from a refreshing and unmistakably Indian perspective. Although the title and the dust jacket would seem to indicate mass market emotionalism in the "Bury My Heart At Wounded Knee" tradition, *The Only Land They Knew* is instead a thoroughly-researched ethnohistory of the major southern tribes from "prehistory" to the American Revolution. Wright is particularly good in discussing trade relations, competing belief systems, and the African and Indian influences on the culture of the "Old South."

Richard Beale Davis, in Volume I of his *Intellectual Life in the Colonial South, 1585-1753* [8], presents an excellent overview of "The Indian as Image and Factor in Southern Colonial Life." Although obviously not intended as an analysis of contact relations, this essay recognizes the centrality of the Native American experience in southern history.

For better or worse, the colonial South is not perceived or studied as a unit as is traditional with New England. In terms of sub-regions, then, analyses of colonial Anglo-Indian relations have largely focused on seventeenth-century Virginia in recent years. This revitalized interest was long overdue, for, as with New England studies, early intercultural contacts in the Chesapeake produced some enduring and erroneous myths about the "savage" frontier. The "new social history" has also recently focused on Virginia, illuminating previously dark corners of the past.

Edmund S. Morgan, informed and stimulated by recent historiographical trends, produced a major reinterpretation of colonial Virginia in *American Slavery–American Freedom* [28]. In the early chapters he tested the validity of English goals for establishing a harmonious, bicultural and agricultural colony against the realities of often bloody Anglo-Indian conflicts in the seventeenth century. He argued that the process by which Englishmen failed to be "gods" and the Indians ceased being "noble" in the initial contact experiences may have sown the seeds of racism, which would fully flower by century's end. Morgan at his best provided an important thematic framework for future interpretations; at his worst, as in his sociocultural analysis of the Virginia Algonquians, he helped determine that those future interpretations would be more strongly grounded in ethnohistorical methods.

In "The Amerindian in English Promotional Literature, 1575-

1625" [32], Loren E. Pennington found, contrary to Morgan, that the English were never very "sympathetic" towards the Indians of Virginia, never developed any deep-seated philosophical commitment to them, and featured them prominently in propaganda only briefly, when it was expedient for fund-raising efforts. Pennington saw the English trapped by a dilemma of their own making: To emphasize Indian savagery justified conquest and dispossession, but implied the difficulty of Christian conversion, while to emphasize the Indian as potential convert raised funds but made it difficult to justify conquest and dispossession.

The English in Virginia had little difficulty justifying dispossession or military retaliation following the fatal rejection of their physical presence and cultural "presents" by the Powhatans in the famous uprising of 1622. That massive and near-disastrous attack was a significant turning point in Anglo-Indian relations, though not entirely or exclusively in the ways claimed by Alden T. Vaughan in "'Expulsion of the Savages': English Policy and the Virginia Massacre of 1622" [57]. While London policymakers may have regarded "all natives as foes" in the aftermath of the uprising, the colonists certainly did not, finding as they always had that they were incapable of surviving or prospering without considerable native assistance. Although Vaughan claimed he was "not . . . attempting fully to analyze early Indian-white relations from an Indian perspective" (p. 57n), his errors of fact and emphasis demonstrated that even traditional white-focused English policy studies could be substantially improved by a fuller awareness of both cultures in contact.

The first largescale ethnohistory of Anglo-Indian relations in Virginia was J. Frederick Fausz's "Powhatan Uprising of 1622" [10], a revisionist account of that event within a broad cultural and chronological context. He analyzed the attitudes and actions of the homeland-English, the Virginia-English, and the various tidewater Algonquian tribes within the Powhatan chiefdom from the 1580s through the 1620s and found that relations among all were far more subtle, complex, and ideologically-focused than had previously been assumed. Both in his dissertation and in "Opechancanough: Indian Resistance Leader" [12], Fausz contended that a nativist revitalization movement arose among the Powhatans by the early 1620s to challenge and thwart English missionary efforts and that this ideological confrontation proved more significant for precipitating the 1622 uprising than the dispossession of Indian lands or other factors. Using the same sources and studying the same principals, Carl Bridenbaugh arrived at conclusions different in content and emphasis in his "Opechancanough: A Native American Patriot" [6]. In the course of his analysis, Bridenbaugh erroneously and eccentrically shuffled the factual cards on Powhatan "prehistory," inserting Eurocentrism in the most curious place of all—i.e., in the supposed Spanish experiences and Catholic education of Opechancanough himself. The decade-long war that followed the Powhatan Uprising was the subject of Fausz, "Fighting 'Fire' with Firearms" [11], in which he revealed how one phase of the acculturation process was pursued with deadly earnestness, i.e., in the adoption of English flintlock muskets by Indian warriors and in the mastery of the tactics of woodland warfare by the colonists.

The brutal, bloody confrontations in Virginia spilled over into what was not yet Maryland and largely predetermined subsequent (and very different) Anglo-Indian relations in that colony after 1634. James H. Merrell, in "Cultural Continuity Among the Piscataway Indians of Colonial Maryland" [26], found that contact did not always have to imply a submit or die proposition as it sometimes did in Virginia, arguing that the Piscataways managed to retain much of their traditional cultural identity even after decades of harmonious interaction with Whites. Merrell's essay revealed that even for peoples living along the same bay, the special needs and experiences of particular indigenous and intruding groups could result in vastly different patterns of interaction.

In "Indians and Frontiers in Seventeenth-Century Maryland" [20], Francis Jennings used the experiences of the Susquehannocks to demonstrate how artificial legal "boundaries" could be and how important cultural ones were for certain centrally-located Amerindian groups. The Susquehannock Nation, which would not survive the seventeenth century intact, had to contend with the French, Swedes, Dutch, Virginia-English, Maryland-English, Delawares, and League Iroquois in an era full of changes and challenges.

Recent studies of contact in the lower South, although relatively few in number, indicate that this will be a significant "growth area" for ethnohistorical interpretation in the near future, and the forthcoming Southeast volume of the *Handbook of North American Indians* may be a catalyst to that end. In the last three decades, scholars have largely researched "prehistoric"/sixteenth-century topics or the late eighteenth- and early nineteenth-century developments that set the stage for removal of the "Five Civilized Tribes." With only a few exceptions, such as Verner Crane's 1928 classic, *The Southern Frontier, 1670-1732*, historians have not exploited the rich potential that exists for comparative analysis of Spanish, French, and English relations with numerous Amerindian groups in this diverse region.

The Cherokees of the colonial era have received more attention than most native peoples of the lower South. An excellent integration of historical geography and ecological anthropology is Gary C. Goodwin's *Cherokees in Transition* [13], which presents a detailed analysis of environmental and cultural adjustments from precontact to the late eighteenth century. John Phillip Reid, *A Better Kind of Hatchet* [38], innovatively investigates continuity and change among the Cherokees by focusing on their legal, trade, and diplomatic relations with the English in the late seventeenth and early eighteenth century. He finds that by 1725 the Cherokees still preserved much of their traditional culture, because they were accepted as valuable trading partners on their terms by the South Carolinians. However, the Cherokees' very success in obtaining "a better kind of hatchet" (i.e., English firearms), gradually forced them into dependency on English laws and trade goods. In a later essay, "A Perilous Rule: The Law of International Homicide" [39], Reid demonstrates how the Cherokees' continued reliance upon traditional legal customs proved dysfunctional and deadly when applied against the English in an eighteenth-century colonial context.

Relatively little research has been done since 1975 on non-Cherokee groups in the Carolinas. Two notable exceptions are Gene Waddell, *Indians of the South Carolina Lowcountry, 1562-1751* [60], and James H. Merrell, "Natives in a New World: The Catawba Indians of Carolina, 1650-1800" [27]. Waddell's book is a valuable collection (without analysis) of important ethnographic and historical sources for a period that should receive increased attention in the years ahead. Waddell's ethnohistory–in–the–rough satisfies the researcher's need for thoroughly-mined nuggets of information, while Merrell's work supplies the scholarly community with a much-desired and fully-refined gem of interpretation. Focusing largely on the eighteenth century, Merrell demonstrates how the Catawbas adapted and adjusted to colonization—by coalescing once-independent groups to offset depopulation, developing new strategies for securing trade goods, and allying with their white neighbors in the American Revolution. By the late eighteenth century, the Catawbas had outwardly conformed and appeared to be a degraded remnant of a once-proud people, but as Merrell shows, they retained many of their core values and continued to enculturate their young in traditional customs that gave meaning to their lives.

The flexibility of the Catawbas in adapting and persisting in a strange postcontact new world was not unlike the strategy adopted by imported Africans, who also had to cope with a different environment not of their making. Indians and slaves alike accommodated themselves to the white masters by presenting one side of themselves to English observers to show how they had been acculturated and were conforming, while in the slave quarters or the Indian villages they perpetuated a native subculture of traditional values and beliefs to confirm their uniqueness.

An altered set of generalizations results when Indians assume the role of plantation masters over African slaves, a subject recently studied by R. Halliburton, Jr., *Red Over Black: Black Slavery Among the Cherokee Indians* [15], and Theda Perdue, *Slavery and the Evolution of Cherokee Society, 1540-1866* [33]. Although both books concentrate on "red-black" relationships that extended well into the nineteenth century, they interpret African slavery as an important acculturative institution that evolved in the colonial era from the Cherokees' traditional practice of slave holding and Anglo-American plantation economics. Halliburton contends that the Cherokees adopted the English model of plantation slavery, complete with racial prejudices, and that this aided the Indians' evolution into a "civilized nation." Perdue, on the other hand, emphasizes some major differences in the ways in which Whites and Indians treated their slaves and contends that plantation slavery had a destructive impact on Cherokee society, introducing economic competition and tribal factionalism that would leave the nation ill-prepared for dealing with the crises of the removal era.

These studies constitute only the tentative beginning in the interpretation of "red-black" interaction, which in all its implications and permutations, promises to emerge as an exciting field for future research. In 1920 Carter Woodson observed that "one of the longest unwritten chapters in the history of the United States is that treating of the relations of the Negroes and the Indians." A half-century later Nash, in *Red, White, and Black* [30], challenged scholars to interpret the development of the South in a holistic way, taking account of the complex cultural interaction of all ethnic groups. Even more recently, Wright, in *The Only Land They Knew* [62], suggested that historians take another look at the so-called African cultural retentions in the Old South, contending that many may in fact have been Indian customs and traditions that were adopted by black slaves and thereafter erroneously associated with them by Whites.

The challenge for the future is to have ethnohistorians, as they rediscover and reinterpret the role of Indians in the colonial South, take account of the long-ignored, "other" frontier of African-Indian relations. But it is also a challenge for Afro-American and Native American specialists to work together, for in their interests and in their recent methodologies, both groups have been "doing" ethnohistory along similar lines. For the past three decades, "Black History" and "Indian History" have evolved along common interpretive paths. Prior to the 1950s Blacks and Indians were generally portrayed as being the beneficiaries of white "civilization," imparted through slavery and colonization. Then in the 1950s and early 1960s, scholars began condemning the cruelty of slavery and colonization while expressing sympathy for the unfortunate victims of these prejudicial policies. With the social activism and ethnic awareness of the late 1960s and 1970s came interpretations that emphasized the slave "rebels" and Indian "patriots" (almost self-consciously modeled after Black Panthers and Wounded Knee combatants) who had violently resisted oppression and acculturation. In the quieter contemporary racial climate of the late 1970s, scholars began stressing how both groups had creatively adapted and outwardly conformed to white society while retaining the crucial core values and cultural traditions that prevented them from totally "melting" in the assimilationist "pot." The current emphasis on African history and African retentions *and* Indian prehistory and Indian retentions are indicative of this interpretive trend and also of the importance of acculturation for both Afro-American and Native American studies.

The quest to comprehend the ethnic heritage of North America has prompted scholars to be more innovative and sophisticated in their research. Today spiritual beliefs and world views, and disease and microbic influences are receiving the attention of "red" and "black" ethnohistorians alike in their efforts to explain the motivations and expectations of Africans and Indians.

The rich and rewarding work of the last few years has brought us closer to the day when American History will be fully and sensitively portrayed as ethnic history. Colonial America is no longer interpreted within the narrow context of a struggle between the Whites of Whitehall and the Whites of the "wilderness," for Indian land, African labor, and the cultures of all are now credited with sharing in the creation of a hybrid North American world. In confronting the challenges of this "New World" that was familiar to none and new to all, the racially and culturally distinct peoples of America interacted individually and collectively and produced a shared legacy of uncommon vitality, creative adjustment, and perpetual renewal.

ALPHABETICAL LIST

[1] Axtell, James. 1981. *The European and the Indian: Essays in the Ethnohistory of Colonial North America*. New York: Oxford University Press.

[2] ———, ed. 1981. *The Indian Peoples of Eastern America: A Documentary History of the Sexes*. New York: Oxford University Press.

[3] Berkhofer, Robert F., Jr. 1978. *The White Man's Indian: Images of the American Indian from Columbus to the Present*. New York: Alfred A. Knopf.

[4] Bowden, Henry Warner. 1981. *American Indians and Christian Missions: Studies in Cultural Conflict*. Chicago History of American Religion Series. Chicago: University of Chicago Press.

[5] Bowden, Henry W., and James P. Ronda, eds. 1980. *John Eliot's Indian Dialogues: A Study in Cultural Interaction*. Westport, Conn.: Greenwood Press.

[6] Bridenbaugh, Carl. 1981. "Opechancanough: A Native American Patriot." In *Early Americans*, pp. 50-76. New York: Oxford University Press.

[7] Ceci, Lynn. 1977. "The Effect of European Contact and Trade on

the Settlement Pattern of Indians in Coastal New York, 1524-1665: The Archaeological and Documentary Evidence." Ph.D. dissertation, City University of New York. Ann Arbor: University Microfilms.

[8] Davis, Richard Beale. 1978. "The Indian as Image and Factor in Southern Colonial Life." In *Intellectual Life in the Colonial South, 1585-1763*. Vol. I, pp. 103-256. Knoxville: University of Tennessee Press.

[9] Drinnon, Richard. 1980. *Facing West: The Metaphysics of Indian-Hating and Empire-Building*. Minneapolis: University of Minnesota Press; New York: New American Library.

[10] Fausz, J. Frederick. 1977. "The Powhatan Uprising of 1622: A Historical Study of Ethnocentrism and Cultural Conflict." Ph.D. dissertation, College of William and Mary. Ann Arbor: University Microfilms.

[11] ———. 1979. "Fighting 'Fire' With Firearms: The Anglo-Powhatan Arms Race in Early Virginia." *American Indian Culture and Research Journal* 3(4):33-50.

[12] ———. 1981. "Opechancanough: Indian Resistance Leader." In *Struggle and Survival in Colonial America*, ed. David G. Sweet and Gary B. Nash, pp. 21-37. Berkeley: University of California Press.

[13] Goodwin, Gary C. 1977. *Cherokees in Transition: A Study of Changing Culture and Environment Prior to 1775*. Chicago: University of Chicago Department of Geography.

[14] Haan, Richard L. 1977. "The Covenant Chain: Iroquois Diplomacy on the Niagara Frontier, 1697-1730." Ph.D. dissertation, University of California, Santa Barbara. Ann Arbor: University Microfilms.

[15] Halliburton, R., Jr. 1977. *Red Over Black: Black Slavery Among the Cherokee Indians*. Westport, Conn.: Greenwood Press.

[16] Haviland, William A., and Marjory W. Power. 1981. *The Original Vermonters: Native Inhabitants Past and Present*. Hanover and London: University Press of New England.

[17] Hudson, Charles. 1976. *The Southeastern Indians*. Knoxville: University of Tennessee Press.

[18] Jennings, Francis. 1975. *The Invasion of America: Indians, Colonialism, and the Cant of Conquest*. Chapel Hill: University of North Carolina Press for the Institute of Early American History and Culture. Reprinted, New York: W. W. Norton.

[19] ———. 1976. "The Indians' Revolution." In *The American Revolution: Explorations in the History of American Radicalism*, ed. Alfred F. Young, pp. 319-48. DeKalb: Northern Illinois University Press.

[20] ———. 1982. "Indians and Frontiers of Seventeenth-Century Maryland." In *Early Maryland in a Wider World*, ed. David B. Quinn, pp. 216-241. Detroit: Wayne State University Press.

[21] Johnson, Richard R. 1977. "The Search for a Usable Indian: An

Aspect of the Defense of Colonial New England." *Journal of American History* 64:623-51.

[22] Koehler, Lyle. 1979. "Red-White Power Relations and Justice in the Courts of Seventeenth-Century New England." *American Indian Culture and Research Journal* 3(4):1-31.

[23] Kupperman, Karen Ordahl. 1980. *Settling With The Indians: The Meeting of English and Indian Cultures in America, 1580-1640*. Totowa, N. J.: Rowman and Littlefield.

[24] Larrabee, Edward McM. 1976. "Recurrent Themes and Sequences in North American Indian-European Culture Contact." In American Philosophical Society, *Transactions* 66(7):3-52.

[25] Martin, Calvin. 1978. *Keepers of the Game: Indian-Animal Relationships and the Fur Trade*. Berkeley: University of California Press.

[26] Merrell, James H. 1979. "Cultural Continuity Among the Piscataway Indians of Colonial Maryland." *William and Mary Quarterly*, 3rd ser., 36:548-70.

[27] ———. 1982. "Natives in a New World: The Catawba Indians of Carolina, 1650-1800." Ph.D. dissertation, The Johns Hopkins University. Ann Arbor: University Microfilms.

[28] Morgan, Edmund S. 1975. *American Slavery–American Freedom: The Ordeal of Colonial Virginia*. New York: W. W. Norton.

[29] Morrison, Kenneth M. 1975. "The People of the Dawn: The Abnaki and Their Relations with New England and New France, 1600-1727." Ph.D. dissertation, University of Maine. Ann Arbor: University Microfilms.

[30] Nash, Gary B. 1974. *Red, White, and Black: The Peoples of Early America*. Englewood Cliffs, N.J.: Prentice-Hall. 2d ed., 1982.

[31] ———. 1979. "Perspectives on the History of Seventeenth–Century Missionary Activity in Colonial America." *Terrae Incognitae* (The Annals of the Society for the History of Discoveries) 11:17-27.

[32] Pennington, Loren E. 1978. "The Amerindian in English Promotional Literature, 1575-1625." In *The Westward Enterprise: English Activities in Ireland, the Atlantic, and America, 1480-1650*, ed. K. R. Andrews, N. P. Canny, and P. E. H. Hair, pp. 175-194. Liverpool: Liverpool University Press. Reprinted, Detroit: Wayne State University Press, 1980.

[33] Perdue, Theda. 1979. *Slavery and the Evolution of Cherokee Society, 1540-1866*. Knoxville: University of Tennessee Press.

[34] Porter, H. C. 1979. *The Inconstant Savage: England and the North American Indian, 1500-1660*. London: Gerald Duckworth.

[35] Quinn, David Beers. 1977. *North America from Earliest Discovery to First Settlements: The Norse Voyages to 1612*. New York: Harper and Row.

[36] ———, ed. 1979. *New American World: A Documentary History of North America to 1612*. With the assistance of Alison M. Quinn and Susan Hillier. 5 vols. New York: Arno Press and Hector Bye, Inc.

[37] ———. 1981. *Sources for the Ethnography of Northeastern North America to 1611*. National Museum of Man, Mercury Series, *Canadian Ethnology Service Paper* 76. Ottawa: National Museum of Man.

[38] Reid, John Phillip. 1976. *A Better Kind of Hatchet: Law, Trade and Diplomacy in the Cherokee Nation During the Early Years of European Contact*. University Park: Pennsylvania State University Press.

[39] ———. 1979. "A Perilous Rule: The Law of International Homicide." In *The Cherokee Indian Nation: A Troubled History*, ed. Duane H. King, pp. 33-45. Knoxville: University of Tennessee Press.

[40] Robinson, W. Stitt. 1979. *The Southern Colonial Frontier, 1607-1763*. Histories of the American Frontier Series. Albuquerque: University of New Mexico Press.

[41] Ronda, James P. 1977. "'We Are Well As We Are': An Indian Critique of Seventeenth-Century Christian Missions." *William and Mary Quarterly*, 3rd ser., 34:66-82.

[42] ———. 1981. "Generations of Faith: The Christian Indians of Martha's Vineyard." *William and Mary Quarterly*, 3rd ser., 38:369-94.

[43] Russell, Howard S. 1980. *Indian New England Before the Mayflower*. Hanover and London: University Press of New England.

[44] Salisbury, Neal. 1974. "Red Puritans: The 'Praying Indians' of Massachusetts Bay and John Eliot." *William and Mary Quarterly*, 3rd ser., 31:27-54.

[45] ———. 1981. "Squanto: Last of the Patuxets." In *Struggle and Survival in Colonial America*, ed. David G. Sweet and Gary B. Nash, pp. 228-46. Berkeley: University of California Press.

[46] ———. 1982. *Manitou and Providence: Indians, Europeans, and the Making of New England, 1500-1643*. New York: Oxford University Press.

[47] Sheehan, Bernard. 1980. *Savagism and Civility: Indians and Englishmen in Colonial Virginia*. Cambridge and New York: Cambridge University Press.

[48] Simmons, William Scranton. 1976. "Southern New England Shamanism: An Ethnographic Reconstruction." In *Papers of the Seventh Algonquian Conference, 1975*, ed. William Cowan, pp. 217-56. Ottawa: Carleton University.

[49] ———. 1979. "Conversion from Indian to Puritan." *New England Quarterly* 52:197-218.

[50] ———. 1979. "The Great Awakening and Indian Conversion in Southern New England." In *Papers of the Tenth Algonquian Conference, 1978*, ed. William Cowan, pp. 25-36. Ottawa: Carleton University.

[51] ———. 1981. "Cultural Bias in the New England Puritans' Perception of Indians." *William and Mary Quarterly*, 3rd ser., 38:56-72.

[52] Simmons, William Scranton, and Cheryl L. Simmons, eds. 1982. *Old Light on Separate Ways: The Narragansett Diary of Joseph Fish, 1765-1776*. Hanover and London: University Press of New England.

[53] Thomas, Peter Allen. 1976. "Contrastive Subsistence Strategies and Land Use as Factors for Understanding Indian-White Relations in New England." *Ethnohistory* 23:1-18.
[54] ———. 1979. "In the Malestrom of Change: The Indian Trade and Cultural Process in the Middle Connecticut River Valley, 1635-1665." Ph.D. dissertation, University of Massachusetts.
[55] Trigger, Bruce G. 1976. *The Children of Aataentsic: A History of the Huron People to 1660*. 2 vols. Montreal and London: McGill-Queen's University Press.
[56] ———, ed. 1978. *Northeast*. Vol. 15 of *Handbook of North American Indians*, gen. ed. William C. Sturtevant. Washington: Government Printing Office for the Smithsonian Institution.
[57] Vaughan, Alden T. 1978. "'Expulsion of the Salvages': English Policy and the Virginia Massacre of 1622." *William and Mary Quarterly*, 3rd ser., 35:57-84.
[58] ———. 1979. *New England Frontier: Puritans and Indians, 1620-1675*. Rev. ed. of 1965 orig. New York: W. W. Norton.
[59] Vaughan, Alden T., and Daniel K. Richter. 1980. "Crossing the Cultural Divide: Indians and New Englanders, 1605-1763." American Antiquarian Society, *Proceedings* 90:23-99.
[60] Waddell, Gene. 1980. *Indians of the South Carolina Lowcountry, 1562-1751*. Spartanburg, S. C.: The Reprint Company.
[61] Washburn, Wilcomb E. 1975. *The Indian in America*. New American Nation Series. New York: Harper and Row.
[62] Wright, J. Leitch, Jr. 1981. *The Only Land They Knew: The Tragic Story of the Indians in the Old South*. New York: Free Press.

Indian-White Relations: 1790-1900

FREDERICK E. HOXIE

D'Arcy McNickle Center for the History of the American Indian

The Newberry Library

A DECADE AGO, signs announcing works in "Indian-White Relations" directed the interested student to a quiet corner of political history where a small group of scholars examined the formulation of federal policy. The work was steady, the questions were clear, and the historians managed to keep the depredations of intruding social scientists to a minimum.

That quiet enclave no longer exists. During the 1970s marauding anthropologists, recalcitrant social historians and an irrepressible band of tribal scholars ransacked the place, permanently jangling the nerves of its previous tenants. These scholars unmasked federal policy as only one aspect of Indian-White relations, and suggested that we should study the cultural, religious, economic, legal, educational and even environmental relationships between the two groups. Indeed, they even attacked the idea that "policy" dominated cultural interaction. In the aftermath of these raids, that quiet refuge grew until it encompassed a broad area of cross-cultural interaction. Its practitioners now hail from a variety of disciplines and happily, the accompanying noise level is on the upswing.

In light of this recent history it should not be surprising that so much has been published in Indian-White relations since 1975. For this essay, a search of the major bibliographies and indexes produced 130 titles with little difficulty. These works discussed activities from schooling and legal affairs to missions and trading. Clearly, federal policy has been joined by a host of rival subjects; "Indian-White relations" now covers many new topics. As a result, even when confined to the nineteenth century, it seems that the items listed below have only a tangential relationship to one another. The field shows signs of outgrowing itself.

But the changes and innovations may not be as great as they seem. A careful look at the fifty-odd most important titles selected for the following list reveals some familiar patterns. Nearly half the works cited address themselves primarily to the post-Civil War period. Furthermore, when we eliminate studies of removal, there are fewer than half a dozen studies of the "Middle Period," the years between the election of Andrew Jackson and the end of the Civil War. (If we eliminate Civil War books, the number shrinks to two or three.) There are no purely quantitative conclusions here, only the observation that the periods traditionally interesting to frontier and political historians—the era of trans-Appalachian conquest and the "winning" of the West—have continued to attract us. The relatively quiet middle years seem less appealing.

There are no doubt many reasons for this skewed distribution (including the reviewer's selection habits), but two explanations are most likely: habit and a persistent reliance on federal policy. Scholars congregate around familiar problems: frontier diplomacy and the War of 1812, removal, Indian wars and allotment. There is nothing wrong with that habit (re-examining complex questions inevitably produces a fuller understanding of them), but it may suggest that we are overlooking other important areas. In addition, each of the "interesting" eras begins with a federal policy—war, removal, assimilation programs—and accepts implicitly the idea that government action is the underlying determinant of relations between Native Americans and Whites. Perhaps we are not as free from old patterns as we thought.

Turning to the subjects of the works listed below, the distribution is more even. Education appears to be as interesting as economics; there are as many studies of reform activity as there are biographies of central figures, and broad discussions of the Indians' image are neatly balanced by local studies of tribes and agencies. Here the activity of the past decade is most evident. The only discontinuity appears when one separates books and articles. There are eighteen books on the list; none of them is on education, missions or treatymaking. The only book on legal relations is Russell Barsh and James Youngblood Henderson's *The Road* [6], a general study of the Indian's place in American law. There are three book-length case studies (Hagan [17], Berthrong [8], Miner and Unrau [32]), but all of them are concerned primarily with the administration of federal policy. There are four books on images of the Indian. My categories may be idiosyncratic, but there appear to be more books on traditional subjects—military affairs, and federal policy—and more scholarly articles on "newer" concerns: education, legal affairs, missions.

Perhaps like numberless Indian agents in the past, we have been premature in announcing a "new day" for Indian-White relations. While scholars have embarked on a number of forays into fresh subjects, they seem to have confined themselves to familiar problems and time periods. And most authors who have departed from the traditional concerns of the field have published brief articles rather than full-length monographs. What does this signify? To pursue the question we must turn from crude generalizations to a discussion of the works on the list.

Images

Six works examine images of the Indian: Berkhofer [7], Dippie [12], Drinnon [13], William Nichols [36], Rydell [41], and Tyler [50]. All of these owe a debt to Roy Harvey Pearce's *The Savages of America: A Study of the Indian and the Idea of Civilization* (1953), for they share with Pearce a conviction that what one race *believed* about the other was as important as what was actually true. Beliefs shaped actions and played a major role in the formulation of policy. But these works have propelled us into a new stage of understanding for they provide a comprehensive overview of the various images and their impact: Berkhofer and Drinnon cover the colonial era to the present, while Dippie and Tyler discuss the nineteenth and twentieth centuries and the articles by Nichols and Rydell examine two case studies taken from either end of the 1800s.

Nevertheless, it would be a mistake to confuse the common ancestry and purpose of these "image studies" with homogeneity. They offer different assessments of what the images were, and suggest different uses for Pearce's thirty-year-old insights. For Drinnon, white images of the Indian have been both uniform and negative. "Indian hating" has dominated public perceptions, driven policymaking, and answered the American culture's need to dominate exotic peoples. Dippie and Berkhofer agree that there is a relationship between the "need" of white people and their image of Indians, but where Drinnon sees hatred they see ambivalence. Dippie describes the persistence of the idea that Native Americans are a vanishing race and argues that this image captures both the ethnocentrism and paternalistic benevolence of intellectuals and politicians. Berkhofer's view is more complex. He traces a paradoxical attitude of hatred and fascination through time. That attitude takes different forms in different eras, but it is always bipolar and expressive of white values. Together, these works make a persuasive case that the Indian policies of the nineteenth century expressed widely felt attitudes and expectations. White actions were democratic in the sense that they accurately represented the dominant culture's wishes.

The articles in the Tyler collection, as well as the essays by Rydell and Nichols, point in other directions. *Red Men and Hat Wearers*, edited by Daniel Tyler [50], contains essays by Donald Berthrong, John Ewers and Joseph Cash that describe Indian images of Whites and suggest that native actions might well reflect not only their culture, but their image of white men. Their contributions call a number of old assumptions into question. The complexity of mutual image-making is further underlined by William Nichols's fascinating essay on Lewis and Clark [36]. His description of the explorers' winter in the Pacific Northwest hints at just how difficult it is to descend from the grand canvas of American civilization to the details of cross-cultural interaction. It is important to note as well that neither Nichols nor the contributors to the Tyler collection are directly concerned with policy. On the other hand, Rydell's description of the Omaha exposition of 1898 [41] gives us a concrete example of image–serving policy (in this case imperialism and assimilation). It leaves us wanting to know more exactly how specific ideas affect particular actions.

Policy

Federal policy is the principal concern of works by David A. Nichols [35], Stuart [45], Smith and Kvasnicka [44], Hoxie [22], Satz [42] and Williams [52]. While the subjects of their work range across the nineteenth century, these authors exhibit a common concern for the relationship between Indian policy and broader issues and themes in American culture. Three of them examine how Indian affairs "play out" into other concerns. Walter Williams [52] traces the links between the debate over the annexation of the Philippines in the aftermath of the Spanish-American War and earlier discussions about the "plight" of the red man. Paul Stuart [45] shows how the myriad responsibilities heaped on the Indian Office in the late nineteenth century conspired to produce a modern bureaucracy similar to those springing up in other parts of Washington at the same time. Neither study seeks to excuse either imperialism or the official rigidities of the Bureau of Indian Affairs, but both urge us to look beyond the familiar landscape when describing federal actions. Ronald Satz [42] makes a similar suggestion by depicting removal in the Old Northwest as an extension of the southeastern removals of the 1820s and the 1830s.

Events external to Indian affairs "play in" to policy in my piece [22] as well as in the Nichols [35] and Smith and Kvasnicka [44] volumes. I examined the complex pressures affecting government policymakers through a quantitative analysis of voting behavior in the United States Senate. Nichols's definitive study of federal action during the Lincoln administration describes vividly how political pressure, the inertia of corruption, and the demands of the Civil War combined to produce a "policy" that was deeply imbedded in the political culture of its time. *Indian-White Relations: A Persistent Paradox* was published in 1976 under the editorship of Jane F. Smith and Robert M. Kvasnicka, but it contains the proceedings of a conference sponsored by the National Archives in 1972. While rich in subject matter (papers ranged from descriptions of archival collections to discussions of assimilation), the bulk of the book examines the nineteenth century. And throughout the collection runs a concern for understanding the impact of historical context on particular events. That concern is evident in the essays on new research strategies as well as in the examinations of "Ethnocentric Reform" and "The Frontier Army" by, respectively, Henry Fritz and Robert Utley.

Legal Relations

When scholars turn from image and policy studies to legal and treaty relations between Native Americans and Whites, the focus often shifts from broad context to narrow case study. With the exception of Barsh and Henderson's *The Road* [6], all the titles in this area explore particular instances of legal or diplomatic interaction. *The Road* is a general work, but its overview of Indian tribes' shifting legal status is important to an understanding of the contours of the nineteenth century. Part Two of the book traces the progressive deterioration of the legal notion of tribal sovereignty and provokes an inevitable response: how did this process operate in a specific tribe? Raymond DeMallie [11] asks the question more directly in his description of the cultural context in which treatymaking occurred on the Great Plains. Six other titles—Edmunds [15], Ferguson [16], Zanger [55], McLoughlin [26, 27], and Young [54]—provide some answers.

According to R. David Edmunds [15], the treaty negotiated at Vincennes in 1792 was both unplanned and ineffective as an instrument of federal policy. Meanwhile, according to Clyde R. Ferguson [16], deep divisions existed between Federalists and nascent Jeffersonians on the Georgia frontier. Both authors demonstrate that policy in the Early Republic was governed in large part by local pressures and *ad hoc* decision making. Martin Zanger's [55] description of three young Winnebagoes' encounter with American law in 1821 reveals similar pressures and a similarly haphazard system. Warriors seeking "justice" by killing two soldiers found themselves facing a white hangman. In the end, one man was released, one died in jail, and a third was executed as federal authorities—inconsistent to the end—paid compensation to the tribesmen's families. Edmunds, Ferguson and Zanger provoke us by tossing fascinating monkey wrenches into the conventional understanding of a deliberate and expansionist government policy; the two essays by William McLoughlin contain another, more systematic argument: treatymaking stimulated rather than undermined Indian nationalism. First, McLoughlin [26] describes how the 1806 agreement between the United States and the Cherokees galvanized the leadership's opposition to future land cessions; his 1981 article [27] indicates that the failure of a grant of United States citizenship contained in a 1817 treaty convinced the tribe that integration with Anglo-Americans was impossible. Mary Young's piece on Cherokee nationalism [54] ranges far beyond treatymaking, but her conclusions generally follow McLoughlin. All of these case studies suggest rich avenues for future work.

Case Studies

Ironically, the titles that are more comprehensive case studies are not quite so compelling. Donald Berthrong [8] and William T. Hagan [17] have produced important monographs on reservation life. Their books on the Southern Cheyenne and Arapaho and Kiowa-Comanche agencies examine public affairs: legal conflicts, efforts to introduce agriculture, and the corrosive impact of American capitalism on traditional societies. Their detailed descriptions offer a unique perspective, but their broad focus raises new questions: what was the relationship of private life (family structure, sex roles, religious beliefs) to these public tragedies? How did social and political beliefs change and evolve in a reservation environment? The Berthrong and Hagan volumes suggest some significant answers to these questions; unfortunately, the case studies of Miner and Unrau [32] on Kansas, Burton Smith [43] on the Flatheads, Edward Barry [5] on Fort Belknap, and Stephen McCluskey [29] on the Hopis do not. These surveys provide important information about specific tribal experiences and they offer impressive lessons in how one might carry out a narrowly focused project, but they leave us wanting a more comprehensive picture of policy's impact on tribal cultures.

Military Relations

It is somewhat surprising that the two titles emphasizing military affairs by James L. Haley [18] and Gerald Thompson [46] are also successful case studies. Apparently heeding the calls of Robert Utley and Richard Ellis to see the frontier army in three dimensions and to view its relations with Native Americans as the product of mutual aggression, Haley and Thompson have produced two excellent works on incidents that are a part of our folklore: the Red River War and the Navajo incarceration at Bosque Redondo respectively. While Haley makes some inexcusable generalizations about "primitive" tribes that exhibited a "lack of sophistication," his book, like Thompson's, demonstrates that military confrontation could provoke deep divisions on both ends of the battlefield. Issues of authority, leadership and cultural identity plagued both General Carleton and his Navajo subjects.

Biographies

There are three biographies on this list—Drury [14], Moulton [34], and McQuaid [28]—and one biographical collection: Kvasnicka's *Commissioners of Indian Affairs* [24]. They present the lives of individuals who stood between Anglo society and the native world, and are legitimate contributions to the history of Indian-White relations. The Kvasnicka volume [24] is an important reference work that will prove immensely valuable. Nevertheless, all of these titles attend to public affairs and leave the reader wondering about other aspects of the subject's relationships with Indian people. Gary E. Moulton's biography of John Ross [34] goes farthest by offering a fascinating portrait of a trader's son who owned slaves, married a Quaker, sent his children to an eastern preparatory school and devoted himself to a cause he must have known was doomed. His book suggests a framework for future work in which individuals will be described "in the round" and we will learn how they were both the objects and the subjects of cultural interaction.

Reformers and Missionaries

Despite the pervasiveness of mission and reform activity in the nineteenth century, most of the scholarship in this area has confined itself to the period after the Civil War. Of this activity, the most significant general study is Francis Paul Prucha's *American Indian Policy in Crisis* [39], a general study of Christian reformers and policy formulation from 1865 to 1900. Based on extensive research in government documents, contemporary periodicals and the archives of major reform groups, Prucha's book offers an exhaustive survey of the subject as well as a powerful argument that reformers were pivotal figures who acted out of a rich Protestant evangelical tradition.

According to Prucha, reformers faced the problems of their day "with honesty and the best of intentions" (p. 404). Wilbert Ahern [3] agrees that the reformers were both important and honest, but he calls their insistence that native "progress" be defined in Anglo-American terms "assimilationist racism." Chandler's profile of attitudes in California offers a similar view of the reformers and their supporters [10].

Despite the disagreements over the reformers' virtues, however, recent discussion of their work and studies of missionary endeavor—like the new titles on policy and legal relations—shun simple moralizing. Here too the concern is with context: the sources of belief and the motives for action. The "reform" subgroup also shares an interest in case studies. Milner [30], Hinckley [21], Norwood [37] and Zwink [56] examine particular missions and agencies. Like the detailed studies of treatymaking, their work reveals how important the values and experience of the Indian groups were to the outcome of their encounter with strangers who wanted to "save them." Milner's study—the most developed and sophisticated of the group—examines the details of Quaker agents' activities with the Pawnees, Otos and Omahas. He illustrates how good intentions could be lost amidst the cultural conflict and confusion of reservation life. Similarly, Zwink's description of Lawrie Tatum illustrates both the impact and the limits of the "peace policy" at the Kiowa agency. Hinckley's study of John Brady's work with the Tlingits in the 1880s and 1890s, on the other hand, is a story of "success." These authors demonstrate that explaining different outcomes requires more than an examination of missionary character; it demands an understanding of both sides of the cultural confrontation. Finally, Valerie Mathes's survey [25] of Indian women in the Catholic church makes a similar point about "successful" missions when she speculates that individuals from cultures where women had important religious roles were likely to become Catholic converts and nuns.

Perhaps the two "newest" areas of scholarly activity in the field of Indian-White relations are education and the economic interaction between Native Americans and Whites. While the topics are hardly new, the systematic investigation of them is. They have attracted people from a variety of disciplines (economics, anthropology, geography) who have turned up new sources and explored new questions.

Education

Works on Indian education fall into two categories: studies of educational policy and profiles of institutions. Irving Hendrick's article on California [20] and Ronald Rayman's on the adoption of the Lancastrian technique at early schools for the civilized tribes [40] are of the former type, while Adams [1, 2], Moranian [33] and Trennert [47, 49] explore the latter. It is interesting that while Rayman and Hendrick describe very different situations, their theses are quite similar: the efforts of white teachers neither bridged the cultural gaps between the races nor succeeded in reducing the economic exploitation of native groups. These two articles suggest that Indians realized better than their "friends" the shortcomings of classroom instruction.

As in other areas, the complex relationship between Indians and Whites comes through most vividly in case studies. The articles that examine particular schools or agencies probe the details of that relationship and offer somewhat paradoxical conclusions. On the one hand, all the authors agree that education occurred in an atmosphere of antagonism: the teachers were ethnocentric and the students resistant (Moranian says teachers practiced "ethnocide"). On the other hand, several writers note that Indian students used the schools for their own ends. The experience had a profound impact on the individuals subjected to it. Adams's article on "Schooling the Hopi" [2], Trennert's on "Educating Indian Girls" [49], and Moranian's on Wisconsin [33] all suggest that returned students were more open to federal programs, more likely to take jobs with the Bureau of Indian Affairs or other white employers, and probably ended up at odds with their uneducated kinsmen. The authors usually call these results "failures." But if we take seriously the critique of nineteenth century educational policy contained in the other titles in this section, we might revise our conclusions. Schools that defined ethnocentrism and the exploitation of American capitalism as "progressive" were likely to be proud of producing tormented graduates who lived in society's lower ranks. In short, as the work on schooling moves beyond discussions of general policy, the real impact of the schools and the precise nature of their educational program comes more sharply into focus.

Economic Relations

The final cluster of titles examines the economic ties between Indians and Whites. As in the area of education, this is not so much a "new" subject as it is a newly explored one. Scholars have examined in greater detail the federal policies that affected the economic life of Native Americans, as well as the role of Indian traders, and the impact of white contact on native land use.

Carlson [9], Hauptman [19], Miner [31] and Pennington [38] tackle different aspects of government economic policy. Carlson's is the only general work; it examines the impact of the Dawes Act on Indian farming. Carlson [9] brings an economist's precision to an old generalization: the allotment law had a disastrous effect on Native American agriculture. In the process he demonstrates the extent to which the introduction of agriculture had been successful prior to the passage of the severalty act and catalogues the many ways the new policy undermined that success. Hauptman, Pennington and Miner present a similar view in their case studies. Pennington [38] describes the beginning of farming on the Cheyenne and Arapaho reservation in the late nineteenth century, and Miner's book [31] describes the economic dismemberment of the Indian Territory. Both emphasize the profound changes in economic life brought on by contact with white society. For the Cheyennes and Arapahoes those changes were rapid and forced by federal action, while for the civilized tribes the invasion of the corporation marked the last stage of a long, slow process. Miner also argues that tribal leaders played a substantial role in encouraging non-Indian economic interests to enter the tribal preserves. In both instances the authors share Carlson's view that tribes were not uniformly resistant to economic change. Hauptman [19] would probably agree with that position, for in his description of the Senecas' fight to protect their reservation from allotment, he shows that they were already farming successfully when allotment was proposed. Luckily, they were able to mobilize both themselves and their political allies to fend off this dubious reform.

Two titles, Trennert's *Indian Traders of the Middle Border* [48], and Gary Anderson's essay on the upper Mississippi prior to 1812 [4], examine economic relations from the perspective of the merchant's counter. Their work is provocative, for it makes clear how central traders were to a tribe's relations with the outside world. Anderson shows how important economic power was on the northwestern frontier. Tribal leaders were not as impressed by forts and military hardware as they were by quality merchandise. Loyalty and good service won Indian allies; erratic bluster did not. These axioms worked against American interests before 1812, but afterwards—as Trennert's monograph on the House of Ewing shows—persistent American businessmen benefited from them. The Ewing brothers were in the Indian business, supplying government agencies and offering cash for native trade goods. Over three decades they exercised enormous influence over midwestern Indian policy and the internal politics of several tribes. Despite Trennert's protest that his book is "not a study of Indians," he teaches us a great deal about an important area of Indian-White relations. One hopes his book will soon be joined by others.

Perhaps the most unusual of the economic case studies are the three titles on land use. Knack [23], VanStone [51] and Wilms [53] focus on the relationship between Native Americans and their natural environment. Gone is the old notion that Indians dwelled passively in their world. In its place is the assertion that tribesmen—like all people—shaped their environment through land use practices. Building on that insight, these authors ask, "how did contact with non-Indians affect the tribal environment; how did changes in culture produce changes in land use?" All three describe a rise in commercial activity and substantial Indian participation in new economic patterns. Knack's description of Pyramid Lake in Nevada shows this process occurring very rapidly, while VanStone's essay on the Yukon River Ingalik and Wilms's on the Cherokee indicate that profound changes occurred even when federal officials were absent or indifferent. Their studies introduce new methodologies (Wilms is a geographer, VanStone an anthropologist), and offer a fresh approach to descriptions of Indian-White contact.

Conclusions

Three closing conclusions suggest themselves. First, despite the depredations and raids, government policy will not disappear as a subject for scholarly study. Nor should it. Examinations of government action have grown more sophisticated and complex, and the definition of public policy has expanded to include new areas; none of these authors would argue that the subject is unimportant. During the nineteenth century, as Anglo-Americans consolidated their control over the continent, the actions of their government became increasingly important to the lives of Native Americans. While Indian people continued to find meaning and continuity in their own cultures, they experienced an environment—political, economic, even natural—that was being shaped by outsiders. New methodologies cannot cancel that reality; they can make us more conscious of its complexity.

Second, in each area of activity there appears to be a symbiotic relationship between general studies and examinations of particular tribes and agencies. Broad treatments examine the relationship between Indian affairs and other dimensions of American life, while individual cases either test these generalizations or demonstrate how national concerns affected (or bypassed) the relations of individual Indians and Whites. Inquiry in one sphere seems necessary for the health of the other.

And third, dozens of subjects remain to be explored. In addition to the suggestions made in the discussion above, readers should notice that there are no comparative studies on this list. How do Indian–White relations in the United States differ from native-

European relations in Russia or Argentina or, indeed with Black-White or Asian-White relations in the United States? There are also only a few titles here that draw on social scientific research. Unlike Afro-Americanists or historians of the family, students of Indian-White relations have been reluctant to venture into other disciplines for help. Revitalization movements now win ready recognition, but the substantial literature in areas such as assimilation, modernization, or religious conversion remain unexploited. Perhaps this will be a form of exploitation we can endorse!

ALPHABETICAL LIST

[1] Adams, David Wallace. 1977. "Education in Hues: Red and Black at Hampton Institute: 1878-1893." *South Atlantic Quarterly* 76:159-76.

[2] ———. 1979. "Schooling the Hopi: Federal Indian Policy Writ Small, 1887-1917." *Pacific Historical Review* 48:335-56.

[3] Ahern, Wilbert H. 1976. "Assimilationist Racism: The Case of the 'Friends of the Indian'." *Journal of Ethnic Studies* 4:23-33.

[4] Anderson, Gary. 1980. "American Agents vs. British Traders: Prelude to the War of 1812 in the Far West." In *The American West: Essays in Honor of W. Eugene Hollon*, ed. Ronald Lora, pp. 3-24. Toledo: University of Toledo Press.

[5] Barry, Edward E., Jr. 1976. "From Buffalo to Beef: Assimilation on the Fort Belknap Reservation." *Montana, The Magazine of Western History* 26:38-51.

[6] Barsh, Russel Lawrence, and James Youngblood Henderson. 1980. *The Road: Indian Tribes and Political Liberty*. Berkeley: University of California Press.

[7] Berkhofer, Robert F., Jr. 1978. *The White Man's Indian: Images of the American Indian from Columbus to the Present*. New York: Alfred A. Knopf.

[8] Berthrong, Donald J. 1976. *The Cheyenne and Arapaho Ordeal: Reservation and Agency Life in the Indian Territory, 1875-1907*. Norman: University of Oklahoma Press.

[9] Carlson, Leonard A. 1981. *Indians, Bureaucrats and Land: The Dawes Act and the Decline of Indian Farming*. Westport: Greenwood Press.

[10] Chandler Robert. 1980. "The Failure of Reform: White Attitudes and Indian Response in California During the Civil War Era." *Pacific Historian* 24:284-94.

[11] DeMallie, Raymond J. 1980. "Touching the Pen: Plains Indian

Treaty Councils in Ethnohistorical Perspective." In *Ethnicity on the Great Plains*, ed. Frederick C. Luebke, pp. 38-53. Lincoln: University of Nebraska Press.

[12] Dippie, Brian W. 1982. *The Vanishing American: White Attitudes and U.S. Indian Policy*. Middletown: Wesleyan University Press.

[13] Drinnon, Richard. 1980. *Facing West: The Metaphysics of Indian-Hating and Empire-Building*. Minneapolis: University of Minnesota Press.

[14] Drury, Clifford M. 1979. *Chief Lawyer of the Nez Perce Indians, 1796-1876*. Glendale, California: Arthur H. Clark Company.

[15] Edmunds, R. David. 1978. "'Nothing Has Been Effected': The Vincennes Treaty of 1792." *Indiana Magazine of History* 74:23-25.

[16] Ferguson, Clyde R. 1979. "Confrontation at Coleraine: Creeks, Georgians and Federalist Indian Policy." *South Atlantic Quarterly* 78:224-43.

[17] Hagan, William T. 1976. *United States-Comanche Relations: The Reservation Years*. New Haven: Yale University Press.

[18] Haley, James L. 1976. *The Buffalo War: The History of the Red River Indian Uprising of 1874*. Garden City: Doubleday.

[19] Hauptman, Laurence M. 1977. "Senecas and Subdividers: Resistance to Allotment of Indian Lands in New York, 1875-1906." *Prologue* 9:105-16.

[20] Hendrick, Irving G. 1976. "Federal Policy Affecting the Education of Indians in California, 1849-1934." *History of Education Quarterly* 16:163-85.

[21] Hinckley, Ted C. 1980. "'We Are More Truly Heathen Than the Natives': John G. Brady and the Assimilation of Alaska's Tlingit Indians." *Western Historical Quarterly* 11:37-55.

[22] Hoxie, Frederick E. 1977. "The End of the Savage: Indian Policy in the United States Senate, 1880-1900." *Chronicles of Oklahoma* 55:157-79.

[23] Knack, Martha C. 1977. "A Short Resource History of Pyramid Lake, Nevada." *Ethnohistory* 24:47-63.

[24] Kvasnicka, Robert M., et al. 1979. *The Commissioners of Indian Affairs, 1824-1977*. Lincoln: University of Nebraska Press.

[25] Mathes, Valerie Sherer. 1980. "American Indian Women and the Catholic Church." *North Dakota History* 47:20-25.

[26] McLoughlin, William G. 1975. "Thomas Jefferson and the Beginning of Cherokee Nationalism, 1806-1809," *William and Mary Quarterly*, 3rd ser. 32:547-80.

[27] ———. 1981. "Experiment in Cherokee Citizenship, 1817-1829." *American Quarterly* 33:3-25.

[28] McQuaid, Kim. 1977. "William Apes, Pequot: An Indian Reformer in the Jackson Era." *New England Quarterly* 50:605-25.

[29] McCluskey, Stephen C. 1980. "Evangelists, Educators, Ethnog-

raphers, and the Establishment of the Hopi Reservation." *Journal of Arizona History* 21:363-90.

[30] Milner, Clyde A. II. 1982. *With Good Intentions: Quaker Work Among the Pawnees, Otos and Omahas in the 1870s*. Lincoln: University of Nebraska Press.

[31] Miner, H. Craig. 1976. *The Corporation and the Indian: Tribal Sovereignty and Industrial Civilization in Indian Territory, 1865-1907*. Columbia: University of Missouri Press.

[32] Miner, H. Craig, and William E. Unrau. 1978. *The End of Indian Kansas: A Study of Cultural Revolution, 1854-1871*. Lawrence: Regents Press of Kansas.

[33] Moranian, Suzanne Elizabeth. 1981. "Ethnocide in the Schoolhouse: Missionary Efforts to Educate Indian Youth in Pre-Reservation Wisconsin." *Wisconsin Magazine of History* 64:243-60.

[34] Moulton, Gary E. 1978. *John Ross, Cherokee Chief*. Athens: University of Georgia Press.

[35] Nichols, David A. 1978. *Lincoln and the Indian: Civil War Policy and Politics*. Columbia: University of Missouri Press.

[36] Nichols, William. 1979-80. "Lewis and Clark Probe the Darkness." *American Scholar* 49:94-101.

[37] Norwood, Frederick A. 1979. "Conflict of Cultures: Methodist Efforts with the Ojibway, 1830-1880." *Religion in Life* 48:360-76.

[38] Pennington, William D. 1979. Government Policy and Indian Farming on the Cheyenne and Arapaho Reservations, 1869-1880." *Chronicles of Oklahoma* 57:171-89.

[39] Prucha, Francis Paul. 1976. *American Indian Policy in Crisis: Christian Reformers and the Indian, 1865-1900*. Norman: University of Oklahoma Press.

[40] Rayman, Ronald. 1981. "Joseph Lancaster's Monitorial System of Instruction and American Indian Education, 1815-1838." *History of Education Quarterly* 21:395-410.

[41] Rydell, Robert W. 1981. "The Trans-Mississippi and International Exposition: 'To Work Out the Problem of Universal Civilization'." *American Quarterly* 33:587-607.

[42] Satz, Ronald N. 1976. "Indian Policy in the Jacksonian Era: The Old Northwest as a Test Case." *Michigan History* 60:71-93.

[43] Smith, Burton M. 1979. "The Politics of Allotment: The Flathead Indian Reservation as a Test Case." *Pacific Northwest Quarterly* 70:131-40.

[44] Smith, Jane F., and Robert M. Kvasnicka. 1976. *Indian-White Relations: A Persistent Paradox*. Washington, D.C.: Howard University Press.

[45] Stuart, Paul. 1979. *The Indian Office: Growth and Development of an American Institution*. Ann Arbor: University of Michigan Research Press.

[46] Thompson, Gerald. 1976. *The Army and the Navaho*. Tucson: University of Arizona Press.

[47] Trennert, Robert A. 1979. "Peaceably If They Will, Forcibly If They Must: The Phoenix Indian School, 1890-1901." *Journal of Arizona History* 20:297-322.

[48] ———. 1981. *Indian Traders of the Middle Border: The House of Ewing, 1827-54*. Lincoln: University of Nebraska Press.

[49] ———. 1982. "Educating Indian Girls at Nonreservation Boarding Schools, 1878-1920." *Western Historical Quarterly* 13:271-90.

[50] Tyler, Daniel, ed. 1976. *Red Men and Hat Wearers: Viewpoints in Indian History*. Boulder Colorado: Pruett Publishing.

[51] Van Stone, James W. 1976. "The Yukon River Ingalik: Subsistence, the Fur Trade, and a Changing Resource Base." *Ethnohistory* 23:199-212.

[52] Williams, Walter L. 1980. "United States Indian Policy and the Debate over Philippine Annexation: Implications for the Origins of American Imperialism." *Journal of American History* 66:810-31.

[53] Wilms, Douglas C. 1978. "Cherokee Acculturation and Changing Land Use Practices." *Chronicles of Oklahoma* 56:331-43.

[54] Young, Mary. 1981. "The Cherokee Nation: Mirror of the Republic." *American Quarterly* 33:502-24.

[55] Zanger, Martin. 1980. "Conflicting Concepts of Justice: A Winnebago Murder Trial on the Illinois Frontier." *Journal of the Illinois State Historical Society* 73:263-76.

[56] Zwink, T. Ashley. 1978-79. "On the White Man's Road: Lawrie Tatum and the Formative Years of the Kiowa Agency, 1869-1873." *Chronicles of Oklahoma* 56:431-41.

Twentieth Century Federal Indian Policy

DONALD L. FIXICO

University of Wisconsin, Milwaukee

The literature on federal Indian policy since 1900 focuses on various topics within the wide scope of federal-tribal relations. A precarious range of subjects are covered consisting mainly of books, law review articles and dissertations. Much of the literature affects the current status of Native Americans, including water rights and the legalities involving other natural resources on reservation lands. Other subject areas cover health, education, claims cases and particular legislation that has influenced federal Indian policy during this century. Because of the topics' contemporary nature, legal scholars have produced much of the literature while humanists have focused on topics relating to the early decades.

Two attorneys, Russel Barsh and James Henderson, in *The Road: Indian Tribes and Political Liberty* [8], legally interpret pertinent legislation and court decisions while noting the haphazard legal status of tribal sovereignty. *The Road* is beyond the comprehension of the lay individual and it is best suited to the needs of the law student and legal scholar. Vine Deloria, Jr. and Clifford Lytle have co-authored *American Indians, American Justice* [28], a text directed to the needs of classroom use. It is an overview of federal Indian law, covering the legal and political rights of contemporary Indians. The ambiguity of Indian policy and its legalities are also explored in Michael Dorris's "The Grass Still Grows, the Rivers Still Flow: Contemporary Native Americans" [31]. Dorris's message is clear: the legal basis for Indian rights is embedded in federal-Indian treaties.

The most comprehensive survey of federal Indian policy regarding land is Imre Sutton, *Indian Land Tenure: Bibliographic Essays and a Guide to the Literature* [118]. This bibliography covers the full gamut of literature prior to 1900 and afterwards. It covers a wide range of topics, with discussion sections on colonial land policy, treaty land cessions, utilization of reservations, allotment and natural resources on Indian lands. Differences between Euroamerican land and Indian land relationships are distinguished at length in Francis E. Ackerman, "A Conflict Over Land" [1]. Anglo-American and Native American attitudes toward land are clarified, corroborating that different philosophies of land utilization existed among these two peoples. By comprehending these historical land relationships, the premises of twentieth-century Indian policy are better understood.

Paul Stuart, "United States Indian Policy: From the Dawes Act to the American Indian Policy Review Commission" [117] paints a full picture of federal Indian policy in the twentieth century. Stuart stresses that the Dawes and Indian Reorganization acts failed as revolutionary concepts during their times, and he points out their shortcomings. Records of the last ninety years reveal errors in the allotment and reorganization experiments due to inadequate federal support. At the time of completing his study, Stuart thought that the American Indian Policy Review Commission (AIPRC) in the 1970s would recommend a final solution and effect a better policy. The origin of the AIPRC is briefly told in Kirke Kickingbird, "The American Indian Policy Review Commission: A Prospect for Future Change in Federal Indian Policy" [66]. On July 16, 1973, Senator James Abourezk introduced Senate Joint Resolution 133, a measure that proposed the Commission. Kickingbird excerpted Congressional discussions to explain how the resolution became Public Law 93-580 and created the AIPRC.

A special issue of the *American Indian Culture and Research Journal*, entitled "New Directions in Federal Indian Policy, A Review of the American Indian Policy Review Commission," analyzes the AIPRC. The edition consists of essays by ten authors. Mark Thompson's "Nurturing the Forked Tree: Conception and Formation of the American Indian Policy Review Commission" [122] and Donald A. Grinde's "Politics and the American Indian Policy Review Commission" [44] examine the political and legal problems during the Commission's troubled beginnings when the National Congress of American Indians filed a suit against the AIPRC. The Commission's errors in health investigation are cited in Susan Guyette, "Suggestions for Priority Alcohol and Drug Abuse Research: A Comment on the Recommendations of Task Force Eleven of the American Indian Policy Review Commission" [47] and Cecelia Gallerito, "Indian Health, Federal or Tribally Determined: Health Recommendations of the American Indian Policy Review Commission" [37]. Numerous statistics prove that the Commission grossly overlooked Indian use of alcohol and drugs, as noted in Margaret B. Cooper's "Task Force Eleven of the American Indian Policy Review Commission: A Developmental Overview" [25]. Grayson Noley reiterates the Commission's shortcomings in "Summary and Critique of the Report on Indian Education of the American Indian Policy Review Commission" [86].

The Commission relied on previously collected data rather than gathering its own facts. Insufficient design of methodological research is noted in David Beaulieu, "A Critical Review of the Urban Indian Task Force of the American Indian Policy Review Commission" [10]. Joseph H. Stauss, in "A Critique of Task Force Eight, Final Report to the American Indian Policy Review Commission: Urban and Rural Non-Reservation Indians" [113] noted that most findings on urban Indians were not scientifically substantiated and the Commission failed to address the unique needs of non-reservation Indians. Improving Indian conditions requires action in both law and policy as Jerry Muskrat points out in "Recommendations of the American Indian Policy Review Commission and the Supreme Court" [83]. Al Logan Slagle's "The American Indian Policy Review Commission: Repercussions and Aftermath" [111] surmises that AIPRC recommendations caused controversy within the Indian community, thereby threatening the autonomy of Indian groups and undermining the self-determination policy.

As Indians entered the twentieth century, legal problems as well as socio-economic problems engulfed them. Water rights affecting western reservations climaxed in 1908 with the "Winters Decision." Norris Hundley has written two exceptional articles exposing the ambiguity surrounding Indian water rights. "The Dark and Bloody Ground of Indian Water Rights: Confusion Elevated to Principle" [57] supplies a helpful historical backdrop of the landmark water case. The origin of "reserve right" which legally guaranteed water from the Milk River for the Fort Belknap Reservation is thoroughly analyzed. In "The 'Winters' Decision and Indian Water Rights: A Mystery Reexamined" [58], the debate over Indian water rights and the complexity involved in the landmark case are restated. How the Court interprets quantum of water usage by Indians, legitimate users of water and the priority of Indian rights is carefully examined. The essence is that Indian water rights remain a cloudy issue with many questions for the Court to address.

The ambiguous Winters case has attracted the attention of several scholars, leading them to study various water related issues on reservations—surface rights, riparian water, water quantity and ground water. The last is the subject in Gwendolyn Griffith's "Indian Claims to Groundwater: Reserved Rights or Beneficial Interest?" [43] Griffith concurs with Hundley that Indian water rights are complex and need to be settled. The prevailing Indian "reserve right" doctrine empowers tribal people on reservations to claim original right to water, whether they use it or not, hence making non-Indians junior appropriators. As the water table drops, increasing scarcity of groundwater, especially in the West during droughts, competition intensifies for this valuable resource that is taken for granted.

Belinda K. Orem forewarns that the demand for western water will exceed current supplies in "Paleface, Redskin and the Great White Chiefs in Washington: Drawing the Battle Lines over Western Water Rights" [88]. Orem notes that William Veeder and other proponents of Indian water rights have been supported by the federal government in its fiduciary role which opposes western states' interests whose economies depend very much on water. To protect state interests, Congress will likely need to revise the law. In this process Indians stand to lose the most.

A 147-page study paper, "The Winters Doctrine: Seventy Years of Application of 'Reserved' Water Rights to Indian Reservations" [84], produced by Michael C. Nelson with the assistance of Bradley L. Booke, is the most comprehensive bibliographic source on Indian water rights. The rationale of federal Indian policy in regard to western reservations is preserving a sufficient water supply for irrigation and program development, else the arid Indians lands will become valueless. Beginning with the Winters Doctrine, all of the court cases on the subject of Indian water rights are reviewed and a synopsis accompanies each.

H. A. Ranquist, "The *Winters* Doctrine and How it Grew: Federal Reservation of Rights to the Use of Water" [102], traces the events leading up to the famous case. The "theoretical function" of other types of federally-reserved rights are examined and a revised federal structure for supervising Indian water pertaining to state jurisdiction over reserved water claims is recommended. Indian skepticism of state courts and administrative agencies is the focus of R. S. Pelcyger's "Indian Water Rights: Some Emerging Frontiers" [92]. Pelcyger divides the water issue into surface water and ground water, and he suggests an intricate federal policy is needed to manage the water usage for upstream and downstream users to avoid further disputes with state interests. A specific tribal water case involving theoretical rights is addressed in M. E. Price and G. D. Weatherford's "Indian Water Rights in Theory and Practice: Navajo Experience in the Colorado River Basin" [100]. The Navajo struggle to use the Winters case in negotiating for the Navajo Generating Station at Page, Arizona and the Navajo Irrigation Project near Farmington, New Mexico focuses on a new area for litigation.

Indian water authority William H. Veeder, in "Water Rights in the Coal Fields of the Yellowstone River Basin" [127] and "Confiscation of Indian Water Rights in the Upper Missouri River Basin" [126], exemplifies the unfair practice of the federal government in monopolizing control over Indian water. Water needed for developing coal and other natural resources on tribal lands is dominated by the government which competes against reservation developments in Montana and Wyoming.

Anne E. Ross, "Water Rights: Aboriginal Water Use and Water Law in the Southwestern United States: Why the Reserved Rights Doctrine was Inappropriate" [107], addresses inherent Indian water rights. Ross criticizes the American legal system for not acknowledging that southwestern Indian groups, in particular, were "full-fledged riparians and prior appropriators, builders of [water] diversion works." Although local white interests should not be disregarded, the doctrine of aboriginal land title protects Indian water.

Michael S. Laird predicts in "Water Rights: The Winters Cloud

Over the Rockies: Indian Water Rights and the Development of Western Energy Resources" [68], that in the 1980s, the Rocky Mountain area will receive significant attention. National need to develop energy resources in the West and water required for the process mandates defining the "quantity" of Indian water rights; but, until then, a cloud of uncertainty hangs over the region. In 1976, a judicial decree in *Colorado River Water Jurisdiction v. United States* held that state courts have jurisdiction over tribal "reserve" water rights. In "Water Rights: The McCarren Amendment and Indian Tribes: Reserved Water Rights" [74], Elizabeth McCallister explains that the Court based its decision on the 1970 McCarran Amendment, two cases in 1971 and the Colorado judicial system of water rights. As Indian usage competes with local needs, McCallister deems that aboriginal Indian rights should be acknowledged instead of the Winters Doctrine interpretation of "reserved rights."

What will happen to Indian water rights if they are not resolved in the courts and enforced? A horrifying example has already occurred and it is told vividly in Michael L. Lawson, *Dammed Indians: The Pick-Sloan Plan and the Missouri River Sioux, 1944-1980* [69]. Without respect for traditional Indian lands, the machination of the federal bureaucracy allowed the government to bulldoze and flood more than 202,000 acres of Sioux lands. Some 580 families on the Standing Rock, Cheyenne River, Lower Brule and Yankton reservations were evacuated.

Uncertainties about Indian water rights is but one of the many paradoxes of federal-Indian relations from the late nineteenth century to the present. The Indian had his supporters in the staunch critics of the General Allotment Act, but this heavy siege of criticism obscured other relevant issues such as health. Living conditions on reservations were largely ignored and therefore improvement was gradual. Appalling health conditions and diseases are revealed in Diane Putney's "Fighting the Scourge: American Indian Morbidity and Federal Policy, 1897-1928" [101]. The federal government's response to Native American morbidity and the development of Indian medical services are described. Unimaginable statistics resulting from numerous cases of tuberculosis, trachoma, measles, and whooping cough led to a 32.42 percent death rate of every 1,000 Indians.

Scholars have reluctantly viewed Indian health as a subject in pursuing federal Indian policy studies. Rather, scholars concentrate largely on the Americanization process of "civilizing" Indian peoples and Indian land held in trust with the government. Land has been the bonding element of federal-tribal relations. Reformers in the first two decades of the twentieth century pursued an unrealistic goal of assimilating Indians into American society. Bureaucratic reformers known as "'Friends of the Indian,'' who met at Lake Mohonk Resort from 1893 to 1913, erroneously believed that the "Indian Problem" could be resolved through land allotment. The Mohonk reformers, or "Old Campaigners" as John F. Berens refers to them in "'Old Campaigners,' New Realities: Indian Policy Reform in the Progressive Era, 1900-1912" [12], applied rhetorical arguments to morally justify their actions as doing the Lord's work. "The existing state of Indian domestic life was a violation of God's established social order, so Indians were obliged to adopt both civilian morality and Christian family life."

The solution to the "Indian Problem" was believed resolved in 1887 with the Dawes Act. Allotting Indians lands would lead to farming which would individualize them; Christianization would follow. Oversight of the dangerous repercussions from the allotment program resulted in huge Indian land losses. Janet McDonnell accurately noted in "The Disintegration of the Indian Estate: Indian Land Policy, 1913-1929" [78] that reservation lands decreased sharply from 138 to 47 million acres. The blame falls to federal officials like Indian Commissioners Cato Sells and Charles Burke who possessed an agrarian mentality.

The transformation of the American nation from an agrarian to an industrial society became known as "Progressivism." A parallel between Indian and national reforms is substantiated in Thomas M. Holm, "Indians and Progressives: From Vanishing Policy to the Indian New Deal" [54]. Little relationship existed between the two reform efforts. Of more importance, Indianness survived both the Depression and federal efforts to assimilate Indians into the mainstream. Progressive thought focused on urban concerns while Indian reform concentrated on reservations. Still, the land allotment program continued.

In "Competency Commissions and Indian Land Policy, 1913-

1920," Janet McDonnell contends that anxious federal officials, especially Secretary of Interior Franklin Lane and Commissioner Cato Sells, created a "Competency Commission," then selected the Montana Flathead Reservation as their first test case to issue Indian allotment patents. McDonnell exposes in "Competency Commissions and Indian Land Policy, 1913-1920" [77] the manipulation and corruption of Lane and Sells, who persuaded and cajoled illiterate and non-English speaking Indians to take the "new medicine" during an elaborate ritual. Each Indian "stepped from a tepee and shot an arrow to signify that he was leaving his Indian way of life. He placed his hands on a plow," indicating the decision to live from then on as a "white man," then the Secretary of Interior presented him a "purse as a reminder that he must save what he earned." From 1913 to 1920, Sells and Lane were responsible for issuing 20,000 patents, covering over one million acres, most of which the Indians lost, thus accelerating impoverishment.

The origin of Indian guardianship is accounted for in Nancy C. Carter, "Race and Power Politics As Aspects of Federal Guardianship Over American Indians: Land-Related Cases, 1887-1924" [19]. The "guardianship" concept was first introduced in the Court of Claims and applied in the federal district courts. What followed was unfortunate. Contempt for Native American cultures exposed white racist beliefs that Indian people were inferior. Graft and corruption involving guardians in Indian allotments during the early decades of this century was exposed in a valuable, now-classic work written by Angie Debo and printed under the title, *And Still the Waters Run: The Betrayal of the Five Civilized Tribes* (1940). Legal scholar Rennard Strickland critiqued Debo's book and Francis Paul Prucha's more recent *Americanizing the American Indian* (1973) in "Friends and Enemies of the American Indian: An Essay Review on Native American Law and Public Policy" [116]. In assessing both works as worthy contributions, Strickland concludes that the Dawes Allotment program failed, Native Americans survived a terrible ordeal, and nothing will return to Indians the lands that they lost.

At the national level of progressivism, Indian identity survived both societal changes and the Great Depression. Certain tribes like the Rosebud Sioux and the Iroquois remained indifferent to the white man's march of progress. Application of the Indian Reorganization Act under John Collier, Bureau of Indian Affairs field agents and anthropologists is covered in Graham Taylor's "Anthropologists, Reformers and the Indian New Deal" [120]. Failure and limited success of Indian progress did not result from B.I.A. lack of information. Young anthropologists provided the Bureau with facts and they even worked for the government during the Great Depression. These social scientists and the respective tribes with whom they worked included Oliver La Farge-Hopi; Morris E. Opler-Apache, Kiowa and Comanche; H. S. Meekel-Dakota Sioux; Gordon MacGregor-Plains tribes; and, Oscar Lewis, John Harrington and Ruth Underhill who worked with the Navajo, Papago and Pima. Taylor maintains that B.I.A. field officials were impatient to introduce the I.R.A. to tribal communities, and irreparable damage occurred among the tribes. Of the tribes that voted for referendums to accept the I.R.A., 174 voted "yes" and 78 rejected it.

A thorough examination of the I.R.A. is provided by Lawrence Kelly in "The Indian Reorganization Act: The Dream and the Reality" [64]. Kelly dissects and explains the legislative measure section by section. Originally, the Wheeler-Howard Bill was 48 typewritten pages, but Congressional amendments undermined Collier's plan for total reform. Kelly concludes that scholars have been too optimistic in portraying the I.R.A. as a panacea for Indians when actually the act fell short of Collier's expected revolutionary changes. The theme of unrelenting tribal opposition to the I.R.A. was first introduced by Kelly in *The Navajo Indians and Federal Indian Policy, 1900-1935* (1968), thus paving the way for other New Deal tribal studies. Kelly examined the reasons for Navajo opposition to the I.R.A. in focusing on their efforts to add more acreage to their inadequate land base. Multiple factors for Navajo opposition are analyzed by Donald Parman in *The Navajos and the New Deal* [90]. Educated tribal leaders, conservation measures, economic change, vocational training, depression conditions and the successful adoption of sheep worked against Navajo acceptance of the I.R.A.

Indian communities faced tremendous pressures from Indian New Dealers. Micro-studies about how tribal groups responded to the I.R.A. have been completed. These include Richmond Clow, "The Rosebud Sioux: The Federal Government and the Reservation Years, 1878-1940" [24]; Roger Bromert, "The Sioux and the Indian

New Deal, 1933-1944" [16]; Steven Crum, "The Western Shoshone of Nevada and the Indian New Deal" [26]; Charles Weeks, "The Eastern Cherokee and the New Deal" [130]; Laurence M. Hauptman, *The Iroquois and the New Deal* [50]; and Kenneth R. Philp, "The New Deal and Alaskan Natives, 1936-1945" [97].

Clow and Bromert view the Sioux similarly. The federal government sought to strip the Sioux people of their romantic Plains culture and then incorporate them into the American mainstream. Reluctance to farm allotments and limited success of the cattle herd program enabled the tribe's native identity to survive. All of this occurred in spite of educational efforts to rehabilitate the Siouian political structure, while factions within the tribe disagreed over whether or not to accept the I.R.A. legislation.

Endurance of tribal nativism among the Sioux is similar to the experiences of other groups that have been studied during this critical period. Charles Weeks notes that 970 members of a "white Indian" faction among the Eastern Cherokee opposed New Deal programs. Although the Civilian Conservation Corps provided the Cherokees with jobs, as with the Sioux, the I.R.A. brought no radical changes to the Eastern Cherokees. In a more positive light, Steven Crum takes the position that the Western Shoshone reorganized four tribal communities and four separate tribal organizations, although the I.R.A. limited the political autonomy of the groups.

Weeks, Clow and Bromert focus on tribal politics plagued by the decision to accept the Indian New Deal. This level of federal-tribal politics has been given a new dimension by Hauptman in *The Iroquois and the New Deal.* Federal-Iroquois politics is examined in philosophical depth. Iroquoian interpretation of "sovereignty" conflicted with the limited sovereignty imposed under I.R.A. guidelines. In spite of this difference, the New Deal enabled the tribespeople to flourish into vibrant communities in modern Indian America.

A different Native American opposition to the Collier New Deal was cited in Kenneth Philp, "The New Deal and Alaskan Natives, 1936-1945." After chronicling the history of Alaska Natives, the coming of statehood in 1958, and the enactment of the Indian Claims Commission in 1946, Philp explains why the Alaska Natives were excluded from the I.R.A. in 1934. With the assistance of politician Anthony J. Dimond, the Alaska Native Brotherhood opposed the I.R.A. on the grounds that it hindered them from assimilating into the mainstream. This response persisted until villages needed federal loans for development.

Graham Taylor's *The New Deal and American Indian Tribalism* [121] is a pragmatic study of the I.R.A. among all tribes who accepted it. Political ramifications included factionalized tribes who were reluctant to accept the Collier philosophy of restructuring tribal governments according to federal guidelines. The I.R.A. amplified intra-tribal problems and caused new ones. Over–optimism mesmerized tribes inasmuch as they failed to revise their governments according to Collier's high expectations.

John Collier's liberal approach towards Indian reform has made him a controversial figure. Scholars continue to examine his philosophy of the Indian New Deal, and they have analyzed the man. The first full-length biography of the obstinate Commissioner is Kenneth R. Philp, *John Collier's Crusade for Indian Reform, 1920-1954* [96]. This work concentrates on what motivated the idealistic reformer and how Collier's programs and philosophies have affected federal-Indian relations from the 1930s to the present.

Another biography on John Collier is Lawrence Kelly's first of a two-volume study, *The Assault on Assimilation: John Collier and the Origins of Indian Policy Reform* [65]. Collier's life and career are covered up to 1928. His humanistic ideas that led to his program of Indian reform have been extracted by Kelly from numerous archival sources. Kelly characterizes Collier as a dynamic and strong-willed leader who refused to compromise or accept defeat in pursuing idealistic goals. Keen insight into this extraordinary humanist reformer is achieved, with a second volume to come.

A separate aspect of the Indian New Deal is studied in Robert F. Schrader, *The Indian Arts and Crafts Board; An Aspect of New Deal Indian Policy* [108]. An effort to defend Native American arts and crafts led to creation of the Arts and Crafts Board, a government agency that protected the interests of Native American artists and craftspersons. Strict federal regulations prevented entrepreneurs from undermining opportunities for Indians to make profits from selling their works. White American and Japanese imitations of Indian arts and crafts competed for sales, thus forcing Native American artists of Alaska, the Plains and the Southwest to form protective associations. After World War II, the Board ignored the termination policy of assimilation, and pushed to establish the Institute of American Indian Arts and Crafts in Santa Fe, New Mexico in 1962.

The effects of the I.R.A. have continued since the 1930s to the present, but World War II interrupted its legacy as a continuous policy. "Termination" evolved as a new policy during the late 1940s and it persisted until the early 1960s. Two studies attempt to explain the transition from Indian New Dealism to termination: Clayton R. Koppes, "From New Deal to Termination: Liberalism and Indian Policy, 1933-1953" [67] and Kenneth Philp, "Termination: A Legacy of the Indian New Deal" [98]. Koppes maintains that the dominant society criticized Indian communal living and promoted modern individualism during the nation's transition from Roosevelt's New Deal to Truman's Fair Deal. Societal intolerance of community lifestyle deviating from mainstream values during the Cold War and intolerance associated with McCarthyism contributed to the termination policy. Conservative federal officials like Nevada Senator George Malone equated Indian communalism with socialism. Philp hypothesizes that termination was a congressional response to I.R.A. failures. And, rapid Indian assimilation into the mainstream became the new directive of the termination policy.

Much of the termination policy originated from the Zimmerman Plan of 1946 to dissolve federal-Indian trust relationships. Commissioner of Indian Affairs William Zimmerman's plan categorized three groups of Indian tribes based on their economic readiness for total independence from federal relations. During the same year, the Congress enacted the Indian Claims Commission Act (ICCA) to settle once and for all tribal claims brought against the United States. Two studies, Harvey D. Rosenthal, "Their Day in Court: A History of the Indian Claims Commission" [106] and Nancy O. Lurie, "The Indian Claims Commission" [72], address this important measure that had profound socio-economic effects on native groups. Rosenthal's monograph is the more complete study of the ICCA, showing the development of the legislation and the adjudicating process of filing claims against the United States.

Lurie responded to the impact of the claims awards twenty years later. Having testified herself in claims cases, Lurie asserts that the Commission turned deaf ears to hearing all Indian grievances. And the Indian population did not actually benefit from the per capita distributions. Chicanery was common as per capita money quickly changed hands from Indians to opportunists. In 1974, the government designated that twenty percent of each claims award had to be used for tribal program development. Rosenthal concurs that the I.C.C. failed in its primary objective, and he concludes that technically, the tribes and their attorneys had "their day in court" when 613 claims were presented, even though 57 percent were awarded by "appellate bodies."

In "Barmecide Revisited: The Gratuitous Offset in Indian Claims Cases" [133], John White reports that Congress designed the I.C.C. to protect the U. S. Government against an outrageous $3 billion estimated sum that the tribes would collect. Only $130 million was awarded due to "gratuitous offsets" that reduced the actual amounts paid to tribes.

Since Gary Orfield's pioneer study on termination, entitled *A Study of the Termination Policy* (1965), there have been few additional works on federal termination policy. Charles F. Wilkinson and Eric R. Biggs collaborated in presenting the historical development of the termination policy in "The Evolution of the Termination Policy" [134]. A wide range of termination events is covered in this overview, presenting to readers the full impact on Indians when federal trust relations and government services were ended. Termination was not widely debated in Congress, but was uncharacteristically handled in subcommittees and hastily approved. No ulterior motives were suggested, although it would be interesting to learn the relationships between the congressmen and their constituents who might have gained from termination of Indian trust lands.

Susan Work analyzed the reduction of Oklahoma's Five Civilized Tribes' political powers, especially the Seminole. In "The 'Terminated' Five Tribes of Oklahoma: The Effect of Federal Legislation and Administrative Treatment on the Government of the Seminole Nation" [135], a chronology of occurrences supplements her argument that the federal government usurped the Five Tribes of their governments. Legal analysis exposes B.I.A. control, a phenomenon Work labels "bureaucratic imperialism."

Scholarship on termination languished until 1974 when Larry J. Hasse's dissertation, "Termination and Assimilation: Federal Indian

Policy, 1943 to 1961," sparked new interest for major studies. In 1979, Larry W. Burt completed a dissertation that led to the publication, *Tribalism in Crisis: Federal Indian Policy, 1953-1961* [17]. A year later, Donald L. Fixico completed a similar dissertation study, "Termination and Relocation: Federal Indian Policy in the 1950s" [34]. Both works note that the termination policy had negative effects on Indian groups. While both studies also focus on federal Indian policy across the nation, Burt concentrates on the Eisenhower era when Glenn L. Emmons was Commissioner of Indian Affairs for eight years. Commissioner Emmons is also the subject of Debra R. Boender, "Termination and the Administration of Glenn L. Emmons as Commissioner of Indian Affairs, 1953-1961" [15]. Boender asserts that Emmons did not fully understand termination while Burt contends that the Commissioner devised a gradual withdrawal plan in 1956 that focused on industrial improvement on the reservations to sever dependence on federal assistance. Fixico maintains that Emmons was not the culprit, but rather bureaucrats like Utah Senator Arthur Watkins and previous Indian Commissioner Dillon S. Myer were to blame for assimilating Indians at the cost of government services and their native identities.

During the termination years, the "relocation program" was a federal effort to ultimately end individual Indian dependence on federal services. Fewer monographs exist on relocation than on termination since scholars have been more interested in the insensitive termination policy of liquidating federal-Indian relations. Three social scientists, James H. Gundlach, P. Nelson Reid and Alden E. Roberts point out that relocated Indians in cities have a higher income than their reservation brethren. Their brief article, "Native American Indian Migration and Relocation" [46], corroborates an obvious point that reservation Indians were poorer than urban Indians.

A similar work, "Urban Relocation Reconsidered: Antecedents of Employment Among Indian Males" [23], by Lawrence Clinton, Bruce A. Chadwick and Howard M. Bahr focuses on the economic success of Indian migrants in urban areas. Successful Indian relocation is identified with economic improvement. Employment was relevant to adapting to urban living but the more important issue was social and cultural adjustment to a metropolitan lifestyle. This study noted a direct relationship between education and employment for successful adjustment. More work needs to be done on relocation and more studies are needed on the urban Indian. Unfortunate consequences of alcoholism, high unemployment, numerous arrests, broken marriages and continual return to reservations remain a paradox for scholars to contemplate.

Tribes hiring attorneys to represent them is another aspect of federal-Indian relations, especially after World War II. Only three studies address the subject and two of them focus on the Pyramid Lake Paiutes. Faun M. Dixon, "Native American Property Rights: The Pyramid Lake Reservation Land Controversy" [30] consists of two parts: an analysis of the constitutional rights of Native Americans and the struggle of the Pyramid Lake Tribe from 1861 to 1979 to maintain its reservation boundaries among hostile Nevada interests. Congress was a nest of hostile bureaucrats according to Stanley J. Underal in "On the Road Toward Termination: The Pyramid Lake Paiutes and the Indian Attorney Controversy of the 1950s" [124]. Early in this century the federal government constructed several dams on the Truckee River which flowed from Lake Tahoe into Pyramid Lake. Water diversion to irrigate farms dropped the water level of the lake, thus destroying the trout population that supplemented the Indians' livelihood. A defensive front consisting of attorneys, the Paiute Tribe and lobbyists won the battle against federal termination.

The most active role of attorneys involved in federal-Indian affairs was in representing suits before the Indian Claims Commission. John Gamino has written a brief work entitled, "Indian Claims Commission: Discretion and Limitation in the Allowance of Attorneys' Fees" [38]. The thrust of the study is explaining how the ten percent figure for attorney fees was arrived at in charging tribes for legal services. A statute mandated a ceiling on fees only in cases where the approved attorney contract does not set a fee either higher or lower than ten percent, but Court decisions have interpreted the law as establishing the maximum percentage fee in all cases.

The model tribe for the termination experiment was the Wisconsin Menominee. Stephen J. Herzberg has authored "The Menominee Indians: Termination to Restoration" [53] and "The

Menominee Indians: From Treaty to Termination" [52]. The latter is a historical survey of Menominee-federal relations; the former is concerned mainly with the termination of the Menominees beginning in the 1950s. Inclusion of Public Law 280 and its "withdrawal" of services to the tribe is covered as well. Herzberg notes that federal pressure was applied to cajole the Menominees into accepting termination, thus prompting the demise of Wisconsin's largest and richest tribal group.

A major study of the Menominee termination is Nicholas C. Peroff's *Menominee Drums: From Tribal Termination to Restoration, 1953-1973* [93]. This work is a political analysis of Menominee factions from the termination years to restoration of their tribal recognition by the federal government in 1971. The interacting dynamics of traditionalism versus progressivism among political organizations like DRUMS (Determination of Rights and Unity for Menominee Shareholders) is the essence of this case study of tribal politics.

Public Law 280 was a significant part of federal Indian policy during the 1950s. Basically the law authorized five states—Oregon, Washington, Wisconsin, Minnesota and Nebraska (and later Alaska)—to assume criminal and civil jurisdiction over reservations within their state boundaries. Since 1975 three noteworthy studies on P.L. 280 have been published: Allan Baris, "Washington's Public Law 280 — Jurisdiction on Indian Reservations" [6]; Carol E. Goldberg, "Public Law 280: The Limits of State Jurisdiction Over Reservation Indians" [39]; and, Louis D. Persons II, "Jurisdiction: Public Law 280—Local Regulation of Protected Indian Lands" [94]. Each of these works dissected the law and explained its legal limitations. Persons noted the judiciary's uncertainty in interpreting P.L. 280, even though the Court deemed that Congress protected Indians until their ultimate integration into society. By using the state of Washington as an example, Baris concluded the same, but from another viewpoint. Ambiguity of the law allowed states to assimilate Indians into the mainstream. P.L. 280 contradicted the Indian self-determination policy and Goldberg warned against various state interpretations of P.L. 280 which affected Indian hunting and fishing rights, regulation of land use and taxing power. In the light of tribal progress, Goldberg suggested that P.L. 280 was not compatible with the tribes. Her assumption proved correct in that the law was outdated and it hindered reservation development. In 1968, Congress enacted the Indian Civil Rights Act, thereby negating P.L. 280.

Two former Commissioners of Indian Affairs have written about federal-Indian affairs since World War II. Raymond V. Butler, a Blackfeet Indian, Acting Commissioner in 1977, produced "The Bureau of Indian Affairs: Activities Since 1945" [18] and James E. Officer, a professor of anthropology, who served as Associate Commissioner from 1962-67, wrote "The Bureau of Indian Affairs Since 1945: An Assessment" [87]. Both former officials criticize the termination policy. Butler also highlights Commissioner Philleo Nash's emphasis on economic development on reservations through the Office of Economic Opportunity. The complexity of federal policy in the 1970s during the Nixon administration is Officer's concern, and he warns that tribal sovereignty will become a crucial issue. Both authors assert that the role of the B.I.A. has become more complex and it is a technical advisor rather than a policy maker.

Bureau actions during the termination years of the 1950s provoked a strong tribal response. William T. Hagan explained in "Tribalism Rejuvenated: The Native American since the Era of Termination" [48] how Indian tribalism survived during this negative period for Native American groups. Hagan hypothesizes in this 1981 article that current tribalism flourishes from Red Power pride, opposition to termination and growing tribal memberships.

The turbulence of the civil rights movement during the 1960s has necessitated a reexamination of federal-Indian relations. The Indian Civil Rights Act of 1968 and promotion of Indian self-determination changed the legal status of Indian Americans. James F. Blake discusses the history and complexity of defining Indian status under federal law in "Federal Legal Status of the American Indian" [13]. Individual and tribal identification of an "Indian" have been complicated by citizenship and wardship responsibilities. Blake states that the "Indian" definition is whatever "the law legislatively defines, or judicially determined him to be."

Two brief works, Cliff A. Jones, "Remedies: Tribal Deprivation of Civil Rights: Should Indians Have a Cause of Action Under 42 U.S.C. § 1983?" [61] and Carl Stevens, "Remedies: Indian Civil Rights Act— Exhaustion of Tribal Remedies Prior to Removal to Federal Court" [115], elaborate on how Indian rights are protected.

Stevens recommends that tribal leaders must begin planning and developing remedies at the tribal level to protect Indian rights in the ICRA. Jones warns that the tribes will need to lobby for legislation to further define their legal roles.

Individual rights of American Indians are defined in *American Indian Civil Rights Handbook* [2] and in Stephen L. Pevar, *The Rights of Indians and Tribes* [95]. The former is a short non-scholarly effort that is divided into sections: "fair treatment" by police, courts, equal employment and education opportunities, rights pertaining to students, housing, private property, public facilities and voting rights. The handbook serves best in alerting readers to various problems of the Indian citizenry. The latter work is more comprehensive than the former. It serves as an authoritative guide to the legal bases of Indian personal rights and tribal rights, including explanations of trust responsibilities involving treaties, federal and state authority that affect criminal and civil jurisdiction in Indian country. Taxation, hunting and fishing rights and government services are covered as well.

Laws affecting the general Native American population are covered in Vine Deloria, Jr., "Legislation and Litigation Concerning American Indians" [27]. Deloria notes the absence of legislative direction in policy regarding Native Americans from 1957 to 1977. During this twenty year period, insufficient legislation permitted ambiguous interpretations of Indian rights and legal status. In the 1960s minority protests led to the civil rights movement and resulted in the Civil Rights Act of 1964 (ICRA). Specific Indian civil rights legislation occurred four years later. Dennis R. Holmes in "Political Rights under the Indian Civil Rights Act" [55], addresses the political implications of tribal rights and sovereignty, noting that the courts recognized tribes as sovereign "distinct communities."

A similar legal argument in support of the distinctiveness of Indianness is in C. L. Stetson's "Tribal Sovereignty . . . 146 Years Later" [114]. The ICRA had a two-fold purpose, "to protect individual Indian citizens from infringement on their rights by the tribal governments, but also to promote Indian self-determination." The federal government would not undermine tribal authority. Continuity of traditions is important for developing self-determination although Julia Martinez's discrimination suit was upheld in *Martinez v. Santa Clara Pueblo*.

Legal sexual discrimination against Martinez is covered in Andra Pearldaughter, "Constitutional Law: Equal Protection: *Martinez v. Santa Clara Pueblo*—Sexual Equality Under the Indian Civil Rights Act" [91]. Santa Clara Pueblo is criticized for employing a sex-based criteria for determining tribal membership. This case of double jeopardy involves tribal responsibility for sexual discrimination and tribal membership without federal interference. Vieno Lindstrom maintains in "Constitutional Law: *Santa Clara Pueblo v. Martinez:* Tribal Membership and the Indian Civil Rights Act" [71] that the ICRA aided in initiating Santa Clara tribal policy. In fact, the American judicial system defended Santa Clara policy as determined by the tribal council. Lindstrom notes that the federal government was correct in deferring to the Santa Clara government, since the latter was better equipped to handle the Martinez issue.

Another legal scholar, John T. Hardin, in "Santa Clara Pueblo v. Martinez: Tribal Sovereignty and the Indian Civil Rights Act of 1968" [49], asked several penetrating questions about the ICRA legislation. Did the government have the authority to impose the ICRA on an Indian tribe and authorize the judicial branch to interfere in a tribe's internal affairs? And, what guidelines under the U.S. Constitution existed for such judicial intervention? Hardin deems that the federal government has created a dichotomy in Indian policy of assimilation and sovereignty. Such confusion has made federal-Indian relations unclear and has undermined the concept of tribal sovereignty. The judicial system is left with the responsibility of clarifying an ambiguous federal Indian policy, thus causing uncertainties in federal Indian law.

Such ambiguity in federal Indian policy has also been confirmed in Scott N. Singer, "Federal Indian Law: The Bureau of Indian Affairs" [110]. His two-part study surveys recent developments in federal Indian law to define the functions of the B.I.A. The first part examines B.I.A. administration of policy and the limitations imposed by Congress on the Bureau. The second part analyzes additional limitations imposed by the judiciary. This study makes clear that the Indian Bureau is actually a liaison that supervises policy as it is defined by Congress.

Red Power activism in the late 1960s and American Indian Movement militancy in the early 1970s endangered federal-Indian relations. Only a few books presently exist on this period. The more important of these are Jack D. Forbes, *Native Americans and Nixon: Presidential Politics and Minority Self-Determination 1969-1972* [35]; Peter Matthiesen, *In The Spirit of Crazy Horse* [81]; Bill Zimmerman, *Airlift to Wounded Knee* [138] and Rex Weyler, *Blood of the Land: The Government and Corporate War Against the American Indian Movement* [132]. Forbes's monograph is a slim volume that chronologically discusses Indian protests during this volatile period. The high point is the Trail of Broken Treaties march and the takeover of the Indian Bureau in Washington in 1972. Forbes is sensitive to the Indians' position in their confrontation with federal officials.

Matthiesen's book is a lengthy chronology based largely on interviews. It spans the years, 1968-1981, in an attempt to answer questions such as did the American government and the F.B.I. subvert AIM? Did the government perceive AIM as a political threat? And, how does the government view the rise of proficient self-determined tribal governments? Short on analysis, the book provides interesting reading via Indian voices in presenting their side of turbulent federal-Indian relations. Those interested in Wounded Knee will find Matthiesen's and Zimmerman's books of interest. The latter is a narrative of the occupation of Wounded Knee. Interviews and notes enable Zimmerman to elaborate in detail about his airlifting food and supplies to the Indians in the occupation camp encircled by armed F.B.I. agents. More recent AIM activism is the subject of Weyler's *Blood of the Land*. Survival of AIM despite federal attempts to subvert its existence since the early 1970s is the essence of this work.

The Nixon years produced reform measures like the Alaska Native Claims Settlement Act of 1971, return of Taos Blue Lake in 1972 and the Indian Education Act of 1972. The Alaska Native Claims Settlement Act (ANCSA) has received considerable attention from scholars. Lauren L. Fuller argues that ANCSA attempted to assimilate Alaska Native Americans in a manner reminiscent of the Dawes Act of 1887. Supposedly both legislative measures deemed desegregation was best for Native Americans. Her study, "Alaska Native Claims Settlement Act: Analysis of the Protective Clauses of the Act Through a Comparison with the Dawes Act of 1887" [36], is brief and without strong evidence for citing parallels between the two acts.

Prelude to the ANCSA was the famous "Tee-Hit-Ton" decision. Its history is expertly told in Steven J. Bloxham, "Aboriginal Title, Alaska Native Property Rights, and the Case of the Tee-Hit-Ton Indians" [14]. The decision has no direct relation to Indian policy, but how Congress and the Court have dealt with the case is pertinent. An overview of the Alaska Native situation enables one to see how the ANCSA logically followed Tee-Hit-Ton. Sarah Arnott cites the criticism of ANCSA in "Legislation: The Alaska Native Claims Settlement Act: Legislation Appropriate to the Past and the Future" [4]. The Act has not been a panacea for Alaska Natives. Instead, repercussions from windfall dollars have disturbed the Alaskan economy and the native lifestyle. Trying to hang on to dollars while eager opportunists are at hand has been a problem for the Alaska Natives.

Another struggle for Native Americans is covered in Jerry Kammer's *The Second Long Walk: The Navajo-Hopi Land Dispute* [63]. Congress authorized a federal court in 1974 to divide equally between the Navajo and Hopi tribes 1.8 million acres of land in Arizona. The part of the Joint Use Area awarded to the Hopi forced several thousand Navajos to relocate elsewhere. Kammer, a journalist, has investigated how the land dispute has affected both tribespeoples. And he is convinced that relocating Navajo families was not worth the cost of human suffering involved. Goodman and Thompson [41] are two geographers who have presented the complex Hopi-Navajo dispute from a sympathetic, yet analytical point of view. They show empathetic insight into the two tribes' perceptions of the Joint Use Area. The two authors set out to present a simplified view of the major issues involved in the dispute and they have done that.

The Politics of American Indian Policy [11] is the title of a recent book by anthropologist Robert L. Bee. The dynamics of federal Indian policy are examined, not from the perspective of a tribal community, but from the author's observation of policy decision-making in Washington. A similar study is Brian Porto, "The Policy Process in American Indian Affairs; Patterns of Interaction Between American Indian Interest Groups, The Bureau of Indian Affairs, and the Indian Affairs Committees of the Congress" [99]. Porto analyzes the interaction of Indian organizations like the National Tribal Chairman's Association with government policy makers. Bee concentrates specifically on the "Washington Connection" while Porto emphasized the working relationship between bureaucrats and Indian organizations.

A related study is J. McIver Weatherford, *Tribes on the Hill: An Investigation into the Rituals and Realities of an Endangered American Tribe*. [129]. This work concentrates on the Congress where policy is established by law. The high turnover rate among congressmen and the lack of informed congressional members who make policy remind us that people without knowledge of Indians are frequently in control of federal-Indian relations. The aftermath of Indian Civil Rights and Red Power activism in the 1970s has finally convinced government officials of the importance of sovereignty to the tribes. Keith M. Werhan, in "The Sovereignty of Indian Tribes: A Reaffirmation and Strengthening in the 1970's" [131], describes the essence of "sovereignty" and how the concept applies to Native American groups. This concept has caused conflicts of legal interpretation in federal-tribal relations. The Supreme Court reaffirmed in 1977 the doctrine of "tribal sovereignty," first articulated by Chief Justice John Marshall in the 1830s.

A superb examination of the Self-Determination and Education Assistance Act is Michael P. Gross, "Indian Self-Determination and Tribal Sovereignty: An Analysis of Recent Federal Indian Policy" [45]. Gross emphasizes that the Act has become the fundamental vehicle for Indian self-rule, and he explores the strengths and weaknesses of the measure. Thomas P. Flannery attempts to produce a similar analysis in "The Indian Self-Determination Act: An Analysis of Federal Policy" [33]. Limitations in the legislation included a lack of B.I.A. involvement in specific problems, vulnerability of Indian individual rights and the B.I.A. failure to comport itself with the self-determination policy.

The provisions under Title 1 of the Act are tested by Russel L. Barsh and Ronald L. Trosper in "Title 1 of the Indian Self-Determination and Education Assistance Act of 1975" [9]. The authors set out to prove that Congress has not learned from its previous mistakes in the history of federal-Indian relations. Basically, Title 1 restored governing powers to the tribes. The authors assert that the federal government will continue blaming Indian poverty on Indian incompetency even though tribes are given more self-governing powers. At the same time, the act protects the B.I.A. by perpetuating the Bureau's power to provide services while endorsing the B.I.A.'s own definition of "trust responsibility."

Tribal governments exercising sovereign powers is addressed optimistically in Daniel H. Israel, "The Reemergence of Tribal Nationalism and Its Impact on Reservation Resource Development" [59]. Israel maintains that reservation governments have revitalized tribal nationalism since about 1965, and they are expanding their sovereign powers. After World War II, Indian fears triggered protest and tribal nationalism followed. Israel optimistically contends that during the 1970s, tribal governments acquired expertise to negotiate usage of natural resources. The question of tribal readiness must be carefully considered. Are the tribes educated sufficiently in white ways to compete successfully? Indian education is a key area for speculating answers. Since 1975, three published studies shed light on this area: Robert J. Havighurst, "Indian Education Since 1960" [51]; Margaret C. Szasz, "Federal Boarding Schools and the Indian Child: 1920-1960" [119]; and Daniel M. Rosenfelt, "Toward a More Coherent Policy for Funding Indian Education" [105].

Szasz describes Indian children struggling in boarding schools during a forty-year period. In the early years, the schools were controversial because sending Indian youths away to schools weakened students' family ties. Even with Collier's New Deal Indian policy, designed to revitalize Indian cultures, the boarding schools remained Anglo-oriented. The thrust of Szasz's portrayal is the chronology of change in supervision of the federal boarding schools. Indian education since 1960 has become a dualistic system according to Robert Havighurst. He contends that contemporary Indian students face a dilemma of assimilating into Anglo society or coexisting with the mainstream on the basis of tribal traditions. Cultural pluralism became an alternative while mandatory school attendance acted as a catalyst enforcing the issue. Rosenfelt suggests that numerous federal endeavors have improved Indian education to a respectable level. Since the late 1960s, the federal government has approved the Indian Education Act of 1972, the Indian Self-Determination and Education Assistance Act, revised the Johnson-O'Malley regulations and improved the administration of Title 1. Such assistance has enabled tribal communities to exercise self-determination in educational programs and supervise them in a more flexible and responsive manner.

The judiciary plays an important role in defending and interpreting the self-determination policy. And, the role of the Court in establishing Indian self-determination is becoming more imperative. Debate over Indian sovereignty has largely occupied the courts within the last several years. William D. Holyoak, "Tribal Sovereignty and the Supreme Court's 1977-1978 Term" [56]; Reid Peyton Chambers, "Judicial Enforcement of the Federal Trust Responsibility to Indians" [20]; and, Frederick J. Martone, "American Indian Tribal Self-Government in the Federal System: Inherent Right or Congressional License?" [80] exemplify the importance of the judiciary in federal Indian policy. Holyoak and Martone differ in their views on who actually determines tribal sovereignty and its legal status. Holyoak takes the position that Indian groups have "limited tribal sovereignty" with Congress possessing plenary power to define tribal governing powers. Martone argues that the Constitution is not designed to address tribes' status and Congress has suffered from changing tides of opinion that influence Indian legislation during the history of policy reform.

Reid Chambers covers two areas where policy is determined. First, he notes that the Court's participation in its fiduciary responsibilities is imperative for making policy consistent as Indian groups advance in achieving sovereignty. Second, the Congress has a vital role in formulating policy via legislation. Chambers asserts that Congress has actually deferred to executive federal officials in deciding policy, and it has passed their recommended bills.

Another area of ambiguous interpretation and conflict of interest is taxation involving Indian lands. Federal Indian policy has been affirmed to assist Native Americans and to protect their rights all-the-while encouraging self-determination. Are tribes allowed to tax non-tribal members on their lands? The extent of legal authority and problems of such taxation are covered in Carol Goldberg, "A Dynamic View of Tribal Jurisdiction to Tax Non-Indians" [40]. In Jim Noble, Jr., "Tribal Power to Tax Non-Indian Mineral Lessees" [85], the tribes may be able to use inherent sovereign powers to tax non-Indian leases. Congress has also authorized states to exercise exclusive power to tax all land within their boundaries, except on reservations. Tribes do not have the same power since the federal government does not equate states and reservations as polities of the same status.

A related unsettled area is federal taxation of Indian income derived from restricted lands. James R. McCurdy, "Federal Income Taxation and the Great Sioux Nation" [76] and Terry N. Fiske and Robert F. Wilson, "Federal Taxation of Indian Income from Restricted Indian Lands" [32] address the subject from legal points of view. McCurdy alerts us that inconsistencies in this area have frustrated bureaucrats as well as Indians. Indians are citizens and subject to income tax laws, but are excluded when treaties and legislation exempt them—usually in Indian country. Interestingly, under the law and federal policy, an Indian person can be assigned restricted land by the tribe and that person could be exempt from paying federal taxes if he is a tribal member. Such possibility could lead to numerous tax issues as suggested in Sharon E. Claassen, "Taxation: State Transaction Privilege Tax: An Interference with Tribal Self-Government" [22]. Claassen contends that flourishing tribal governments and increasing business contact with non-Indians will force this area of federal-Indian law to be resolved. State and tribal tax systems will need to be explored in the near future.

Michael D. Palmer maintains that the progress of business enterprises among Indians in Oklahoma will force the taxation issue. Palmer perceptively notes in "Taxation: Sales Tax Exemption of the Five Civilized Tribes" [89], that the power to tax the Five Tribes depends on their having reorganized according to the Oklahoma Indian Welfare Act of 1936. If the tribes followed the I.R.A. reorganization policy, they are empowered to tax.

Since the late 1970s, the Navajo Nation and some other mineral-rich tribes have been taxing energy companies. Their tribal governments are beginning to exercise the full scope of their limited sovereign powers. Some tribes' incomes now depend on taxing companies who lease rights to mine natural resources on Indian lands. In "Mineral Resources: Tribal Development of Reservation Oil and Gas Resources Through the Use of a Nontaxation-Based Tribal Joint Development Program" [62], Quentin M. Jones warns that tribes must be aware of development alternatives available to them and be aware of possible effects reservation resources will have on the oil and gas industry.

Focusing on another natural resource, Joe D. Dillsaver examines the federal government's Indian timber policy since 1861. In his brief "Natural Resources: Federal Control Over Indian Timber" [29], Dillsaver notes that the future timber policy is only conjecture at the present, and he warns of the risk of serious future environmental consequences. Presently, federal control of Indian timberlands is enforced through statutes, regulations and court decisions.

The need for a federal-Indian timber policy alerts us to other natural resources on Indian lands. Nationwide mining of subsurface minerals has brought about a mandatory national environmental policy. Becky J. Miles Viers in "Environmental Law: Uranium Mining on the Navajo Reservation" [128] and Patti Palmer McGee in "Indian Lands: Coal Development: Environmental/Economic Dilemma for the Modern Indian" [79] address the National Environmental Policy Act (NEPA) as both conflicting with and assuring Indian interests. But in point of fact, the NEPA restricts the practice of tribal sovereignty. For instance, on the Navajo Reservation, the mining of uranium and coal mandates a balancing of environmental protection of surface lands while the Navajos supply uranium to the U.S. Royalties paid to the tribe and forced reclamation of lands result in both enormous economic gain and environmental consequences which are creating serious dilemmas for tribes.

Upsetting the spiritual balance of the Navajo Reservation is the focus of Karen M. Art in "Natural and Supernatural Resources: Mining on Navajo Land and the American Indian Religious Freedom Act" [5]. Traditional concepts about land come into conflict with modern economic projects, especially the mining of natural resources on the reservation. Traditionalists who are opposed to mining are supported by the American Indian Religious Freedom Act. Art emphasizes that the decision to mine natural resources has factionalized the Navajos.

Traditional land relationships are addressed in Ruby Sooktis and Anne Terry Straus, "A Rock and a Hard Place: Mineral Resources on the Northern Cheyenne Reservation" [112] and Barrik Van Winkle and Robert Poor, "The Opposition of Nevada Indians to the MX System" [125]. In both cases, the dilemma for protecting traditional interests becomes greater. Sooktis and Straus point out that the Northern Cheyennes' economic survival depends on negotiating leases with ARCO to mine coal on the reservation. Van Winkle and Poor maintain that the previously dispersed Western Shoshone have united against the MX project. As a result, tribal communities are developing into political organizations to oppose the government and energy companies.

With the increasing demands for natural resources on reservation lands, the trust relationship of federal Indian policy will need revision in the near future. Lise Young forewarns in "What Price Progress? Uranium Production on Indian Lands in the San Juan Basin" [137] that uranium on Indian lands is high on the list for energy demands. Other Indian organizations like the Council of Energy Resource Tribes will be drawn into the crucible of the energy crisis involving Indian lands, calling for major changes in Indian policy.

Inconsistency in federal-Indian policy has produced instability. In dissecting such inconsistency, several key areas have been found to be vulnerable to dissension between Indians and federal officials. Defining "tribal sovereignty" is one of the problem areas and it is analyzed in Robert G. McCoy, "The Doctrine of Tribal Sovereignty: Accommodating Tribal, State, and Federal Interests" [75]. The Supreme Court has conceived the doctrine of tribal sovereignty as "Indian tribes who are independent political communities." McCoy suggests that the unique status of the tribes can best be understood by examining tribal-federal relations, tribal-state relations and tribal powers of self-government. But, when treaties and statutes do not render answers, then the Court should safeguard tribal interests.

Professional humanists have provided different views on Indian sovereignty from those of legal scholars. A collection of essays edited by William R. Swagerty from a conference on "Indian Sovereignty" presents largely a non-legal perspective. The papers include Francis Jennings, "Sovereignty in Anglo-American History" [60]; Arthur Lazarus Jr., "Tribal Sovereignty under United States Law" [70]; Wendell Chino, "Relations Between Indian Tribes and the Nation" [21]; and, John Redhouse, "Preservation of Tribal Culture and Identity" [103].

Jennings distinguishes between the legal theory of sovereignty and its use in history. Lazarus presents the legal interpretation and theoretical applications of sovereignty. The implication of tribal sovereignty as interpreted by law is his concern. Inherent rights of Indian people should not be overlooked according to Chino. Sovereignty, in his view, equates feelings of spirituality that are translated to mean freedom. Redhouse reminded the audience of the pressing energy crisis and its demands for natural resources on tribal lands. How the varying interpretations of sovereignty affect Indian people was the upshot of the conference. Such humanistic concerns are usually discarded when interpretations are put forth by the judiciary and legal scholars.

Earl Mettler postulates a comprehensive theory of sovereignty in "A Unified Theory of Indian Tribal Sovereignty" [82]. Mettler contends that sovereignty is a legal status held in varying degrees by tribes in American Indian law. Every political action of a tribe's power must be facilitated by a federal treaty or statute, and therefore, such autonomy is delimited by a federal government action.

A related doctrine, "sovereign immunity," compounds the confusion over the question of Indian sovereignty. Douglas R. Wright thoroughly addresses the two concepts in "Sovereignty: Indian Sovereignty and Tribal Immunity From Suit" [136]. The courts have employed tribal immunity, thus delimiting Indian sovereignty and the self-determination policy. Tribal immunity does not actually derive from sovereignty, but rather from the federal trust relationship. Indian tribes are distinct political entities in light of faltering federal support. In recent years, the federal government has pretended to recognize tribal sovereignty while purporting a self-determination policy.

Clifford M. Lytle, in "The Supreme Court, Tribal Sovereignty, and Continuing Problems of State Encroachment into Indian Country" [73], argues that the flow of Supreme Court decisions has not protected the tribes from state intrusion as guaranteed in *Worcester v. Georgia*. This may indicate a change in the relationship between Indian reservations and white communities. Dario F. Robertson notes in "A New Constitutional Approach to the Doctrine of Tribal Sovereignty" [104], that the doctrine of tribal sovereignty is unique within the concept of sovereignty. After justifying tribal sovereignty as a principle of natural law, a principle of international law, and as a principle of constitutional law, Robertson stresses the need for constitutionalizing tribal sovereignty.

The legal history of Indian sovereignty is traced in Jessie D. Green and Susan Work, "Inherent Indian Sovereignty" [42]. The development of Indian sovereignty is presented as it has been affected by constitutional restrictions, congressional plenary power, constitutional sources of plenary power, treaty-making and assimilation policy. This useful study helps the reader to understand the legal history and complications surrounding Indian sovereignty. Efforts to define tribal sovereignty have been almost a one-sided view from the federal government's position. J. S. Thomson explores the view of tribal sovereignty from this position and that of international law in "Federal Indian Policy": A Violation of International Treaty Law" [123]. Federal Indian policy has been based upon political and judicial expediency, supported at best by the application of questionable legal tenets. Trial nations' asserting a valid claim to full, rather than restricted sovereignty is a possibility. Should this happen, the principles of international law would apply to all American Indian policy and the United States would be shown to have breached many international principles, giving tribes the right to demand reparations.

Judith L. Andress and James E. Falkowski concur with Thomson in "Self-Determination: Indians and the United Nations—the Anomalous Status of America's 'Domestic Dependent Nations'" [3]. The two authors claim that the U. S. Government as trustee has failed to protect Indian interests. The proposed solution for tribes is to apply for United Nations charters since the international trust system promotes accountability. Current domestic trust over tribes appears inadequate. Furthermore, the self-determination policy is misguided and can easily be disguised as termination.

Charles Scott notes in "Administrative Law: Self-Determination and Consent Power: The Role of the Government in Indian Decisions" [109] that Congress has intervened too much in Indian decision-making. The basis and scope of tribal consent power is delimited by congressional plenary power. Tribal powers are also limited by the Secretary of the Interior's overabundance of power. Tribal development in self-determination and internal sovereignty is therefore hindered. Scott recommends that the federal government's authority in Indian affairs should be changed to an advisory capacity.

Russel Barsh has cited a series of deliberate superficial changes that were made in the Bureau of Indian Affairs within recent years. In "The BIA Reorganization Follies of 1978: A Lesson in Bureaucratic Self-Defense" [7], Barsh claims that during the 1970s, when federal agencies like the BIA were recognized to be ineffective, they were expanded for improvement. The Indian Service became the largest subdivision of the Interior Department and consisted of some 15,000 employees and a billion-dollar budget. Barsh also notes that the Bureau hid behind its own bureaucracy and maneuvered to avoid major changes in its structure.

The literature made available since 1975 on twentieth-century federal Indian policy reveals unresolved issues that have historically plagued federal officials and Indians. The full scope of federal Indian policy since 1900 covers numerous and diverse topics that will keep scholars busy for years to come. Old policies like assimilation and termination have failed to solve Indian problems. In the likelihood of new, trial-and-error efforts, current Indian needs should be kept in mind. A carefully defined philosophy is mandatory to assure continuity of a modernized policy that should be incorporated into the Constitution. In light of the complexity of federal Indian policy, future literature on the subject will flourish.

ALPHABETICAL LIST

[1] Ackerman, Francis E. 1980. "A Conflict Over Land." *American Indian Law Review* 8:259-98.

[2] *American Indian Civil Rights Handbook*. 1980. Washington: U. S. Government Printing Office.

[3] Andress, Judith L., and James E. Falkowski. 1979. "Self-Determination: Indians and the United Nations—The Anomalous Status of America's 'Domestic Dependent Nations'." *American Indian Law Review* 8:97-116.

[4] Arnott, Sarah. 1983. "Legislation: The Alaska Native Claims Settlement Act: Legislation Appropriate to the Past and the Future." *American Indian Law Review* 9:135-60.

[5] Art, Karen M. 1981. "Natural and Supernatural Resources: Mining on Navajo Land and the American Indian Religious Fredom Act." *Chicago Anthropology Exchange*, Special Issue, "Native American Land" 14:4-26.

[6] Baris, Allan. 1978. "Washington's Public Law 280 Jurisdiction on Indian Reservations." *Washington Law Review* 53:701-27.

[7] Barsh, Russel L. 1979. "The BIA Reorganization Follies of 1978: A Lesson in Bureaucratic Self Defense." *American Indian Law Review* 7:1-50.

[8] Barsh, Russel L., and James Y. Henderson. 1980. *The Road: Indian Tribes and Political Liberty*. Berkeley: University of California Press.

[9] Barsh, Russel L., and Ronald L. Trosper. 1975. "Title 1 of the Indian Self-Determination and Education Assistance Act of 1975." *American Indian Law Review* 3:361-95.

[10] Beaulieu, David L. 1979. A Critical Review of the Urban Indian Task Force of the American Indian Policy Review Commission." *New Directions in Federal Indian Policy: A Review of the American Indian Policy Review Commission*, Contemporary American Indian Issues Series, 1:75-85. Los Angeles: American Indian Studies Center, University of California, Los Angeles.

[11] Bee, Robert L. 1982. *The Politics of American Indian Policy*. Cambridge: Schenkan Publishing Company.

[12] Berens, John F. 1977. "'Old Campaigners,' New Realities: Indian Policy Reform in the Progressive Era, 1900-1912." *Mid-America* 59:51-64.

[13] Blake, James F. 1976. "Federal Legal Status of the American Indian." *Rendezvous* 11:17-27.

[14] Bloxham, Steven J. 1980. "Aboriginal Title, Alaska Native Property Rights, and the Case of the Tee-Hit-Ton Indians." *American Indian Law Review* 8:299-331.

[15] Boender, Debra R. 1979. "Termination and the Administration of Glenn L. Emmons as Commissioner of Indian Affairs, 1953-1961." *New Mexico Historical Review* 54:287-304.

[16] Bromert, Roger. 1980. "The Sioux and the Indian New Deal, 1933-1944." Ph.D. dissertation, University of Toledo. Ann Arbor: University Microfilms International.

[17] Burt, Larry W. 1982. *Tribalism in Crisis: Federal Indian Policy, 1953-1961*. Albuquerque: University of New Mexico Press.

[18] Butler, Raymond V. 1978. "The Bureau of Indian Affairs: Activities Since 1945." *Annals of the American Academy of Political and Social Science* 436:50-60.

[19] Carter, Nancy C. 1976. "Race and Power Politics as Aspects of Federal Guardianship Over American Indians: Land-Related Cases, 1887-1924." *American Indian Law Review* 4:197-248.

[20] Chambers, Reid P. 1975. "Judicial Enforcement of the Federal Trust Responsibility to Indians." *Stanford Law Review* 27:1213-48.

[21] Chino, Wendell. 1979. "Relations Between Indian Tribes and the Nation." In *Indian Sovereignty, Proceedings of the Second Annual Conference on Problems and Issues Concerning American Indians Today*, ed. William R. Swagerty. Newberry Library Center for the History of the American Indian, *Occasional Papers* 2:85-102.

[22] Claassen, Sharon E. 1979. "Taxation: State Transaction Privilege Tax: An Interference with Tribal Self-Government." *American Indian Law Review* 7:319-33.

[23] Clinton, Lawrence, Bruce A. Chadwick, and Howard M. Bahr. 1975. "Urban Relocation Reconsidered: Antecedents of Employment Among Indian Males." *Rural Sociology* 40:117-33.

[24] Clow, Richmond. L. 1977. "The Rosebud Sioux: The Federal Government and the Reservation Years, 1878-1940." Ph.D. dissertation, University of New Mexico. Ann Arbor: University Microfilms International.

[25] Cooper, Margaret B. 1979. "Task Force Eleven of the American Indian Policy Review Commission: A Developmental Overview." *New Directions in Federal Indian Policy: A Review of the American Indian Policy Review Commission*, Contemporary American Indian Issues Series, 1:53-56. Los Angeles: American Indian Studies Center, University of California, Los Angeles.

[26] Crum, Steven. 1983. "The Western Shoshone of Nevada and the Indian New Deal." Ph.D. dissertation, University of Utah. Ann Arbor: University Microfilms International.

[27] Deloria, Vine Jr. 1978. "Legislation and Litigation Concerning American Indians." *Annals of the American Academy of Political and Social Science* 436:86-96.

[28] Deloria, Vine, Jr., and Clifford M. Lytle. 1983. *American Indians, American Justice*. Austin: University of Texas Press.

[29] Dillsaver, Joe D. 1977. "Natural Resources: Federal Control Over Indian Timber." *American Indian Law Review* 5:415-22.

[30] Dixon, Faun M. 1981. "Native American Property Rights: The Pyramid Lake Reservation Land Controversy." Ph.D. dissertation, University of Nevada. Ann Arbor: University Microfilms International.

[31] Dorris, Michael. 1981. "The Grass Still Grows, the Rivers Still Flow: Contemporary Native Americans." *Daedalus, The Journal of the American Academy of Arts and Sciences* 110:43-69.

[32] Fiske, Terry N., and Robert F. Wilson. 1975. "Federal Taxation of Indian Income from Restricted Indian Lands." *Land and Water Law Review* 10:63-92.

[33] Flannery, Thomas P., Jr. 1980. "The Indian Self-Determination Act: An Analysis of Federal Policy." Ph.D. dissertation, Northwestern University.

[34] Fixico, Donald L. 1980. "Termination and Relocation: Federal In-

dian Policy in the 1950s." Ph.D. dissertation, University of Oklahoma. Ann Arbor: University Microfilms International.

[35] Forbes, Jack D. 1981. *Native Americans and Nixon: Presidential Politics and Minority Self-Determination 1969-1972.*" Los Angeles: U.C.L.A. American Indian Studies Center.

[36] Fuller, Lauren L. 1976. "Alaska Native Claims Settlement Act: Analysis of the Protective Clauses of the Act Through a Comparison with the Dawes Act of 1887." *American Indian Law Review* 4:269-278.

[37] Gallerito, Cecelia. 1979. "Indian Health, Federally or Tribally Determined? Health Recommendations of the American Indian Policy Review Commission." *New Directions in Federal Indian Policy: A Review of the American Indian Policy Review Commission*, Contemporary American Indian Issues Series, 1:29-43. Los Angeles: American Indian Studies Center, University of California, Los Angeles.

[38] Gamino, John. 1975. "Indian Claims Commission: Discretion and Limitation in the Allowance of Attorneys' Fees." *American Indian Law Review* 3:115-35.

[39] Goldberg, Carol E. 1975. "Public Law 280: The Limits of State Jurisdiction Over Reservation Indians." *UCLA Law Review* 22:535-94.

[40] ———. 1976. "A Dynamic View of Tribal Jurisdiction To Tax Non-Indians." *Law and Contemporary Problems* 40:166-89.

[41] Goodman, James M., and Gary L. Thompson. 1975. "The Hopi-Navajo Land Dispute." *American Indian Law Review* 3:397-417.

[42] Green, Jessie D., and Susan Work. 1976. "Comment: Inherent Indian Sovereignty." *American Indian Law Review*. 4:311-42.

[43] Griffith, Gwendolyn. 1980. "Indian Claims to Groundwater: Reserved Rights or Beneficial Interest?" *Stanford Law Review* 33:103-30.

[44] Grinde, Donald A., Jr. 1979. "Politics and the American Indian Policy Review Commission." *New Directions in Federal Indian Policy: A Review of the American Indian Policy Review Commission*, Contemporary American Indian Issues Series, 1:19-28. Los Angeles: American Indian Studies Center, University of California, Los Angeles.

[45] Gross, Michael P. 1978. "Indian Self-Determination and Tribal Sovereignty: An Analysis of Recent Federal Indian Policy." *Texas Law Review* 56:1195-1244.

[46] Gundlach, James H., P. Nelson Reid, and Alden E. Roberts. 1978. "Native American Indian Migration and Relocation." *Pacific Sociological Review* 21:117-27.

[47] Guyette, Susan. 1979. "Suggestions for Priority Alcohol and Drug Abuse Research: A Comment on the Recommendations of Task Force Eleven of the American Indian Policy Review Commission." *New Directions in Federal Indian Policy: A Review of the American Indian*

Policy Review Commission, Contemporary American Indian Issues Series, 1:45-52. Los Angeles: American Indian Studies Center, Univesity of California, Los Angeles.

[48] Hagan, William T. 1981. "Tribalism Rejuvenated: The Native American since the Era of Termination." *Western Historical Quarterly* 12:5-16.

[49] Hardin, John T. 1979. "Santa Clara Pueblo v. Martinez: Tribal Sovereignty and the Indian Civil Rights Act of 1968." *Arkansas Law Review* 33:399-421.

[50] Hauptman, Laurence M. 1981. *The Iroquois and the New Deal*. Syracuse: Syracuse University Press.

[51] Havighurst, Robert J. 1978. "Indian Education Since 1960." *Annals of the American Academy of Political and Social Science* 436:13-26.

[52] Herzberg, Stephen J. 1977. "The Menominee Indians: From Treaty to Termination." *Wisconsin Magazine of History* 60:267-329.

[53] ———. 1977. "The Menominee Indians: Termination to Restoration." *American Indian Law Review* 6:143-86.

[54] Holm, Thomas M. 1978. "Indians and Progressives: From Vanishing Policy to the Indian New Deal." Ph.D dissertation, University of Oklahoma. Ann Arbor: University Microfilms International.

[55] Holmes, Dennis R. 1979. "Political Rights under the Indian Civil Rights Act." *South Dakota Law Review* 24: 419-46.

[56] Holyoak, William D. 1978. "Tribal Sovereignty and the Supreme Court's 1977-78 Term." *Brigham Young University Law Review* 1978: 911-36.

[57] Hundley, Norris Jr. 1978. "The Dark and Bloody Ground of Indian Water Rights: Confusion Elevated to Principles." *Western Historical Quarterly* 9:455-82.

[58] ———. 1982. "The 'Winters' Decision and Indian Water Rights: A Mystery Reexamined." *Western Historical Quarterly* 13:17-42.

[59] Israel, Daniel H. 1976. "The Reemergence of Tribal Nationalism and Its Impact on Reservation Resource Development." *University of Colorado Law Review* 47:617-52.

[60] Jennings, Francis. 1979. "Sovereignty in Anglo-American History." In *Indian Sovereignty, Proceedings of the Second Annual Conference on Problems and Issues Concerning American Indians Today,* ed. William R. Swagerty. The Newberry Library Center for the History of the American Indian, *Occasional Papers* 2:2-21.

[61] Jones, Cliff A. 1975. "Remedies: Tribal Deprivation of Civil Rights: Should Indians Have a Cause of Action Under 42 U. S. C. § 1983?" *American Indian Law Review* 3:183-95.

[62] Jones, Quentin M. 1983. "Mineral Resources: Tribal Development of Reservation Oil and Gas Resources Through the Use of a Nontaxation-Based Tribal Joint Development Program." *American Indian Law Review* 9:161-94.

[63] Kammer, Jerry. 1980. *The Second Long Walk: The Navajo-Hopi Land Dispute*. Albuquerque: University of New Mexico Press.

[64] Kelly, Lawrence C. 1975. "The Indian Reorganization Act: The Dream and the Reality." *Pacific Historical Review* 44:291-312.

[65] ———. 1983. *The Assault on Assimilation: John Collier and the Origins of Indian Policy Reform.* Albuquerque: University of New Mexico Press.

[66] Kickingbird, Kirke. 1975. "The American Indian Policy Review Commission: A Prospect for Future Change in Federal Indian Policy." *American Indian Law Review* 3:243-53.

[67] Koppes, Clayton R. 1977. "From New Deal to Termination: Liberalism and Indian Policy, 1933-1953. *Pacific Historical Review* 46:543-66.

[68] Laird, Michael S. 1979. "Water Rights: The Winters Cloud Over the Rockies: Indian Water Rights and the Development of Western Energy Resources." *American Indian Law Review* 7:155-69.

[69] Lawson, Michael. 1982. *Dammed Indians: The Pick-Sloan Plan and the Missouri River Sioux, 1944-1980*. Norman: University of Oklahoma Press.

[70] Lazarus, Arthur, Jr. 1979. "Tribal Sovereignty under United States Law." In *Indian Sovereignty, Proceedings of the Second Annual Conference on Problems and Issues Concerning American Indians Today*, ed. William R. Swagerty, Newberry Library Center for the History of the American Indian, *Occasional Papers* 2:28-46.

[71] Lindstrom, Vieno. 1978. "Constitutional Law: *Santa Clara Pueblo v. Martinez:* Tribal Membership and the Indian Civil Rights Act." *American Indian Law Review* 6:205-16.

[72] Lurie, Nancy O. 1978. "The Indian Claims Commission." *Annals of the American Academy of Political and Social Science* 436:97-110.

[73] Lytle, Clifford M. 1979. "The Supreme Court, Tribal Sovereignty, and Continuing Problems of State Encroachment into Indian Country." *American Indian Law Review* 8:65-77.

[74] McCallister, Elizabeth. 1976. "Water Rights: The McCarren Amendment and Indian Tribes: Reserved Water Rights." *American Indian Law Review* 4:303-10.

[75] McCoy, Robert G. 1978. "The Doctrine of Tribal Sovereignty: Accommodating Tribal, State, and Federal Interests." *Harvard Civil Rights Review* 13:357-423.

[76] McCurdy, James R. 1977. "Federal Income Taxation and the Great Sioux Nation." *South Dakota Law Review* 22:296-321.

[77] McDonnell, Janet A. 1980. "Competency Commissions and Indian Land Policy, 1913-1920." *South Dakota History* 11:21-34.

[78] ———. 1980. "The Disintegration of the Indian Estate: Indian Land Policy, 1913-1929." Ph.D. dissertation, Marquette University. Ann Arbor: University of Microfilms International.

[79] McGee, Patti P. 1976. "Indian Lands: Coal Development:

Environmental/Economic Dilemma for the Modern Indian." *American Indian Law Review* 4:279-88.

[80] Martone, Frederick J. 1976. "American Indian Tribal Self-Government in the Federal System: Inherent Right or Congressional License?" *Notre Dame Lawyer* 51:600-35.

[81] Matthiesen, Peter. 1983. *In the Spirit of Crazy Horse*. New York: Viking Press.

[82] Mettler, Earl. 1978. "A Unified Theory of Indian Tribal Sovereignty." *Hastings Law Journal* 30:89-136.

[83] Muskrat, Jerry. 1979. "Recommendations of the American Indian Policy Review Commission and the Supreme Court." *New Directions in Federal Indian Policy: A Review of the American Indian Policy Review Commission,* Contemporary American Indian Issues Series 1:99-114. Los Angeles: American Indian Studies Center, University of California, Los Angeles.

[84] Nelson, Michael C., and Bradley L. Booke. 1977. "The Winters Doctrine: Seventy Years of Application of 'Reserved' Water Rights to Indian Reservations." *Arid Lands Resource Information Paper* No. 9. Tucson: University of Arizona Office of Arid Land Studies.

[85] Noble, Jim Jr. 1979. "Tribal Power to Tax Non-Indian Mineral Lessees." *Natural Resources Journal* 19:969-95.

[86] Noley, Grayson. 1979. "Summary and Critique of the Report on Indian Education of the American Indian Policy Review Commission." *New Directions in Federal Indian Policy: A Review of the American Indian Policy Review Commission*, Contemporary American Indian Issues Series 1:57-73. Los Angeles, American Indian Studies Center, University of California, Los Angeles.

[87] Officer, James. 1978. "The Bureau of Indian Affairs Since 1945: An Assessment." *Annals of the American Academy of Political and Social Science* 436:61-72.

[88] Orem, Belinda K. 1980. "Paleface, Redskin, and the Great White Chiefs in Washington: Drawing the Battle Lines Over Western Water Rights." *San Diego Law Review* 17:449-89.

[89] Palmer, Michael D. 1978. "Taxation: Sales Tax Exemption of the Five Civilized Tribes." *American Indian Law Review* 6:417-27.

[90] Parman, Donald L. 1976. *The Navajos and the New Deal*. New Haven: Yale University Press.

[91] Pearldaughter, Andra. 1978. "Constitutional Law: Equal Protection: *Martinez v. Santa Clara Pueblo* — Sexual Equality Under the Indian Civil Rights Act." *American Indian Law Review* 6:187-204.

[92] Pelcyger, R. S. 1976. "Indian Water Rights: Some Emerging Frontiers." *Rocky Mountain Mineral Law Institute Journal* 21:743-75.

[93] Peroff, Nicholas C. 1982. *Menominee Drums: From Tribal Termination to Restoration, 1953-1973*. Norman: University of Oklahoma Press.

[94] Persons, Louis D. II. 1978. "Jurisdiction: Public Law 280 — Local

Regulation of Protected Indian Lands." *American Indian Law Review* 6:403-15.

[95] Pevar, Stephen L. 1983. *The Rights of Indians and Tribes*. New York: Bantam Books.

[96] Philp, Kenneth R. 1977. *John Collier's Crusade for Indian Reform 1920-1954*. Tucson: University of Arizona Press.

[97] ———. 1981. "The New Deal and Alaskan Natives, 1936-1945." *Pacific Historical Review* 50:309-27.

[98] ———. 1983. "Termination: A Legacy of the Indian New Deal." *Western Historical Quarterly* 14:165-80.

[99] Porto, Brian L. 1979. "The Policy Process in American Indian Affairs; Patterns of Interaction Between American Indian Interest Groups, The Bureau of Indian Affairs, and the Indian Affairs Committees of the Congress." Ph.D. dissertation, Miami University. Ann Arbor: University Microfilms.

[100] Price, M. E., and G. D. Weatherford. 1976. "Indian Water Rights in Theory and Practice: Navajo Experience in the Colorado River Basin." *Law and Contemporary Problems* 40:98-131.

[101] Putney, Diane T. 1980. "Fighting the Scourge: American Indian Morbidity and Federal Policy, 1897-1928." Ph.D. dissertation, Marquette University. Ann Arbor: University Microfilms.

[102] Ranquist, H. A. 1975. "The *Winters* Doctrine and How It Grew: Federal Reservation of Rights to the Use of Water." *Brigham Young University Law Review* (1975): 639-724.

[103] Redhouse, John. 1979. "Preservation of Tribal Culture and Identity." In *Indian Sovereignty, Proceedings of the Second Annual Conference on Problems and Issues Concerning American Indians Today*, ed. William Swagerty. Newberry Library Center for the History of the American Indian, *Occasional Papers* 2:103-07.

[104] Robertson, Dario F. 1978. "A New Constitutional Approach to the Doctrine of Tribal Sovereignty." *American Indian Law Review* 6:371-94.

[105] Rosenfelt, Daniel M. 1976. "Toward a More Coherent Policy for Funding Indian Education." *Law and Contemporary Problems* 40:190-223.

[106] Rosenthal, Harvey D. 1976. "Their Day in Court: A History of the Indian Claims Commission." Ph.D. dissertation, Kent State University. Ann Arbor: University Microfilms.

[107] Ross, Anne E. 1983. "Water Rights: Aboriginal Water Use and Water Law in the Southwestern United States: Why the Reserved Rights Doctrine was Inappropriate." *American Indian Law Review* 9:195-209.

[108] Schrader, Robert F. 1983. *The Indian Arts and Crafts Board: An Aspect of New Deal Indian Policy*. Albuquerque: University of New Mexico Press.

[109] Scott, Charles. 1977. "Administrative Law: Self-Determination and the Consent Power: The Role of the Government in Indian Decisions." *American Indian Law Review* 5:195-215.

[110] Singer, Scott N. 1976. "Federal Indian Law: The Bureau of Indian Affairs." *Annual Survey of American Law* (1976): 41-58.

[111] Slagle, Al Logan. 1979. "The American Indian Policy Review Commission: Repercussions and Aftermath." *New Directions in Federal Indian Policy: A Review of the American Indian Policy Review Commission*, Contemporary American Indian Issues Series 1:115-132. Los Angeles: American Indian Studies Center, University of California, Los Angeles.

[112] Sooktis, Ruby, and Anne Terry Straus. 1981. "A Rock and A Hard Place: Mineral Resources on the Northern Cheyenne Reservation." *Chicago Anthropology Exchange*, Special Issue, "Native American Land" 14:27-35.

[113] Stauss, Joseph H. 1979. "A Critique of Task Force Eight, Final Report to the American Indian Policy Review Commission: Urban and Rural Non-Reservation Indians." *New Directions in Federal Indian Policy: A Review of the American Indian Policy Review Commission*, Contemporary American Indian Issues Series 1:87-98. Los Angeles: American Indian Studies Center, University of California, Los Angeles.

[114] Stetson, C. L. 1980. "Tribal Sovereignty: *Santa Clara Pueblo v. Martinez:* Tribal Sovereignty 146 Years Later." *American Indian Law Review* 8:139-59.

[115] Stevens, Carl. 1975. "Remedies: Indian Civil Rights Act—Exhaustion of Tribal Remedies Prior to Removal to Federal Court." *American Indian Law Review* 3:169-82.

[116] Strickland, Rennard. 1975. "Friends and Enemies of the American Indian: An Essay Review on Native American Law and Public Policy." *American Indian Law Review* 3:313-31.

[117] Stuart, Paul. 1977. "United States Indian Policy: From the Dawes Act to the American Indian Policy Review Commission." *Social Service Review* 51:451-63.

[118] Sutton, Imre. 1975. *Indian Land Tenure: Bibliographic Essays and a Guide to the Literature*. New York: Clearwater Publishing Company.

[119] Szasz, Margaret C. 1977. "Federal Boarding Schools and the Indian Child: 1920-1960." *South Dakota History* 7:371-84.

[120] Taylor, Graham D. 1975. "Anthropologists, Reformers and the Indian New Deal." *Prologue* 7:151-62.

[121] ———. 1980. *The New Deal and American Indian Tribalism, The Administration of the Indian Reorganization Act, 1934-1945*. Lincoln: University of Nebraska Press.

[122] Thompson, Mark. 1979. "Nurturing the Forked Tree: Conception and Formation of the American Indian Policy Review Commis-

sion." *New Directions in Federal Indian Policy: A Review of the American Indian Policy Review Commission*, Contemporary American Indian Issues 1:5-18. Los Angeles: American Indian Studies Center, University of California, Los Angeles.

[123] Thomson, J. S. 1977. "Federal Indian Policy: A Violation of International Treaty Law." *Western State University Law Review* 4:229-71.

[124] Underal, Stanley J. 1977. "On the Road Toward Termination: The Pyramid Lake Paiutes and the Indian Attorney Controversy of the 1950s." Ph.D. dissertation, Columbia University.

[125] Van Winkle, Barrik and Robert Poor. 1981. "The Opposition of Nevada Indians to the MX System." *Chicago Anthropology Exchange*, Special Issue, "Native American Land" 14:36-49.

[126] Veeder, William H. 1976. "Confiscation of Indian Water Rights in the Upper Missouri River Basin." *South Dakota Law Review* 21:282-309.

[127] ———. 1976. "Water Rights in the Coal Fields of the Yellowstone River Basin." *Law and Contemporary Problems* 40:77-96.

[128] Viers, Becky J. M. 1979. "Environmental Law: Uranium Mining on the Navajo Reservation." *American Indian Law Review* 7:115-24.

[129] Weatherford, J. McIver. 1981. *Tribes on the Hill: An Investigation into the Rituals and Realities of an Endangered American Tribe–The Congress of the United States.* New York: Rawson, Wade Publishers.

[130] Weeks, Charles J. 1976. "The Eastern Cherokee and the New Deal." *North Carolina Historical Review* 53:303-19.

[131] Werhan, Keith M. 1978. "The Sovereignty of Indian Tribes: A Reaffirmation and Strengthening in the 1970's." *Notre Dame Lawyer* 54:5-25.

[132] Weyler, Rex. 1982. *Blood of the Land: The Government and Corporate War Against the American Indian Movement*. New York: Everest House Publishers.

[133] White, John. R. 1978. "Barmecide Revisited: The Gratuitous Offset in Indian Claims Cases." *Ethnohistory* 25:179-92.

[134] Wilkinson, Charles F., and Eric R. Biggs. 1977. "The Evolution of the Termination Policy." *American Indian Law Review* 5:139-84.

[135] Work, Susan. 1977. "The 'Terminated' Five Tribes of Oklahoma: The Effect of Federal Legislation and Administrative Treatment on the Government of the Seminole Nation." *American Indian Law Review* 6:81-141.

[136] Wright, Douglas R. 1980. "Sovereignty: Indian Sovereignty and Tribal Immunity From Suit." *American Indian Law Review* 8:401-18.

[137] Young, Lise. 1983. "What Price Progress? Uranium Production on Indian Lands in the San Juan Basin." *American Indian Law Review* 9:1-50.

[138] Zimmerman, Bill. 1976. *Airlift to Wounded Knee*. Athens: Swallow Press.

Contemporary American Indians

RUSSELL THORNTON

University of Minnesota

THE TOPIC "CONTEMPORARY American Indians" is, of course, extremely pervasive and encompasses every facet of the existing life of all Indian peoples today. As such, it is in its broad meaning too encompassing for this single chapter. Consequently, the decision was made to restrict consideration to only certain aspects of the contemporary situation of American Indians. These are: urbanization, family, education, health and mental health, criminal justice system, economic development and government policy, legal status and tribalism. In addition, some general works are discussed at the beginning and some miscellaneous ones at the end. It should also be noted that with only certain exceptions the literature discussed in the two recent bibliographies—Russell Thornton and Mary K. Grasmick, *The Sociology of American Indians* [101], and Russell Thornton, Gary D. Sandefur and Harold G. Grasmick, *The Urbanization of American Indians* [102]—is not included.

General

Several general works on American Indians today have appeared in the scholarly literature of recent years. A bibliography of published works from 1975 to 1980 on historic and contemporary American Indians is *Indian-White Relations in the United States* [83] by Francis Paul Prucha. It is both near-exhaustive and very useful. Two other recent relevant bibliographies covering both historic and contemporary American Indians are Russell Thornton and Mary K. Grasmick's *Bibliography of Social Science Research and Writings on American Indians* [100] and *The Sociology of American Indians* [101].

Some general discussions of the contemporary situations of American Indians may be found in Sar A. Levitan and Barbara Hetrick's *Big Brother's Indian Programs–With Reservations* [59]; Sar A. Levitan and William B. Johnston's *Indian Giving: Federal Programs for Native Americans* [60]; William E. Coffer's *Phoenix: The Decline and Rebirth of the Indian People* [19]; Jack D. Forbes's *Tribes and Masses: Explorations in Red, White and Black* [26]; and, Alvin M. Josephy's *Now That the Buffalo's Gone: A Study of Today's American Indian* [50].

Aside from these considerations of North American Indians as a general population, there have been various examinations of the contemporary situations of specific American Indian groups. These include Karen I. Blu's *The Lumbee Problem: The Making of an American Indian People* [7]; Jerry Kammer's *The Second Long Walk: The Navajo-Hopi Land Dispute* [52]; Loretta Fowler's *Arapahoe Politics, 1851-1978, Symbols in Crises of Authority* [28]; Peter Iverson's *The Navajo Nation* [48]; and, Ethel Nurge's *The Modern Sioux: Social Systems and Reservation Change* [72].

Urbanization

As might be expected, a very large number of books and journal articles on the urbanization of American Indians have appeared in recent years as American Indians have become increasingly urbanized. This literature encompasses not only the topic of urbanization *per se* but also what might be called the relationships of urbanization and other aspects of contemporary American Indian life. Since this literature is so extensive in its total scope, works of the latter type are discussed under the other appropriate headings following this section, and only a few works focusing on urbanization itself are mentioned here.

Existing literature on the broad topic of urbanization of American Indians is examined in the previously cited bibliography, *The Urbanization of American Indians* [102]. Its scope includes not only recent urbanization but also the historic "urbanism" of American Indians of both North and South America.

Much has been written on American Indians and urban institutions. Many of these works are discussed in following sections; however, others may be mentioned here. A broad examination of this topic may be found in John A. Price's "The Development of Urban Ethnic Institutions by United States and Canadian Indians" [77] in which he suggests a sequence of stages in the evolution of American Indian urban living. Shirley J. Fiske, in "Urban Indian Institutions: A Reappraisal from Los Angeles" [25], finds, in contrast, that Price's model does not fit the history of the Los Angeles Indian population. Also dealing with urban institutions, Herbert H. Locklear in "American Indian Myths" [66] illustrates how American Indian centers help with the adjustment process to urban areas. Karen Tranberg Hansen in "Ethnic Group Policy and the Politics of Sex: The Seattle Indian Case" [45] examines the American Indian Women's Service League and Richard E. Gardner in "The Role of the Pan-Indian Church in Urban Indian Life" [35] examines urban Indian churches.

Other works on urban American Indians have also appeared in the past several years. Included here is Theodore D. Graves's "Urban Indian Personality and the 'Culture of Poverty'" [38], a study of the 'culture of poverty' thesis *vis-à-vis* American Indians, and Donald D. Stull's "Native American Adaptation to an Urban Environment: The Papago of Tucson, Arizona" [95], an examination of demographic changes that accompany modernization and urbanization.

Finally, two recent books on urban Canadian Indians may be mentioned: Larry Krotz's *Urban Indians: The Strangers in Canada's Cities* [55], and William T. Stanbury and Jay Siegel's *Success and Failure: Indians in Urban Society* [92].

Family

Two broad, general treatments of the American Indian family have been published recently. These are *The American Indian Family: Strengths and Stresses* [85], edited by John Red Horse, August Shattuck and Fred Hoffman, and *The Destruction of American Indian Families* [103], edited by Steven Unger. Both are collections of papers on various topics relevant to Indian families: the former is the proceedings of a National Institute of Mental Health Conference; the latter is published under the auspices of the Association of American Indian Affairs. Both may serve as introductions to contemporary American Indian families from primarily Indian points of view and are recommended on this basis.

The fertility of contemporary American Indian families is considered in several papers. Two interesting ones are Margot Liberty, Richard Scaglion and David V. Hughey's "Rural and Urban Seminole Indian Fertility" [63] and Margot Liberty, David V. Hughey and Richard Scaglion's "Rural and Urban Omaha Indian Fertility" [62]. The former shows a lower Indian fertility rate with urbanization; the latter shows this is not always the case. Similary, Terry L. Hayne's "Some Factors Related to Contraceptive Behavior Among Wind River Shoshone and Arapahoe Females" [47] compares contraceptive users and non-users and finds differences in age, marital status, pregnancy history and religious beliefs. Finally, James H. Gundlach et al., "Migration, Labor Mobility and Relocation Assistance" [41], is a study of welfare levels among reservation families, families moving to urban areas with Bureau of Indian Affairs assistance and families migrating to urban areas without such assistance.

Education

Recent scholarly treatments of American Indians and education are focused on both the elementary and secondary systems and the higher education system. Generally, works on the former systems revolve around problems urban American Indian youth face in schools, while works on the higher education system revolve around the development of the academic discipline of American Indian studies in colleges and universities of the United States and Canada, though examinations of the problems Indian college students face may also be found in this literature.

In "Indian Education in the City: Correlates of Academic Performance" [13], Bruce Chadwick, Howard Bahr and Joseph Stauss identify five factors which affect the performance of Indian students: self-concept, achievement motivation, cultural conflict, family instability and discrimination. W. James Grainger's "The Urban Indian Student vs. The Integrated School Situation" [37] shows that urban and rural Indian students face many of the same disadvantages, and George M. Guilmet's "Navajo and Caucasian Children's Verbal and Nonverbal-Visual Behavior in the Urban Classroom" [40] illustrates differences in the classroom between these two groups of students.

A very significant amount of scholarly attention has been given in recent years to the development of American Indian studies in the higher educational systems of the United States and Canada. Early papers on this topic include Beatrice Medicine's "The Anthropologist and American Indian Studies Programs" [67]; Frank C. Miller's "Involvement in an Urban University" [69], a discussion of the early development of American Indian studies at the University of Minnesota; Wilcomb Washburn's "American Indian Studies: A Status Report" [108]; and, Morgan G. Otis, Jr.'s "A Native American Studies Program" [74].

More recent examinations of American Indian studies are Russell Thornton's investigation of the disciplinary basis and potential of American Indian studies, in "American Indian Studies as an Academic Discipline" [98, 99]; Ward Churchill and Norbert S. Hill, Jr.'s "Indian Education at the University Level: An Historical Survey" [16] and their "An Historical Survey of Tendencies in Indian Education: Higher Education" [17]; John A. Price's *Native Studies: American and Canadian Indians* [78] and "Native Studies in Canadian Universities and Colleges" [79]. Also pertinent here are Patricia Locke's *A Survey of College and University Programs for American Indians* [65] and U.C.L.A.'s American Indian Studies Center's Symposium on American Indian Studies [104], a discussion of the development and potential of American Indian studies.

Recent concern for this topic culminated in 1980 when U.C.L.A.'s American Indian Studies Center's Fourth Annual Spring Conference on Contemporary American Indian Issues was devoted to "American Indian Issues in Higher Education." Papers presented at the conference focused not only on American Indian studies but also on the issues and problems of the involvement of American Indian students in higher education. These papers were published as a volume entitled *American Indian Issues in Higher Education* [106].

Finally, several other publications on American Indian education have appeared in the past few years, often considering American Indians and American Indian concerns at all levels of the educational system. Included here are Dean Chavers's "New Directions in Indian Education" [15], Laurence French and Charles Hornbuckle's "Cultural Clash in our Educational System: The Need for a Multicultural Philosophy in Higher Education" [31], Laurence French's presentation of objectives and program for a model Indian education project as explained in "The Educational Dilemma Facing Urban Indians" [29], and Duane Champagne and Joy Query's study of the United Tribes Education Training Center, "Urban Education and Training for American Indian Students: Some Correlates of Success" [14]. Also included here are W. T. Stanbury's examination of the educational level of non-reservation Indians in British Columbia, "The Education Gap: Urban Indians in British Columbia" [91], Vincent Little and Larry Rummell's description of an urban Indian education program, "Phoenix Indians Adopt Community Education" [64], and Ann Beuf's paper suggesting changes in the educational system to help American Indians, "The Home of Whose Brave? Problems Confronting Native Americans in Education" [5].

Health and Mental Health

Another grouping of recent publications focuses on the health and mental health status of American Indians. Relatively few papers concerned with the physical health of American Indians were located. One of these is Barbara Carr and Eun Sul Lee's "Navajo Tribal Mortality: A Life Table Analysis of the Leading Causes of Death" [12]. Their data indicate that the greatest increase in the life expectancy of Navajo males would come about through elimination of motor vehicle accidents and the greatest increase in the life expectancy of Navajo females would come about through the elimination of circulatory diseases. Other important works are Donald Stull's "New Data on Accident Victim Rates among the Papago Indians: The Urban Case" [95] and Michael Fuchs and Rashid Bashshur's "Use of Traditional Indian Medicine among Urban Native Americans" [34].

A relatively large number of recent publications on the mental health of American Indians are of note. An important bibliography here is Dianne R. Kelso and Carolyn L. Attneave's *Bibliography of North American Indian Mental Health* [53].

Much of this literature pertains to problems American Indians experience in urban areas. "Neglected Minority: Urban Indians and Mental Health" [9] by Patrick Borunda and James H. Shore focuses on the problems of American Indians in the Portland, Oregon area (one of which is suicide as found by James H. Shore in his "American Indian Suicide—Fact and Fantasy" [89]). "Urban Indians and Mental Health Problems" [2] by Eloise R. Barter and James T. Barter is a discussion of how urban Indians are deprived of many of the health and mental health services available to reservation Indians, and "Indian People and Community Psychiatry in Saskatchewan" [33] by W. B. Fritz indicates less adequate mental health services for Indians than for non-Indians. "Grief Counseling with Native Americans" [46] by Wynne Hanson urges mental health workers to be aware of the unique cultural factors associated with grief for American Indians. In an interesting paper, "Toward a Reconceptualization of American Indian Urbanization: A Chippewa Case" [75], J. Anthony Paredes describes differences in involvement in city life by American Indians without making assumptions about their "success" of urban adaptation.

Comparisons between the mental health of rural Indians and others have been considered in J. Anthony Paredes and Sandra K. Joos's study of the Creek, "Economics, Optimism, and Community History: A Comparison of Rural Minnesotans and Eastern Creek Indians" [76], and in David Liberman and Joel Frank's study of the Miccosukee, "Individuals' Perceptions of Stressful Life Events: A Comparison of Native American, Rural and Urban Samples Using the Social Readjustment Rating Scale" [61]. Paul A. Brinker and Benjamin J. Taylor have studied southern Plains Indians from western Oklahoma who returned to their former homes after having relocated to the city in their paper, "Southern Plains Indian Relocation Returnees" [10]. They suggest ways the returnee rate might be reduced.

Studies focusing on the alcoholism and drinking behavior of American Indians have also been published in the past few years. Important among these works is the volume, *Drinking Behavior Among Southwestern Indians* [107], edited by Jack O. Waddell and Michael W. Everett. Two other recent publications are Thomas Beltrame and David V. McQueen's "Urban and Rural Indian Drinking Patterns: The Special Case of the Lumbee" [4] and Robert F. Kraus and Patricia A. Buffler's "Sociocultural Stress and the American Native in Alaska: An Analysis of Changing Patterns of Psychiatric Illness and Alcohol Abuse among Alaska Natives" [54]. A recent book is edited by John Hamer and is titled *Alcohol and Native Peoples of the North* [44].

Criminal Justice

American Indians and the criminal justice system is a topic which has also received attention in recent years, albeit only a few works were found. American Indians in Seattle, Washington have been studied in this regard by Larry E. Williams, Bruce A. Chadwick and Howard M. Bahr in "Antecedents of Self-Reported Arrest for Indian Americans in Seattle" [109].

Other studies in this category are "Criminal Justice in Rural and Urban Communities: A Study of the Bureaucratization of Justice" [43] by John Hagan; a study of Indians and Whites in Alberta, Canada, "Criminal Justice and the American Indian" [84] by Archie and Bette Randall; "An Analysis of Indian Violence: The Cherokee Example" [32] by Laurence French and Jim Hornbuckle; and, *Indians and Criminal Justice* [30] by Laurence French.

Economic Development

Various issues associated with the economic development of American Indian people have also been studied. *American Indian Economic Development* [93], edited by Sam Stanley, is a recent collection of papers focused on the economic development of specific Indian groups. The tribes considered are the Navajo, the Lummi Indian community, the Morongo Indian Reservation, the Pine Ridge Sioux, the Passamaquoddy, the Oklahoma Cherokee and the Papago.

Other works since the mid-1970s encompass Ernest L. Schusky's "Development by Grantsmanship: Economic Planning in the Lower Brule Sioux Reservation" [88], Robert A. Hackenberg's "Colorado River Basin Development and Its Potential Impact on Tribal Life" [42], Stephen J. Kunitz's "Underdevelopment and Social Services on the Navajo Reservation" [57], Joseph G. Jorgensen's "A Century of

Political Economic Effects on American Indian Society, 1880-1980" [49], Alan L. Sorkin's "The Economic and Social Status of the American Indian, 1940-1970" [90], and Henry F. Dobyns, Richard W. Stoffle and Kristine Jones's "Native American Urbanization and Socio-Economic Integration in the Southwestern United States" [22].

Two books just published on economic development of American Indian tribes are Phillip Reno's *Mother Earth, Father Sky, and Economic Development: Navajo Resources and Their Use* [86] and Michael L. Lawson's *Dammed Indians: The Pick-Sloan Plan and the Missouri River Sioux, 1944-1980* [58].

Government Policy, Legal Status and Tribalism

This grouping of scholarly literature is rather heterogeneous, and includes literature considering the relationships of American Indian tribes and individuals with United States and Canadian governments as well as the nature of tribalism as it exists today. Two bibliographies on government policy have been published recently under the auspices of The Newberry Library Center for the History of the American Indian Bibliographical Series. These are Francis Paul Prucha's *United States Indian Policy* [81] and Robert J. Surtees's *Canadian Indian Policy* [97]. Both serve as quite good introductions to the topic.

Also recently published is Francis Paul Prucha's *Indian Policy in the United States* [82], an update containing basic current literature in this category. *New Directions in Federal Indian Policy: A Review of the American Indian Policy Review Commission* [105] is a compilation of articles from papers presented at the 1978 U.C.L.A. American Indian Studies Center Annual Spring Conference on American Indian Issues. The thrust of the articles seems basically critical of the Commission and its general failure to collect new data on American Indian problems and emphasis on reviewing past federal policy toward American Indians. Published in 1981 under the auspices of U.C.L.A.'s American Indian Studies Center is Jack D. Forbes's *Native Americans and Nixon: Presidential Politics and Minority Self-Determination, 1969-1972* [27]. Published in 1982, Larry W. Burt's *Tribalism in Crisis: Federal Indian Policy, 1953-1961* [11] , is the first indepth history of this period of recent Indian relations with the United States government.

Other examinations of government policy toward American Indians are Vine Deloria, Jr.'s "The Next Three Years: A Time for Change" [20] and John A. Price's "Historical Theory and the Applied Anthropology of United States and Canadian Indians" [80]. Nathan Glazer's "Federalism and Ethnicity: The Experience of the United States" [36] is also relevant here, though it focuses on non-Indian groups in American society.

Three articles in *The Indian Historian* might be broadly defined as considering the issue of the legal status of American Indians. These are Donald B. Murdock's "The Case for Native American Tribal Citizenship" [71], Christopher C. Joyner's "The Historical Status of American Indians under International Law" [51], and Patrick Melendy's "Tax Exemption: The Right of Urban Indians" [68].

Various considerations of what may be viewed as American Indian "tribalism" have appeared in the past several years as well. One of these is Larry R. Stucki's "The Case Against Population Control: The Probable Creation of the First American Indian State" [94]. According to Stucki, population growth is the primary reason for the increased power of the Navajo tribe in recent times. He goes even further to argue that the Navajo Reservation will emerge as the fifty-first state in the future.

Appearing in the mid-1970s were two considerations of resurgent tribalism by George Feaver: "Wounded Knee and the New Tribalism: The American Indians" I and II [23, 24]. Published a few years later were Diane Ainsworth's brief report, "Indians on the Warpath: Can They Still Call Themselves Tribes?" [1], Rachel A. Bonney's "The Role of AIM Leaders in Indian Nationalism" [8], John Howard Clinebell and Jim Thompson's "Americans under International Law" [18], and Jeanne Guillemin's "The Politics of National Integration: A Comparison of the United States and Canadian Indian Administrations" [39]. Finally, Joan W. Moore's "American Minorities and 'New Nation' Perspectives" [70], and Roxanne Dunbar Ortiz's "Wounded Knee 1890 to Wounded Knee 1973" [73] both consider United States' colonialism and American Indian communities.

Miscellaneous

Other recent literature not falling appropriately in one of the topics above should also be mentioned. These are Henry F. Dobyns's "Patterns of Indoamerican Chief Executive Tenure" [21], Robert L. Bee's "To Get Something for the People: The Predicament of the American Indian Leader" [3], C. Jean Rogers and Teresa E. Gallion's "Characteristics of Elderly Pueblo Indians in New Mexico" [87], Stephen J. Kunitz's "Factors Influencing Recent Navajo and Hopi Population Change" [56], and Kendall Blanchard's *The Mississippi Choctaws at Play* [6].

ALPHABETICAL LIST

[1] Ainsworth, Diane. 1978. "Indians on the Warpath: Can They Still Call Themselves Tribes?" *Human Behavior* 7: 36-37.

[2] Barter, Eloise R., and James T. Barter. 1974. "Urban Indians and Mental Health Problems." *Psychiatric Annals* 4: 37-43.

[3] Bee, Robert L. 1979. "To Get Something for the People: The Predicament of the American Indian Leader." *Human Organization* 38: 239-47.

[4] Beltrame, Thomas, and David V. McQueen. 1979. "Urban and Rural Indian Drinking Patterns: The Special Case of the Lumbee." *International Journal of Addiction* 14: 533-48.

[5] Beuf, Ann H. 1976. "The Home of Whose Brave? Problems Confronting Native Americans in Education." *Journal of the NAWDAC* 38: 70-79.

[6] Blanchard, Kendall. 1981. *The Mississippi Choctaws at Play*. Urbana: University of Illinois Press.

[7] Blu, Karen I. 1980. *The Lumbee Problem: The Making of an American Indian People*. New York: Cambridge University Press.

[8] Bonney, Rachel A. 1977. "The Role of AIM Leaders in Indian Nationalism." *American Indian Quarterly* 3: 209-24.

[9] Borunda, Patrick, and James H. Shore. 1978. "Neglected Minority: Urban Indians and Mental Health." *International Journal of Social Psychiatry* 24: 220-24.

[10] Brinker, Paul A., and Benjamin J. Taylor. 1974. "Southern Plains Indian Relocation Returnees." *Human Organization* 33: 139-46.

[11] Burt, Larry W. 1982. *Tribalism in Crisis: Federal Indian Policy, 1953-1961*. Albuquerque: University of New Mexico Press.

[12] Carr, Barbara A., and Eun Sul Lee. 1978. "Navajo Tribal Mortality: A Life Table Analysis of the Leading Causes of Death." *Social Biology* 25: 279-87.
[13] Chadwick, Bruce A., Howard M. Bahr, and Joseph Stauss. 1977. "Indian Education in the City: Correlates of Academic Performance." *Journal of Educational Research* 70: 135-41.
[14] Champagne, Duane, and Joy M. N. Query. 1980. "Urban Education and Training for American Indian Students: Some Correlates of Success." *Urban Education* 15: 93-101.
[15] Chavers, Dean. 1975. "New Directions in Indian Education." *The Indian Historian* 8: 43-46.
[16] Churchill, Ward, and Norbert S. Hill, Jr. 1979. "Indian Education at the University Level: An Historical Survey." *Journal of Ethnic Studies* 7: 37-46.
[17] ———. 1979. "An Historical Survey of Tendencies in Indian Education: Higher Education." *The Indian Historian* 12: 37-46.
[18] Clinebell, John Howard, and Jim Thompson. 1978. "Americans Under International Law." *Buffalo Law Review* 27: 669-714.
[19] Coffer, William E. 1981. *Phoenix: The Decline and Rebirth of the Indian People*. New York: Van Nostrand Reinhold.
[20] Deloria, Vine, Jr. 1974. "The Next Three Years: A Time for Change." *The Indian Historian* 7: 25-27, 53.
[21] Dobyns, Henry F. 1981. "Patterns of Indoamerican Chief Executive Tenure." *Human Organization* 40: 78-80.
[22] Dobyns, Henry F., Richard W. Stoffle, and Kristine Jones. 1975. "Native American Urbanization and Socio-Economic Integration in the Southwestern United States." *Ethnohistory* 22: 155-79.
[23] Feaver, George. 1975. "Wounded Knee and the New Tribalism: The American Indians I." *Encounter* 44: 28-35.
[24] ———. 1975. "Wounded Knee and the New Tribalism: The American Indians II." *Encounter* 44: 16-24.
[25] Fiske, Shirley J. 1979. "Urban Indian Institutions: A Reappraisal from Los Angeles." *Urban Anthropology* 8: 149-71.
[26] Forbes, Jack D. 1978. *Tribes and Masses: Explorations in Red, White and Black*. Davis, California: D-Q University Press.
[27] ———. 1981. *Native Americans and Nixon: Presidential Politics and Minority Self-Determination 1969-1972*." Los Angeles: U.C.L.A. American Indian Studies Center.
[28] Fowler, Loretta. 1982. *Arapahoe Politics, 1851-1978, Symbols in Crises of Authority*. Lincoln: University of Nebraska Press.
[29] French, Laurence. 1979. "The Educational Dilemma Facing Urban Indians." *Journal of American Indian Education* 18: 28-32.
[30] ———. 1982. *Indians and Criminal Justice*. Totowa, New Jersey: Allanheld, Osmun.
[31] French, Laurence, and Charles Hornbuckle. 1977. "Cultural Clash

in Our Educational System: The Need for a Multicultural Philosophy in Higher Education." *The Indian Historian* 10: 33-39.

[32] French, Laurence, and Jim Hornbuckle. 1977-78. "An Analysis of Indian Violence: The Cherokee Example." *American Indian Quarterly* 3: 335-56.

[33] Fritz, W. B. 1978. "Indian People and Community Psychiatry in Saskatchewan." *Canadian Psychiatric Association Journal* 23: 1-7.

[34] Fuchs, Michael, and Rashid Bashshur. 1975. "Use of Traditional Medicine Among Urban Native Americans." *Medical Care* 13: 915-27.

[35] Gardner, Richard E. 1969. "The Role of the Pan-Indian Church in Urban Indian Life." *Anthropology* 1: 14-26.

[36] Glazer, Nathan. 1977. "Federalism and Ethnicity: The Experience of the United States." *Publius* 7: 71-87.

[37] Grainger, W. James. 1978. "The Urban Indian Student vs. The Integrated School Situation." *Northian* 13: 3-5.

[38] Graves, Theodore D. 1974. "Urban Indian Personality and the 'Culture of Poverty'." *American Ethnologist* 1: 65-86.

[39] Guillemin, Jeanne. 1978. "The Politics of National Integration: A Comparison of the United States and Canadian Indian Administrations." *Social Problems* 25: 319-32.

[40] Guilmet, George M. 1978. "Navajo and Caucasian Children's Verbal and Nonverbal-Visual Behavior in the Urban Classroom." *Anthropology and Education Quarterly* 9: 196-215.

[41] Gundlach, James H., P. Nelson Reid, and Alden E. Roberts. 1977. "Migration, Labor Mobility, and Relocation Assistance." *Social Service Review* 51: 464-73.

[42] Hackenberg, Robert A. 1976. "Colorado River Basin Development and Its Potential Impact on Tribal Life." *Human Organization* 35: 303-11.

[43] Hagan, John. 1977. "Criminal Justice in Rural and Urban Communities: A Study of the Bureaucratization of Justice." *Social Forces* 55: 597-612.

[44] Hamer, John, ed. 1982. *Alcohol and Native Peoples of the North*. Lanham, Maryland: University Press of America.

[45] Hansen, Karen Tranberg. 1979. "Ethnic Group Policy and the Politics of Sex: The Seattle Indian Case." *Urban Anthropology* 8: 29-47.

[46] Hanson, Wynne. 1978. "Grief Counseling with Native Americans." *White Cloud Journal* 1: 19-21.

[47] Haynes, Terry L. 1977. "Some Factors Related to Contraceptive Behavior among Wind River Shoshone and Arapahoe Females." *Human Organization* 36: 72-76.

[48] Iverson, Peter. 1981. *The Navajo Nation*. Westport, Connecticut: Greenwood Press.

[49] Jorgensen, Joseph G. 1978. "A Century of Political Economic Effects on American Indian Society, 1880-1980." *Journal of Ethnic Studies* 6: 1-82.

[50] Josephy, Alvin M., Jr. 1982. *Now That the Buffalo's Gone: A Study of Today's American Indians.* New York: Alfred A. Knopf.

[51] Joyner, Christopher C. 1978. "The Historical Status of American Indians under International Law." *The Indian Historian* 11: 30-36.

[52] Kammer, Jerry. 1980. *The Second Long Walk: The Navajo-Hopi Land Dispute*. Albuquerque: University of New Mexico Press.

[53] Kelso, Dianne R., and Carolyn L. Attneave. 1981. *Bibliography of North American Indian Mental Health*. Westport, Connecticut: Greenwood Press.

[54] Kraus, Robert F., and Patricia A. Buffler. 1979. "Sociocultural Stress and the American Native in Alaska: An Analysis of Changing Patterns of Pyschiatric Illness and Alcohol Abuse among Alaska Natives." *Culture, Medicine and Pyschiatry* 3: 111-51.

[55] Krotz, Larry. 1980. *Urban Indians, The Strangers in Canada's Cities*. Edmonton: Hurtig Publishers.

[56] Kunitz, Stephen J. 1974. "Factors Influencing Recent Navajo and Hopi Population Changes." *Human Organization* 33: 7-16.

[57] ———. 1977. "Underdevelopment and Social Services on the Navajo Reservation." *Human Organization* 36: 398-405.

[58] Lawson, Michael L. 1982. *Dammed Indians: The Pick-Sloan Plan and the Missouri River Sioux, 1944-1980*. Norman: University of Oklahoma Press.

[59] Levitan, Sar A., and Barbara Hetrick. 1971. *Big Brother's Indian Programs–With Reservations*. New York: McGraw-Hill.

[60] Levitan, Sar A., and William B. Johnston. 1975. *Indian Giving: Federal Programs for Native Americans*. Baltimore: The Johns Hopkins University Press.

[61] Liberman, David, and Joel Frank. 1980. "Individuals' Perceptions of Stressful Life Events: A Comparison of Native American, Rural, and Urban Samples Using the Social Readjustment Rating Scale." *White Cloud Journal* 1: 15-19.

[62] Liberty, Margot, David V. Hughey, and Richard Scaglion. 1976. "Rural and Urban Omaha Indian Fertility." *Human Biology* 48: 59-71.

[63] Liberty, Margot, Richard Scaglion, and David V. Hughey. 1976. "Rural and Urban Seminole Indian Fertility." *Human Biology* 48: 741-55.

[64] Little, Vincent, and Larry Rummell. 1974. "Phoenix Indians Adopt Community Education." *Community Education Journal* 4: 18-19, 62.

[65] Locke, Patricia. 1978. *A Survey of College and University Programs for American Indians*. Boulder: Western Interstate Higher Education.

[66] Locklear, Herbert H. "American Indian Myths." *Social Work* 17: 72-80.

[67] Medicine, Beatrice. 1971. "The Anthropologist and American Indian Studies Programs." *The Indian Historian* 4: 15-18, 63.
[68] Melendy, Patrick. 1978. "Tax Exemption: The Right of Urban Indians." *The Indian Historian* 11: 29-31, 59.
[69] Miller, Frank C. 1971. "Involvement in an Urban University." In *The American Indian in Urban Society*, ed. Jack O. Waddell and O. Michael Watson. Boston: Little, Brown.
[70] Moore, Joan W. 1976. "American Minorities and 'New Nation' Perspectives." *Pacific Sociological Review* 19: 447-68.
[71] Murdock, Donald B. 1975. "The Case for Native American Tribal Citizenship." *The Indian Historian* 8: 2-5.
[72] Nurge, Ethel, ed. 1970. *The Modern Sioux: Social Systems and Reservation Change*. Lincoln: University of Nebraska Press.
[73] Ortiz, Roxanne Dunbar. 1980. "Wounded Knee 1890 to Wounded Knee 1973: A Study in United States Colonialism." *Journal of Ethnic Studies* 8: 1-15.
[74] Otis, Morgan G., Jr. 1976. "A Native American Studies Program." *The Indian Historian* 9: 14-18.
[75] Paredes, J. Anthony. 1971. "Toward a Reconceptualization of American Indian Urbanization: A Chippewa Case." *Anthropological Quarterly* 44: 256-71.
[76] Paredes, J. Anthony, and Sandra K. Joos. 1980. "Economics, Optimism, and Community History: A Comparison of Rural Minnesotans and Eastern Creek Indians." *Human Organization* 39: 142-52.
[77] Price, John A. 1976. "The Development of Urban Ethnic Institutions by U. S. and Canadian Indians." *Ethnic Groups* 1: 107-31.
[78] ———. 1978. *Native Studies: American and Canadian Indians*. Toronto: McGraw-Hill Ryerson.
[79] ———. 1981. "Native Studies in Canadian Universities and Colleges." *The Canadian Journal of Native Studies* 1: 349-61.
[80] ———. 1982. "Historical Theory and the Applied Anthropology of U. S. and Canadian Indians." *Human Organization* 41: 43-53.
[81] Prucha, Francis Paul. 1977. *United States Indian Policy: A Critical Bibliography*. Bloomington: Indiana University Press for The Newberry Library.
[82] ———. 1981. *Indian Policy in the United States*. Lincoln, Nebraska: University of Nebraska Press.
[83] ———. 1982. *Indian-White Relations in the Untied States: A Bibliography of Works Published 1975-1980*. Lincoln, Nebraska: University of Nebraska Press.
[84] Randall, Archie, and Bette Randall. 1978. "Criminal Justice and the American Indian." *The Indian Historian* 11: 42-48.
[85] Red Horse, John, August Shattuck, and Fred Hoffman, eds. 1981. *The American Indian Family: Strengths and Stresses*. Isleta, New Mexico: American Indian Social Research and Development Associates, Inc.

[86] Reno, Phillip. 1981. *Mother Earth, Father Sky, and Economic Development: Navajo Resources and Their Use*. Albuquerque: University of New Mexico.

[87] Rogers, C. Jean, and Teresa E. Gallion. 1978. "Characteristics of Elderly Pueblo Indians in New Mexico." *The Gerontologist* 18: 482-87.

[88] Schusky, Ernest L. 1975. "Development by Grantsmanship: Economic Planning in the Lower Brule Sioux Reservation." *Human Organization* 34: 227-36.

[89] Shore, James H. 1975. "American Indian Suicide—Fact and Fantasy." *Psychiatry* 38: 86-91.

[90] Sorkin, Alan L. 1976. "The Economic and Social Status of the American Indian, 1940-1970." *The Journal of Negro Education* 45: 432-47.

[91] Stanbury, W. T. 1973. "The Education Gap: Urban Indians in British Columbia." *British Columbia Studies* 19: 21-49.

[92] Stanbury, W. T., and Jay Siegel. 1975. *Success and Failure: Indians in Urban Society*. Vancouver: University of British Columbia Press.

[93] Stanley, Sam, ed. 1978. *American Indian Economic Development*. The Hague: Mouton.

[94] Stucki, Larry R. 1971. "The Case Against Population Control: The Probable Creation of the First American Indian State." *Human Organization* 30: 393-99.

[95] Stull, Donald D. 1977. "New Data on Accident Victim Rates among the Papago Indians: The Urban Case." *Human Organization* 36: 395-97.

[96] ———. 1978. "Native American Adaptation to an Urban Environment: The Papago of Tucson, Arizona." *Urban Anthropology* 7: 117-35.

[97] Surtees, Robert J. 1982. *Canadian Indian Policy: A Critical Bibliography*. Bloomington: Indiana University Press for The Newberry Library.

[98] Thornton, Russell. 1977. "American Indian Studies as an Academic Discipline." *Journal of Ethnic Studies* 5: 1-15.

[99] ———. 1978. "American Indian Studies as an Academic Discipline." *American Indian Culture and Research Journal* 2: 10-19.

[100] Thornton, Russell, and Mary K. Grasmick. 1979. *Bibliography of Social Science Research and Writings on American Indians*. Minneapolis: University of Minnesota, Center for Urban and Regional Affairs.

[101] ———. 1980. *Sociology of American Indians: A Critical Bibliography*. Bloomington: Indiana University Press for The Newberry Library.

[102] Thornton, Russell, Gary D. Sandefur, and Harold G. Grasmick. 1982. *The Urbanization of American Indians: A Critical Bibliography*. Bloomington: Indiana University Press for The Newberry Library.

[103] Unger, Steven, ed. 1977. *The Destruction of American Indian Families*. New York: Association of American Indian Affairs.

[104] University of California, Los Angeles, American Indian Studies Center. 1978. *American Indian Culture and Research Journal*, Volume 2, Numbers 3 and 4.

[105] ———. 1979. *New Directions in Federal Indian Policy: A Review of the American Indian Policy Review Commission*. Los Angeles: U.C.L.A. American Indian Studies Center.

[106] ———. 1981. *American Indian Issues in Higher Education*. Los Angeles: U.C.L.A. American Indian Studies Center.

[107] Waddell, Jack O., and Michael W. Everett, eds. 1980. *Drinking Behavior Among Southwestern Indians*. Tucson: University of Arizona Press.

[108] Washburn, Wilcomb E. 1975. "American Indian Studies: A Status Report." *American Quarterly* 27: 263-74.

[109] Williams, Larry E., Bruce A. Chadwick, and Howard M. Bahr. 1979. "Antecedents of Self-Reported Arrest for Indian Americans in Seattle." *Phylon* 40: 243-52.

Native Americans and the Environment

RICHARD WHITE
University of Utah

Over the last twenty years the amount of scholarship devoted to Indians and their relation to the natural environment has increased dramatically. The genealogy of this scholarship reveals two distinct ancestral branches, popular environmentalism and cultural ecology, whose concerns have sometimes converged in the work of a third, more miscellaneous, group of ethnohistorians concerned with environmental topics.

Cultural ecology forms, perhaps, the purest strain of this scholarship. Attempts to establish relationships between culture and environment have occupied American scholars for much of the last century. The deserved fall of geographical determinists discredited environmental studies for a prolonged period in the mid-twentieth century, but even then geographers such as Carl Sauer and anthropologists and archaeologists such as Waldo Wedel and John Ewers continued to do important work. In the late 1950s and early 1960s, however, spurred in large part by Julian Steward's *Theory of Culture Change* (1955) and the growing importance of ecological science, cultural ecology emerged as a subfield of anthropology and archaeology and complemented the continuing concern of geographers with similar issues. The resulting scholarly literature, while hardly confined to Indian peoples, has devoted a great deal of attention to them, in part because of Steward's stress on the clearer correlations available between environment and culture in less complex societies and his own work on Shoshonean peoples.

The other branch of current scholarship has more popular

roots. As Bernard Sheehan has noted in *Savagism and Civility* [79], the themes of savagism and bestiality run deep in European and American writings on Indians during the seventeenth, eighteenth, and nineteenth centuries. By connecting Indians with nature in such a manner, Whites could by similar rationales justify the "improvement" of each. Even the allied conception of the noble savage represented a device to criticize European society rather than a serious appreciation of either the Indians or the natural world. Savagism so dominated the intellectual climate of nineteenth century writers that, as Robert Sayre has demonstrated in his *Thoreau and the American Indians* [78], a writer as fascinated by nature and the Indians as Thoreau transcended its limits only with difficulty. Scholars have yet to really explain the evolution of the popular image of the Indian into that of a conservationist, but clearly, with the arrival of popular environmentalism in the late 1960s and 1970s, Indians had become synonymous for most Whites with conservation. Since this popular environmentalism has provided the larger cultural context for much recent writing about Indians, its influence should be gauged before returning to cultural ecology.

In the early 1970s scholars who considered Indian peoples to be conservationists and ecologists made the connection with current environmental concerns quite explicit. Wilbur Jacobs began his essay, "The White Man's Frontier in American History: The Impact upon the Land and the Indian" [42], with a bulletin of ecological crisis, and Rennard Strickland in his "The Idea of Environment and the Ideal of the Indian" [82] immediately connected current environmentalism and the growing popularity of American Indians.

At times this association of Indians and contemporary environmentalism came perilously close to a noble savagism more concerned with a deserved critique of American society than with any critical understanding of Indian people's conception of or influence on the environment. Jacobs, for example, stressed the environmental quietism of Indians. It was what they did not do that mattered. They left, he claimed, the land unmarked by any sign of their lives there. In a second article, later retitled "Indians as Ecologists" [43], Jacobs modified his position by devoting some attention to positive alterations of the environment by Indian peoples, but his major concern remained a critique of the environmental destructiveness of white settlement.

It was surprising that the idea of Indians passing over the land, leaving no trace, could maintain any scholarly credibility in the early 1970s. By then not only was some of Carl Sauer's pioneering work almost forty years old, but scholars had also noted and argued over the Indians' role, largely through burning, in shaping the ecology of the eastern forests, midwestern prairies, and the Great Plains. This literature continued to expand during the 1960s and 1970s. Calvin Martin, in "Fire and Forest Structure in the Aboriginal Eastern Forest" [57], stressed the impact of Indian burning on northeastern woodlands and Richard White, in "Indian Land Use and Environmental Change" [97], detailed ways in which Indians shaped the Pacific Northwest. In more ambitious studies, Richard Yarnell discussed ecological modifications in his *Aboriginal Relationships Between Culture and Plant Life in the Upper Great Lakes* [102]; Henry Lewis examined *Patterns of Indian Burning in California* [53], and stressed its ecological consequences, while Henry Dobyns tied together social change and ecological change in analyzing the impact of Indian land use practices in the Sonoran desert in his *From Fire to Flood* [18]. Stephen Pyne recently included much information on Indian modification of the environment in his *Fire in America* [64]. Studies of contemporary Indian fisherman such Fikret Berkes's "Fishery Resource Use in a Subarctic Indian Community" [8] only added evidence on the ways Indians could shape wild fish as well as game populations. The bulk of this research demonstrated that most changes Indians initiated in the environment were benign and ecosystems remained stable, yet the changes were there, and the ecosystems could not be explained without reference to human actions. The cumulative evidence of Indian influence on the land has become so pervasive that it makes use of the word wilderness (in the sense of land unaffected by human use) meaningless for huge areas of North America at the time of contact.

This awareness of Indian activities that shaped the natural world has appeared in more recent writings which portray the Indians as environmentalists, but some scholars still seem uncomfortable with it. J. Donald Hughes in "Forest Indians: The Holy Occupation" [35] acknowledges that Indians changed nature, but then argues that they tried to do so as little as possible. Robert Heizer and Albert Elsasser in *The Natural World of the California Indians* [30] were more willing to come to terms with actual Indian management of the environment. In their conception of "creative stewardship" they attempted to blend conceptions of people actively shaping the natural world and yet at one with it. Charles Bowden reached similar conclusions in his study of the desert Southwest, *Killing the Hidden Waters* [10].

Some environmentalist scholars have, however, been unconcerned with gauging what Indians did to the land because their real interest has been in what Indians thought about nature. Such a concern drew not only on popular environmentalism but also on the older established study of Indian religions. In his "The Contribution of the Study of North American Indian Religions" [36] Ake Hultkrantz, a Swede and probably the leading modern student of Native American religions, welcomed the new enthusiasm environmentalism created for the study of Indian beliefs. Hultkrantz's own work on links between religion and environment predated the environmental movement, but his writings, until recently, were largely scattered in foreign publications. Two new volumes, his *The Religions of the American Indians* [37], and a collection of essays, *Belief and Worship in Native North America* [38], edited with a useful introductory essay by Christopher Vecsey, have made his work far more accessible to American scholars.

At his best Hultkrantz brings to his writing a sophisticated awareness of the intricacy of the connections between culture and nature. This makes his environmental essays stimulating if not always consistent. Hultkrantz analyzes the relationship between the natural world and religious thought in a manner which rewards a careful reading. He struggles with the problems of the primacy of nature or culture in shaping religious thought, and with material and ideological concerns in religious conceptions of nature. Eventually he argues that nature for the Indians was a cultural construct which revealed a supernatural order. The mechanics of the reciprocal play between nature and culture sometimes seem contradictory or imprecise in these essays, and occasionally the ethnography of his sources is dubious, but Hultkrantz's insistence on this interplay, and the very sweep of the attempt to explain it makes his work both rewarding and important.

Although other recent works on the relationship between Indian philosophy and religion on the one hand and nature on the other have shared Hultkrantz's concerns, much of it lacks his depth and erudition. Two essays by Barre Toelken and N. Scott Momaday — "Seeing with a Native Eye" [88] and "Native American Attitudes toward the Environment" [60] — in a collection of the mid-1970s which took its name from Toelken's essay, are, for example, discursive rather than analytical pieces on how differently Whites and Indians perceive and find meaning in nature. Unique Indian perceptions should not, however, be ascribed to passivity. Franchot Ballinger's "The Responsible Center" [7] is useful for its stress on the creative role Navajo and Pueblo beliefs accorded human beings in the natural world.

Christopher Vecsey, who did much to introduce Hultkrantz to American scholars, has both helped edit and contributed to another recent collection, *American Indian Environments* [93], whose title is misleading since many of the essays have more to do with sovereignty than with nature. Vecsey's own essay in this collection, "American Indian Environmental Religion" [92], attempts to cover both the environmental dimensions of Native American religions and the religious dimensions of American Indian environmental relations. After a useful and perceptive survey of contemporary and historical white associations of Indians with nature, however, Vecsey fails to provide a structure, theory, or theme strong enough to support his string of quotations and facts, and the piece collapses under its own weight. Karl Luckert's *The Navajo Hunter Tradition* [55] is another religious study with environmental implications. Luckert contends that there is an archaic hunting religion buried beneath a far different modern Navajo religion. He makes an interesting, if not always convincing, attempt to discover the substrata of hunting rituals and analyzes them in terms of the psychological stresses of hunters who are forced to kill the game on whose existence they depend.

The tendency of scholars influenced by current environmentalism to stress Indian philosophy and religion contrasts strongly with the original concerns of the cultural ecologists, the other major scholarly branch of writings on Indians and the environment. Interested in the ecological factors which influenced Indian social organization, cultural ecologists concentrated on how Indians "adapted" to the environment. If environmentalists sometimes concerned themselves only with thought and belief to the exclusion of actions in the material world, cultural ecologists, in their more mechanistic formulations, made humans merely another biological population seeking its niche, another link in the flow of energy through the ecosystem. Although such a formulation was certainly partially true, it ignored the human ability to conceptualize the world. Humans often act on the basis of their conceptions of nature; they do not simply react to direct stimuli from the physical environment itself. Cultural ecologists also neglected the human ability to modify the environment to a degree unknown in other species. Too often both cultural ecologists and popular environmentalists either ignored or only gave lip service to the reciprocal influences of culture and nature.

The stress of the cultural ecologists on adaptation and the environment almost inevitably turned their attention to the Great Plains where distinctive societies in a special environment had long captured both popular and anthropological attention. In the 1960s three scholars in particular—Fred Eggan, H. Clyde Wilson, and Symmes Oliver—offered ecological explanations as to why tribal groups from different regions developed similar social systems when they moved onto the plains. By later standards their ecological analyses were rudimentary. They focused almost exclusively on two animals, the bison and the horse, but even in so narrow an arena their interpretations differed significantly. Oliver, in his *Ecology and Cultural Continuity . . . of the Plains Indian* [62], regarded the buffalo herds as the primary environmental factor on the plains and viewed the horse as a tool "used to exploit the buffalo efficiently." By making the horse a tool and borrowing Julian Steward's stress on technology, Oliver explained Plains society as a logical consequence of the technological adaptation to the seasonal pattern of the buffalo herds. The differences he found among the nomadic hunters were only remnants of the cultures of these tribes before migration onto the plains. In making this argument, Oliver relied heavily on F. G. Roe's classic study, *The North American Buffalo* [70], which provided not only a wealth of data on the bison and shrewd comments on historical sources, but also a similar, if cruder, belief in the pervasive influence of the bison on Indian culture. Eggan, whose earlier work had influenced Oliver, basically accepted Oliver's position in his "The Cheyenne and the Arapaho: . . . Ecology and Society" [23].

H. Clyde Wilson, in his "An Inquiry into the Nature of Plains

Indian Cultural Development" [100], however, thought the buffalo had been stressed to the neglect of the horse in interpretations of the plains. The horse was not a tool but rather a large animal with biological needs of its own. Wilson argued that the horse provided a new source of energy which allowed Plains culture to flourish. The Plains nomads were better understood as nomadic pastoralists who happened to hunt buffalo rather than as mounted hunters per se. James Downs [21] in his comments on Wilson's article, took this argument to its logical conclusion: as pastoralists the Plains tribes could have survived the demise of the buffalo, switching to cattle, if the Americans had not restricted their access to the grasslands of the Great Plains.

Critiques of these positions have tended to be either partial and flawed, or else they lack the evidentiary base necessary to support their own contentions. Anthony Fisher, for example, argued in his "The Algonquian Plains" [26] that the social systems of the Plains Indians actually arose from the experience of the northern and central Algonquians in the fur trade, not from the plains itself, but the parallels in social organization he drew were too broad and his discussion of the expansion of the fur trade into the plains was weak.

George Arthur attempted a different kind of critique, far better grounded in historical evidence, in his *An Introduction to the Ecology of Early Historic Communal Bison Hunting* [3], a shorter version of which was published as "A Re-Analysis of the Early Historical Plains Indian Bison Drive" as part of *Bison Procurement and Utilization* [4], edited by Leslie Davis and Michael Wilson. Arthur, perhaps overstating his case, argued that neither the historical record nor buffalo ecology supported the thesis advanced by Oliver and innumerable others that the seasonal patterns of the buffalo herds forced Indians to gather in large summer encampments and then split into small bands for the winter. He demonstrated that before the acquisition of the horse this did not seem to be the case on the northern plains. Arthur, however, never attempted to reconcile his evidence with later conditions on the plains nor did he consider the role the horse eventually played.

Such criticisms, however, avoided a central problem of the supposed correlations between environment and social systems on the plains. Why, if environment determined social organization, did the

Theoretical problems plague functionalist versions of cultural ecology almost as severely as does lack of historical evidence. Eugene Ruyle, who pushed an aggressively materialist interpretation of the potlatch in "Slavery, Surplus and Stratification" [76], argues that such functionalism creates a system independent of the concerns of human actors. Thus, for Suttles, a once-in-a-generation failure of a salmon run or a prolonged period of severe weather sparks a search for prestige which fuels the potlatch. The evolution of such a system in which none of the actors have any knowledge of the real purpose which the system serves, is hard to imagine. Marshall Sahlins, from an opposite theoretical perspective, has made similar criticisms of this type of functionalism which treats culture as a mere appendage of biology and makes it purely instrumental. In such interpretations of the Northwest Coast, cultural ecologists strip people's lives both of their meaningful intent and their historical context and reduce them to hidden adaptations to fish and weather.

Theoretical problems with cultural ecology could not vanish simply by changing the region studied, but evidentiary problems were alleviated in the 1960s and 1970s by the growing emphasis (apparent in collections such as Bruce Cox's *Cultural Ecology: Readings on Canadian Indians and Eskimos* [13]) on the surviving hunting cultures of the Subarctic. Cultural ecologists continued to stress "adaptation," but now anthropologists could at least work with a wealth of contemporary data.

Many of these studies of the Subarctic, such as Richard K. Nelson's *Hunters of the Northern Forest* [61], consisted largely of ethnographic description, but a partial and rewarding focus of much of this literature was the structures (really the limits) the environment imposed on territorial and band organizations. Anthony Fisher's "The Cree of Canada" [27], Richard Slobodin's "Variation and Continuity in Kutchin Society" [80], Edward Rogers's *The Quest for Food and Furs* [74] and "The Mistassini Cree" [73], J. G. E. Smith's "Ecological Basis of Chipewyan Socio-Territorial Organization" [81], James VanStone's *Athapaskan Adaptations* [90] and "Changing Patterns of Indian Trapping" [89], Eleanor Leacock's "The Montagnais-Naskapi Band" [52], and June Helm's "The Dogrib Indians" [31] all, to varying degrees, concerned themselves with such topics. Some, like Fisher, continued to reduce social organization to a simple function of ecology, but often the approach was more sophisticated with a recognition of reciprocal influences. By the end of Van Stone's account in *Athapaskan Adaptations*, for instance, it seems that social organization is determining environmental relations rather than the other way around. Similarly, Edward Rogers in his essay, "Natural Environment—Social Organization—Witchcraft" [72] argued for cultural factors as an explanation for different forms of social organization in the same environment.

In studies of the eastern Subarctic, discussions of the relationship between environment and social organization have continued to revolve around a specific and quite old controversy: Frank Speck's assertion of the existence of aboriginal family hunting territories which served to conserve game and Eleanor Leacock's later critique which argued that such territories were products of the fur trade and not aboriginal. Edward Rogers in his *The Hunting Group-Hunting Territory Complex* [71] analyzed the problem in terms of his fieldwork and historical research on the Mistassini Cree. Distinguishing between hunting groups and hunting territories, Rogers denounced the monocausal arguments of both sides and offered a compromise which blended elements of the two classic explanations. More recently scholars have shifted attention from the origins of the hunting territories to their maintenance. Rolf Knight, in his "A Reexamination of Hunting, Trapping, and Territoriality among the Northeastern Algonkian Indians" [48] criticized both Speck and Leacock for their misreading of subarctic ecology. He argued that fixed hunting territories would lead not to conservation but to starvation in subarctic conditions. According to Knight, the real key to the evolution of family hunting territories was the ecological change brought about in the forests through burning. Because of forest fires, moose replaced caribou and the large groups of hunters effective against migratory caribou herds were less suited to hunting solitary moose than were individual hunters armed with rifles. This, in the context of the fur trade, made hunting territories a better adjustment to the environment.

Adrian Tanner, in an important article, "The Significance of Hunting Territories Today" [85], has in turn offered a critique of Knight. He credited Knight with advancing the argument by demonstrating the ecological impossibility of fixed hunting territories.

He argued, however, that Knight's analysis was flawed because it assumed hunting territories were fixed areas exploited by biological families when actually both hunting territories and hunting groups are flexible. The key to the organization of hunting territories and hunting groups, Tanner claimed, was the perceived relationship of successul hunters to spiritual masters of the game.

Tanner's work possessed an importance far beyond its immediate contribution to the old problem of hunting territories. In his article and in his excellent book on the Mistassini Cree, *Bringing Home Animals* [86], he severed the direct relationship between social organization and the environment prevalent in so much cultural ecology and he interposed culture between them. Tanner made culture more than a simple mechanism which adapts humans to the environment; it was a vital and formative factor in its own right. *Bringing Home Animals* stands both as the most sophisticated study of the Subarctic and probably as the best work on Indians and the environment in general.

Tanner did not, however, proceed alone in making ideas and belief systems significant elements in cultural ecology; he is part of a larger, if still a minority, movement within the field. Ideational concerns have become elements in studies of the location of trapping territories and the intensity of trapping as in Robert Jarvenpa's article, "Subarctic Indian Trappers and Band Society" [44], and his monograph, *The Trappers of Patuanak* [45]. Cultural factors are similarly appealed to in Joel Savishinsky's study of the varying degrees of environmental involvement among the Hare Indians: "Trapping, Survival Strategies, and Environmental Involvement" [77]. It is Harvey Feit, however, who has been second only to Tanner in considering the beliefs of Subarctic hunters as explanations for their actions in the natural world. In his "Ethno-Ecology of the Waswanipi Cree" [25] Feit asserted that modern Cree hunters managed their environment. He emphasized, like Tanner, that the basis of Cree conservation lay in spiritual beliefs, but that, nonetheless, this conservation proceeded upon recognizable ecological principles.

Such a position challenged assertions by Rolf Knight in his *Ecological Factors in the Changing Economy and Social Organization among the Rupert House Cree* [49] that conservation was solely the result of Hudson's Bay Company efforts and Edward Roger's claim in his *Hunting Group–Hunting Territory Complex* [71] that there was no evidence for aboriginal conservation. This controversy was notable not only for its substance, which would recur in other arenas later, but also because it could be answered only by historical research. The wealth of contemporary ethnographic detail available in the Subarctic could frame such problems, but it could not resolve them.

Both cultural ecologists and environmentalists have thus found themselves constantly deflected back into history. Environmentalist scholars undertook historical studies in search of an Indian model of correct environmental behavior. Tanner's and Feit's concerns were more sophisticated, but their study of aboriginal ideology, too, begged for a search for historical roots. Mainstream cultural ecologists were interested in neither ideas nor models of conduct, but their insistence that the practices they described were adaptive demanded an historical component (although as Robert Jarvenpa pointed out, they often failed to provide a satisfactory one), othewise there would be no way of determining if behaviors were actually adaptive over time.

This historical emphasis of both environmentalists and cultural ecologists has produced a shaky common ground where the concerns of both groups have influenced the work of a diverse group of ethnohistorians (some of whose work on how Indians shaped the environment has been mentioned already). These ethnohistorical studies sometimes resemble efforts of cultural ecologists, but they often tend to be more positivist in nature, and they lack the reductionist tendencies of so much cultural ecology.

At their best, these ethnohistories with an environmental focus have laid the foundations for new readings of the past. Harold Hickerson's "The Virginia Deer and Intertribal Buffer Zones" [33], for example, casts a new light on the persistence of intertribal warfare. Hickerson explained the chronic warfare between the Sioux and the Chippewa in terms of competition over game. Warfare itself, by creating a buffer between the two peoples, served to regulate and preserve deer. Charles Watrall in "Virginia Deer and the Buffer Zone" [94] claimed that archaeological site distributions in Hickerson's Minnesota and Wisconsin buffer zone substantiated Hickerson's thesis. Robert Rhoades, however, in "Archaeological Use and Abuse of Ecological Concepts" [68] has contended that Hickerson's use of the concept of ecotone was crude and imprecise.

More influential than Hickerson's work were studies by two other scholars who, even though they focused on Latin and South America, provided the inspiration for much of the research on North America which followed them. Henry Dobyns's "Estimating Aboriginal American Population" [17] revised dramatically upwards estimates of pre-Columbian Indian populations and emphasized the catastrophic influence of disease on Indian peoples. Alfred Crosby, Jr.'s *The Columbian Exchange* [15] also focused on Latin America in examining biological exchanges between the hemispheres, but his conclusions on the resulting changes in ecosystems and demographic trends had obvious implications for North America. In a later, perhaps even more important article, "Virgin Soil Epidemics" [16], Crosby emphasized that the depopulation of Indian America was more than a biological event. The unprecedented loss of population could only be understood within the context of European aggression with its impact upon native subsistence and society. The work of both Dobyns and Crosby drove home the point that demography and ecology both had to be understood in their proper historical context.

If Hickerson, Crosby, and Dobyns laid down the foundations for ethnohistorical studies of Indians and the environment, it has been scholars of the fur trade, particularly geographers, who have provided much of the real historical structure of the changing relations of Indians with the natural world. Charles Bishop's *The Northern Ojibwa and the Fur Trade* [9] began with a contemporary Ojibwa community and then worked back, peeling away the various layers of its present and past, to understand the evolution of the community in terms of the subarctic environment and its exploitation in the fur trade. It was Arthur Ray, a geographer, however, who best managed to blend the varying concerns of ethnohistory, ecology, geography, and disease in his innovative study, *Indians in the Fur Trade* [65]. Based on a detailed analysis of Hudson's Bay Company records, Ray merged these elements into a sophisticated and insightful account of the shifting involvement of the Cree, Assiniboine, and Ojibwa in the fur trade. Another geographer, Jeanne Kay, in "Wisconsin Indian Hunting Patterns" [47] analyzed the changing historical ecology of the Menominees as they shifted from subsistence hunting to a greater involvement in the market. Particularly interesting was Kay's explanation of how the Menominees responded to the scarcity brought by overhunting through hunting new species rather than through conservation.

The problem of overhunting, and indeed the whole emphasis on the fur trade in historical ecological studies, has inevitably raised a basic question related to the issues which divided cultural ecologists on the question of aboriginal conservation: Was the Indians' treatment of the environment largely economic in motivation, a simple response to economic incentives? To determine the nature of exchange in the fur trade, Arthur Ray and Donald Freeman in a careful and tentative book analyzed trade relations between the Indians and the Hudson's Bay Company before 1763. In *Give Us Good Measure* [67] they concluded that Indian behavior in the fur trade (and thus by extension their treatment of the environment) cannot be explained without reference to economic factors and rejected interpretations which stressed exclusively the political and ceremonial aspects of the trade. In the body of their work, however, Ray's and Freeman's insistence that the trade represented a compromise between market oriented Europeans and the Indian's own cultural traditions of exchange, as well as their honest recognition that formalist economic theories do not adequately explain their data on the trade, provided much which substantivist scholars might agree with. Indeed Ray, in a later article, "Competition and Conservation in the Early Subarctic Fur Trade" [66], discussed how the failure of Indians to respond to market incentives, as well as the key role played by the Indian middlemen, acted to conserve furbearers.

Give Us Good Measure is far more sophisticated than most analyses by economists of the Indian's treatment of the environment. John McManus in his "An Economic Analysis of Indian Behavior in the Fur Trade" [56] attempted without success to apply formalist economic theory to the behavior of Montagnais and Naskapi trappers. McManus had to predicate a "Good Samaritan constraint," hardly a standard feature of market theory, to make any sense of his data. Far cruder than McManus's effort was a recent article, "Myth, Admonitions, and Rationality: The American Indian as Resource Manager" [5] by John Baden, Richard Stroup and Walter Thurman which argued that cultural attitudes toward the environment are irrelevant in determining the management of resources. What matters are the "proper incentives" (apparently the common biological inheritance of the race) which exist, independent of culture, in the economic man and woman of economists. Knowledge of the proper incentives allows the authors to proceed in their own analysis willfully ignorant of both the anthropological literature of the last twenty years and the specific Indian cultures they discuss. The result is a distorted and often unrecognizable description of Indian actions couched in a market terminology of little relevance to the behavior under examination.

A critique of such formalist explanations of Indian actions in the fur trade was only one of the threads of discussion of the Indians and the environment which Calvin Martin included in his controversial *Keepers of the Game* [58]. This is a book which represents in some ways a summation of the issues that have dominated recent studies of Indians and the environment. Influenced by Tanner and Feit's work on spiritual masters of the game, Dobyns and Crosby's work on historical demography, disease and biological exchange, and the literature on Indian behavior in the fur trade, Martin wove them together into a provocative thesis whose only flaw was the almost total lack of evidence to support it. Martin asserted that overhunting by the northeastern Algonkian-speaking peoples in the fur trade was not motivated by an inordinate desire for European goods. Rather, overhunting represented a war against animals because the Indians believed that beavers, through supernatural means, were causing the epidemics which were killing native peoples. Although the work has won a major historical prize, criticism of it has been telling. Its ethnography, ecology, logic, and evidence have all been questioned in a series of articles edited by Shepard Krech (*Indians, Animals, and the Fur Trade* [50]) which are devoted solely to critiquing Martin. Most of the criticism in the volume, while often devastating to Martin's thesis, is so materialist in orientation, however, that the critics' counter-interpretations fall prey to Martin's equally effective critique of materialist and formalist scholarship's failure to answer fundamental questions about the trade.

Martin's work, both in the epilogue of *Keepers of the Game* and in another article, "The American Indian as Miscast Ecologist" [59], also served to reopen the persistent question of whether Indians were conservationists. After haphazardly citing evidence of historical overhunting by Indians, Martin admitted that aboriginally Indians treated nature differently, but he contended that labeling Indian practices as "conservation" ignored the context of Indian actions. The spiritual beliefs which governed Indian treatment of game were very different from the rationale for twentieth century conservation. Martin argued that profound differences in the cosmologies of Indians and Whites prevent Native Americans from serving as adequate ecological models for modern Whites. Indians obviously have, however, served as ecological models for those who knew them well, and before insisting that this cannot be, it would be better to know more about the sources of Indian influence on modern conservation than we do now.

Martin is, however, correct in insisting that blindly imposing our own cultural designations on Indian actions is not historically useful. It often only obscures the larger questions such as why and how human societies have influenced their environment, and what the social consequences of human induced environmental change have been. These questions, in essence the reverse side of cultural ecology, deserve to be pursued in terms of all Indian peoples, not just hunters and gatherers.

The only published study to examine such questions in detail for agricultural as well as hunting peoples is William Cronon's excellent *Changes in the Land* [14]. Cronon's interdisciplinary study of Indian and white land use in colonial New England is by far the most sophisticated historical work in the field. Cronon, in turn, has relied heavily on Peter Thomas's fine article, "Contrastive Subsistence Strategies" [81], which compared the productivity and environmental requirements of Indian agriculture in New England with that of European colonists. Most other regions of the country lack studies of similar quality. The early scholarly interest in the environmental aspects of Pueblo agriculture has largely lapsed, but Maitland Bradfield's *The Changing Pattern of Hopi Agriculture* [11] does explore the connection between environmental deterioration, technological change, food production and social change. The real value of this solid work could have been increased, however, by research in the Indian Service records. Far more common than analytical studies of Indian agriculture are descriptions of crops and planting cycles which appear both in articles such as G. Melvin Herndon's "Indian

Agriculture in the Southern Colonies" [32] and in general works such as Charles Hudson's *The Southeastern Indians* [34].

Two agricultural groups—the Cherokees and the Navajos—have somewhat escaped this neglect of environmental studies. The literature on the Cherokees is the weaker of the two. Donald Ballas gives a brief description of Eastern Cherokee land use in the late 1950s in his "Notes on the Population, Settlement, and Ecology of the Eastern Cherokee Indians" [6]. In an historical survey, "Cherokee Acculturation and Changing Land Use Practices" [99] Douglas Wilms gives an ultimately unsatisfactory account of the connections between social change and changes in land use. Gary C. Goodwin's *Cherokees in Transition: A Study of Changing Culture and Environment Prior to 1775* [29] is more descriptive than analytical, but Goodwin makes some attempt to connect social and environmental change.

The recent literature on the Navajos is much stronger. It is dominated by the traumatic reduction of Navajo livestock in the 1930s by the federal government, but scholars have also given attention to earlier and later periods. Peter Kunstadter's "Southern Athabaskan Herding Patterns" [51], for example, attempts to explain why the Navajos did and the Apaches did not raise sheep. And James Downs's *Animal Husbandry in Navajo Society and Culture* [20] provides an excellent discussion of post-reduction Navajo herding practices. Downs's combination of perceptive analyses of culture, economics, and the environment is unusual in such a specialized work.

Of the many books which touch on stock reduction, David F. Aberle's excellent *The Peyote Religion among the Navajo* [1] remains the best for reduction's background, its environmental aspects, and for its impact on the Navajos. A briefer, but still useful discussion of reduction and its environmental and social context is L. Schuyler Fonaroff's "Conservation and Stock Reduction on the Navajo Tribal Range" [28].

Stock reduction is just a single example of a new array of environmental problems resulting from conflicts between white and Indian resource use in the twentieth century. Kai Erikson and Christopher Vecsey in their "A Report to the People of Grassy Narrows" [24] perceptively examine the way in which the social disruption of relocation magnified the consequences of mercury poisoning among the Grassy Narrows Ojibwa. *Native Americans and Energy Development* [46] from the Anthropology Resource Center discusses a variety of issues associated with energy development in the West and links environmental problems to the demands of capitalist development. Amelia Irvin pursues similar concerns in her "Energy Development and . . . the Lakota Nation" [41]. In an article reminiscent of the works of nineteenth-century reformers, Gary Libecap and Ronald Johnson's "Legislating the Commons" [54] portrays current overgrazing on the Navajo reservation as the logical outcome of the lack of enforceable private property rights to land among the Navajos. Their stress on property rights and static economic models makes them both uncritical of capitalist development and only superficially interested in the historical roots of overgrazing. In the long run, the most significant environmental concern of both Indians and Whites in the Southwest will be neither land nor energy, but water. Norris Hundley surveys the issue of Indian water rights in both his "Indian Water Rights" [39] and his "The 'Winters' Decision" [40].

The resource issue which has received the widest press and attention in the last few years is Indian hunting and fishing rights. *Uncommon Controversy* [2] by the American Friends Service Committee is a somewhat dated but still useful study of fishing rights in the Pacific Northwest. Going further north, Boyce Richardson's *Strangers Devour the Land* [69] is a sympathetic account of the attempts of Cree hunters in Quebec to protect their lands and way of life from the massive hydroelectric projects planned for that province.

The growing concern with contemporary environmental problems affecting Indians, the newer interdisciplinary concerns among scholars, the controversy raised by recent works in the field, along with the continuing vitality of cultural ecology and popular environmentalism all indicate that the boom in studies of Indians and nature will be more than a scholarly enthusiasm of the 1960s and 1970s. The continuing challenge facing this scholarship will be to avoid dismembering the experience of Indian peoples with nature — not to amputate perceptions of nature, adaptations to the land, and Indian influences upon the land from the body of Indian life and history. The best scholarship will take its inspiration from ecology, not in any mechanistic sense which eliminates culture as a creative force, but rather by stressing the interplay and reciprocal influences between Indian cultures and the natural world.

ALPHABETICAL LIST

[1] Aberle, David F. 1966. *The Peyote Religion among the Navajo*. Viking Fund Publications in Anthropology 42. Chicago: Aldine Publishing Co.

[2] American Friends Service Committee. 1970. *Uncommon Controversy: Fishing Rights of the Muckleshoot, Puyallup, and Nisqually Indians*. Seattle: University of Washington Press.

[3] Arthur, George W. 1975. *An Introduction to the Ecology of Early Historic Communal Bison Hunting among the Northern Plains Indians*. National Museum of Man, Mercury Series, Archaeological Survey of Canada, Paper No. 37. Ottawa: National Museums of Canada.

[4] ———. 1978. "A Re-Analysis of the Early Historic Plains Indian Bison Drive." In *Bison Procurement and Utilization: A Symposium. Plains Anthropologist*, Memoir 14, pt. 2, eds. Leslie B. Davis and Michael Wilson, pp. 23-82.

[5] Baden, John, Richard Stroup, and Walter Thurmon. 1981. "Myths, Admonitions and Rationality: The American Indian as a Resource Manager." *Economic Inquiry* 19:132-43.

[6] Ballas, Donald J. 1960. "Notes on the Population, Settlement, and Ecology of the Eastern Cherokee Indians." *Journal of Geography* 59:238-67.

[7] Ballinger, Franchot. 1978. "The Responsible Center: Man and Nature in Pueblo and Navaho Ritual Songs and Prayers." *American Quarterly* 30:90-107.

[8] Berkes, Fikret. 1977. "Fishery Resource Use in a Subarctic Community." *Human Ecology* 5:289-307.

[9] Bishop, Charles. 1974. *The Northern Ojibwa and the Fur Trade: An Historical and Ecological Study*. Toronto: Holt, Rinehart and Winston of Canada.

[10] Bowden, Charles. 1977. *Killing the Hidden Waters*. Austin: University of Texas Press.

[11] Bradfield, Maitland. 1971. *The Changing Pattern of Hopi Agriculture*. Royal Anthropological Institute, Occasional Paper No. 30. London: Royal Anthropological Institute of Great Britain and Ireland.

[12] Capps, Walter Holden, ed. 1976. *Seeing with a Native Eye: Essays on Native American Religion*. New York: Harper and Row.

[13] Cox, Bruce, ed. 1973. *Cultural Ecology: Readings on Canadian Indians and Eskimos*. Toronto: McClelland and Stewart.

[14] Cronon, William. 1983. *Changes in the Land: Indians, Colonists, and the Ecology of New England*. New York: Hill and Wang.

[15] Crosby, Alfred W., Jr. 1972. *The Columbian Exchange: Biological and Cultural Consequences of 1492*. Westport, Conn.: Greenwood Press.

[16] ———. 1976. "Virgin Soil Epidemics as a Factor in the Aboriginal Depopulation in America." *William and Mary Quarterly* 33:289-99.

[17] Dobyns, Henry F. 1966. "Estimating Aboriginal American Popula-

tion: An Appraisal of Techniques with a New Hemispheric Estimate." *Current Anthropology* 7:395-412.

[18] ———. 1981. *From Fire to Flood: Historic Human Destruction of Sonoran Desert Riverine Oases*. Socorro, New Mexico: Ballena Press.

[19] Donald, Leland, and Donald H. Mitchell. 1975. "Some Correlates of Local Group Rank among the Southern Kwakiutl." *Ethnology* 14:325-46.

[20] Downs, James F. 1964. *Animal Husbandry in Navajo Society and Culture*. Berkeley: University of California Press.

[21] ———. 1964. "Comments on Plains Indian Cultural Development." *American Anthropologist* 66:421-422. Reprinted in *Cultural Ecology*, ed. Bruce Cox, pp. 171-73. See [13].

[22] Drucker, Philip, and Robert F. Heizer. 1967. *To Make My Name Good: A Re-examination of the Southern Kwakiutl Potlatch*. Berkeley: University of California Press.

[23] Eggan, Fred. 1966. "The Cheyenne and the Arapaho in the Perspective of the Plains: Ecology and Society." In *The American Indian: Perspectives for the Study of Social Change* by Fred Eggan. Chicago: Aldine Publishing Co.

[24] Erikson, Kai, and Christopher Vecsey. 1980. "A Report to the People of Grassy Narrows." In *American Indian Environments*, ed. Christopher Vecsey and Robert Venables, pp. 152-161. Syracuse: Syracuse University Press.

[25] Feit, Harvey. 1973. "The Ethno-Ecology of the Waswanipi Cree: Or How Hunters Can Manage Their Resources." In *Cultural Ecology*, ed. Bruce Cox, pp. 115-25. See [13].

[26] Fisher, Anthony. 1968. "The Algonquian Plains?" *Anthropologica* n.s. 10:7-19. Reprinted in *Cultural Ecology*, ed. Bruce Cox, pp. 174-89. See [13].

[27] ———. 1969. "The Cree of Canada: Some Ecological and Evolutionary Consideration." *Western Canadian Journal of Anthropology* 1:7-19. Reprinted in *Cultural Ecology*, ed. Bruce Cox, pp. 126-39. See [13].

[28] Fonaroff, Leonard. 1963. "Conservation and Stock Reduction on the Navajo Tribal Range." *Geographical Review* 53:200-23.

[29] Goodwin, Gary C. 1977. *Cherokees in Transition: A Study of Changing Culture and Environment Prior to 1775*. University of Chicago, Department of Geography, Research Paper 181. Chicago: Department of Geography, University of Chicago.

[30] Heizer, Robert F., and Albert B. Elsasser. 1980. *The Natural World of the California Indians*. Berkeley: University of California Press.

[31] Helm, June. 1972. "The Dogrib Indians." In *Hunters and Gatherers Today: A Socioeconomic Study of Eleven Such Cultures in the Twentieth Century*, ed. M. G. Bicchieri, pp. 51-89. New York: Holt, Rinehart, and Winston.

[32] Herndon, G. Melvin. 1977. "Indian Agriculture in the Southern Colonies." *North Carolina Historical Review* 44:283-97.

[33] Hickerson, Harold. 1965. "The Virginia Deer and Intertribal Buffer Zones in the Upper Mississippi Valley." In *Man, Culture, and Animals: The Role of Animals in Human Ecological Adjustments*, ed. Anthony Leeds and Andrew P. Vayda, pp. 43-66. Publication No. 78 of the American Association for the Advancement of Science. Washington, D.C.: American Association for the Advancement of Science.

[34] Hudson, Charles. 1976. *The Southeastern Indians*. Knoxville, Tenn.: University of Tennessee Press.

[35] Hughes, J. Donald. 1977. "Forest Indians: The Holy Occupation." *Environmental Review* 2:2-13.

[36] Hultkrantz, Ake. 1976. "The Contributions of the Study of North American Indian Religions to the History of Religions." In *Seeing with a Native Eye*, ed. Walter Holden Capps, pp. 86-106. See [12].

[37] ———. 1980. *The Religions of the American Indians*. Berkeley: University of California Press.

[38] ———. 1981. *Belief and Worship in Native North America*, ed. Christopher Vecsey. Syracuse, N.Y.: Syracuse University Press.

[39] Hundley, Norris. 1978. "The Dark and Bloody Ground of Indian Water Rights: Confusion Elevated to Principle." *Western Historical Quarterly* 9:455-82.

[40] ———. 1982. "The 'Winters' Decision and Indian Water Rights: A Mystery Reexamined." *Western Historical Quarterly* 13:17-42.

[41] Irvin, Amelia W. 1982. "Energy Development and the Effects of Mining on the Lakota Nation." *Journal of Ethnic Studies* 10:89-102.

[42] Jacobs, Wilbur. 1972. "The White Man's Frontier in American History: The Impact upon the Land and the Indian." In *Dispossessing the American Indian* by Wilbur Jacobs, pp. 19-30. New York: Charles Scribner's Sons.

[43] ———. 1980. "Indians as Ecologists and Other Environmental Themes in American Frontier History." In *American Indian Environments*, eds. Christopher Vecsey and Robert Venables, pp. 46-64. Originally printed in 1978 as "The Great Despoilation: Environmental Themes in American Frontier History." *Pacific Historical Review* 47:1-26.

[44] Jarvenpa, Robert. 1977. "Subarctic Indian Trappers and Band Society: The Economics of Male Mobility." *Human Ecology* 5:223-59.

[45] ———. 1980. *The Trappers of Patuanak: Toward a Spatial Ecology of Modern Hunters*. National Museum of Man, Mercury Series, Canadian Ethnology Service Paper No. 67. Ottawa: National Museum of Canada.

[46] Jorgenson, Joseph G., Richard O. Clemmer, et al. 1978. *Native Americans and Energy Development*. Cambridge, Mass.: Anthropology Resource Center.

[47] Kay, Jeanne. 1979. "Wisconsin Indian Hunting Patterns, 1634-1836." *Annals of the Association of American Geographers* 69:402-18.

[48] Knight, Rolf. 1965. "A Reexamination of Hunting, Trapping, and Territoriality among the Northeastern Algonkian Indians." In *Man, Culture, and Animals: The Role of Animals in Human Ecological Adjustments*, eds. Anthony Leeds and Andrew Vayda, pp. 27-42. Washington, D.C.: American Association for the Advancement of Science.

[49] ———. 1968. *Ecological Factors in Changing Economy and Social Organization among the Rupert House Cree*. Anthropology Papers, National Museum of Canada No. 15. Ottawa: National Museums of Canada.

[50] Krech, Shepard III, ed. 1981. *Indians, Animals, and the Fur Trade: A Critique of Keepers of the Game*. Athens, Ga.: University of Georgia Press.

[51] Kunstadter, Peter. 1965. "Southern Athabaskan Herding Patterns and Contrasting Social Institutions." In *Man, Culture, and Animals: The Role of Animals in Human Ecological Adjustments*, eds. Anthony Leeds and Andrew Vayda, pp. 67-86. Washington, D.C.: American Association for Advancement of Science.

[52] Leacock, Eleanor. 1973. "The Montagnais-Naskapi Band." In *Cultural Ecology*, ed. Bruce Cox, pp. 81-100. Originally published in *Contributions to Anthropology: Band Societies*, ed. David Damas. National Museum of Canada Bulletin No. 228. Ottawa: National Museums of Canada. 1969.

[53] Lewis, Henry T. 1973. *Patterns of Indian Burning in California: Ecology and Ethnohistory*. Ballena Press Anthropological Papers No. 1. Ramona, Calif.: Ballena Press.

[54] Libecap, Gary, and Ronald Johnson. 1980. "Legislating the Commons: The Navajo Tribal Council and the Navajo Range." *Economic Inquiry* 18:69-86.

[55] Luckert, Karl W. 1975. *The Navajo Hunter Tradition*. Tucson: University of Arizona Press.

[56] McManus, John. 1972. "An Economic Analysis of Indian Behavior in the North American Fur Trade." *Journal of Economic History* 32:36-53.

[57] Martin, Calvin L. 1973. "Fire and Forest Structure in the Aboriginal Eastern Forest." *Indian Historian* 6:38-42, 54.

[58] ———. 1978. *Keepers of the Game: Indian Animal Relationships in the Fur Trade*. Berkeley: University of California Press.

[59] ———. 1981. "The American Indian as Miscast Ecologist." *The History Teacher* 14:243-52.

[60] Momaday, N. Scott. 1976. "Native American Attitudes toward the Environment." In *Seeing with a Native Eye*, ed. Walter Capps, pp. 79-85. See [12].

[61] Nelson, Richard K. 1973. *Hunters of the Northern Forest: Designs for Survival among the Alaska Kutchin*. Chicago: University of Chicago Press.

[62] Oliver, Symmes C. 1962. *Ecology and Cultural Continuity as Contributing Factors in the Social Organization of the Plains Indians*. University of California Publications in American Archaeology and Ethnology 48(1). Berkeley: University of California Press.

[63] Piddocke, Stuart. 1965. "The Potlatch System of the Southern Kwakiutl: A New Perspective." *Southwestern Journal of Anthropology* 21:244-64. Reprinted in *Environment and Cultural Behavior: Ecological Studies in Cultural Anthropology*, ed. Andrew P. Vayda, pp. 130-156. Garden City, N.Y.: The Natural History Press, 1969.

[64] Pyne, Stephen J. 1982. *Fire in America: A Cultural History of Wildland and Rural Fire*. Princeton, N.J.: Princeton University Press.

[65] Ray, Arthur J. 1974. *Indians in the Fur Trade: Their Role as Hunters, Trappers, and Middlemen in the Lands Southwest of Hudson Bay, 1660-1870*. Toronto: University of Toronto Press.

[66] ———. 1978. "Competition and Conservation in the Early Subarctic Fur Trade." *Ethnohistory* 25:347-57.

[67] Ray, Arthur J., and Donald Freeman. 1978. *"Give Us Good Measure:" An Economic Analysis of Relations Between the Indians and the Hudson's Bay Company before 1763*. Toronto: University of Toronto Press.

[68] Rhoades, Robert E. 1978. "Archaeological Use and Abuse of Ecological Concepts and Studies: The Ecotone Example." *American Antiquity* 43:608-14.

[69] Richardson, Boyce. 1976. *Strangers Devour the Land: A Chronicle of the Assault upon the Last Coherent Hunting Culture in North America, the Cree Indians of Northern Quebec and Their Vast Primeval Homeland*. New York: Alfred Knopf.

[70] Roe, Frank G. 1951. *The North American Buffalo: A Critical Study of the Species in Its Wild State*. Toronto: University of Toronto Press. 2nd ed., 1970.

[71] Rogers, Edward S. 1963. *The Hunting Group-Hunting Territory Complex among the Mistassini Indians.* National Museums of Canada Bulletin No. 195. Anthropological Series No. 63. Ottawa: Department of Northern Affairs and National Resources.

[72] ———. 1969. "Natural Environment—Social Organization—Witchcraft: Cree versus Ojibwa—A Test Case." In *Contributions to Anthropology: Ecological Essays*, ed. David Damas, pp. 24-39. National Museums of Canada Bulletin No. 230. Anthropological Series No. 86. Ottawa: National Museums of Canada.

[73] ———. 1972. "The Mistassini Cree." In *Hunters and Gatherers Today: A Socioeconomic Study in Eleven Such Cultures*, ed. M. G. Bicchieri, pp. 90-137. New York: Holt, Rinehart and Winston.

[74] ———. 1973. *The Quest for Foods and Furs, The Mistassini Cree, 1953-54.* National Museum of Man, Publications in Ethnology No. 5. Ottawa: National Museum of Man.

[75] Ruddell, Rosemary. 1973. "Chiefs and Commoners: Nature's Bal-

ance and the Good Life among the Nootka." In *Cultural Ecology*, ed. Bruce Cox, pp. 254-65. See [13].

[76] Ruyle, Eugene. 1973. "Slavery, Surplus and Stratification on the Northwest Coast: The Ethnoenergetics of an Incipient Stratification System." *Current Anthropology* 14:603-30.

[77] Savishinsky, Joel. 1978. "Trapping, Survival Strategies, and Environmental Involvement: A Case Study from the Canadian Sub-Arctic." *Human Ecology* 6:1-25.

[78] Sayre, Robert F. 1977. *Thoreau and the American Indian*. Princeton, N.J.: Princeton University Press.

[79] Sheehan, Bernard W. 1980. *Savagism and Civility: Indians and Englishmen in Colonial Virginia*. Cambridge: Cambridge University Press.

[80] Slobodin, Richard. [1962] 1973. "Variation and Continuity in Kutchin Society." In *Cultural Ecology,* ed. Bruce Cox, pp. 140-51. See [13].

[81] Smith, J. G. E. 1975. "The Ecological Basis of Chipewyan Socio-Territorial Organization." In *Proceedings: Northern Athapaskan Conference, 1971*, ed. A. McFadyen Clark, vol. 2:389-461. National Museum of Man, Mercury Series, Canadian Ethnology Service Paper No. 27. Ottawa: National Museums of Canada.

[82] Strickland, Rennard. 1970. "The Idea of the Environment and the Ideal of the Indian." *Journal of American Indian Education* 10:8-15.

[83] Suttles, Wayne. 1960. "Affinal Ties, Subsistence, and Prestige among the Coast Salish." *American Anthropologist* 62:296-305.

[84] ———. 1968. "Coping with Abundance: Subsistence on the Northwest Coast." In *Man the Hunter*, eds. Richard B. Lee and Irene DeVore, pp. 56-68. Chicago, Aldine Publishing Co.

[85] Tanner, Adrian. 1973. "The Significance of Hunting Territories Today." In *Cultural Ecology*, ed. Bruce Cox, pp. 101-114. See [13].

[86] ———. 1979. *Bringing Home Animals: Religious Ideology and Mode of Production of the Mistassini Cree Hunters*. New York: St. Martins Press.

[87] Thomas, Peter A. 1976. "Contrastive Subsistence Strategies and Land Use as Factors for Understanding Indian-White Relations in New England." *Ethnohistory* 23:1-18.

[88] Toelken, Barre. 1976. "Seeing with a Native Eye: How Many Sheep Will It Hold?" In *Seeing with a Native Eye*, ed. Walter H. Capps, pp. 9-24. See [12].

[89] VanStone, James W. 1963. "Changing Patterns of Indian Trapping in the Canadian Subarctic." *Arctic* 16:159-74.

[90] ———. 1974. *Athapaskan Adaptations: Hunters and Fishermen of the Subarctic Forest*. Chicago: Aldine Publishing Co.

[91] Vayda, Andrew P. 1961. "A Re-Examination of Northwest Coast Economic Systems." *Transactions of the New York Academy of Sciences* (Series 2) 23:618-24.

[92] Vecsey, Christopher. 1980. "American Indian Environmental Religions." In *American Indian Environments,* eds. Christopher Vecsey and Robert Venables, pp. 1-37. See [93].

[93] Vecsey, Christopher, and Robert Venables, eds. 1980. *American Indian Environments: Ecological Issues in Native American History*. Syracuse, N.Y.: Syracuse University Press.

[94] Watrall, Charles. 1968. "Virginia Deer and the Buffer Zone in the Late Prehistoric-Early Protohistoric Periods in Minnesota." *Plains Anthropologist* 13:81-86.

[95] Wedel, Waldo. 1961. *Prehistoric Man on the Great Plains*. Norman: University of Oklahoma Press.

[96] Weinberg, Daniela. [1965] 1973. "Models of Southern Kwakiutl Social Organization." In *Cultural Ecology*, ed. Bruce Cox, pp. 227-53. See [13].

[97] White, Richard. 1975. "Indian Land Use and Environmental Change: Island County, Washington, A Case Study." *Arizona and the West* 17:327-38.

[98] ———. 1982. "The Cultural Landscape of the Pawnees." *Great Plains Quarterly* 2:31-40.

[99] Wilms, Douglas C. 1978. "Cherokee Acculturation and Changing Land Use Practices." *Chronicles of Oklahoma* 56:331-43.

[100] Wilson, H. Clyde. 1963. "An Inquiry into the Nature of Plains Indians Cultural Development." *American Anthropologist* 65:335-69.

[101] Wishart, David J. 1979. "The Dispossession of the Pawnee." *Annals of the Association of American Geographers* 69:382-401.

[102] Yarnell, Richard. 1964. *Aboriginal Relationships between Culture and Plant Life in the Upper Great Lakes Region*. University of Michigan Museum of Anthropology, Anthropological Papers 23. Ann Arbor: University of Michigan Press.

Indian Tribal Histories

PETER IVERSON

University of Wyoming

NEARLY ALL STUDIES OF American Indians involve the consideration of tribe or community. One's tribal affiliation has always been important. Today that identity is still significant, though a modern era has encouraged other kinds of identity as well. But even with urbanism, pan-Indianism, and other more contemporary forces, one's tribe (or tribes) remains critical.

As recently as 1982, in a bibliographical essay written for *Reviews in American History* [28], Reginald Horsman lamented that "while there is a new sensitivity and more solid contributions, traditional areas of interest and traditional methodology still loom large in Native American historiography." Horsman suggested that white perceptions and policies were yet a central focus in the field. Few tribal histories considered the twentieth century in much detail and regional histories rarely had been successful. First-rate Indian biographies were difficult to find.

Though it may be difficult to quarrel with Horsman's essential conclusions, a review of the literature since 1974 reveals an impressive growth in the quality and quantity of work dealing with tribal history. Within an essay of this length, it is impossible to consider the matter exhaustively. Thus, not all tribal histories are included here. For example, the reader may wish to consult the "Indian Tribal Series," essays published in bound form generally about a decade ago. They are brief, reliable introductory texts designed for the general reader. An example from the series is Dale K. McGinnis and Floyd W. Sharrock, *The Crow People* [44].

In addition, extensive bibliographies are now available for those who wish to pursue the history of a particular tribe in greater detail. The Newberry Library Center for the History of the American Indian series provide solid introductions to many Indian communities. The Native American bibliography series published by the Scarecrow Press promises to be an excellent aid; Jack W. Marken and Herbert T. Hoover, *Bibliography of the Sioux* [45] was published as the first volume in this series in 1980. There are other tribal bibliographies independent of the above collections, including W. David Laird's comprehensive Hopi bibliography [42]. A recent bibliography considering works of article length has been compiled by Dwight L. Smith [70]. Other bibliographies give helpful consideration to certain portions of Indian historiography, such as David Brumble's annotated bibliography of American Indian and Eskimo autobiographies [8], and Francis Paul Prucha's bibliography of Indian-White relations [61].

Another vital resource, albeit slow in emerging, is the Smithsonian Institution's *Handbook of North American Indians.* A proposed twenty volumes, the *Handbook* will be a landmark addition to the literature when it is finally completed. While some more contemporary articles inevitably will be dated, given the long gap between their submission and final publication, the *Handbook* in sum will represent an indispensable addition to any serious library holding. To date, five of the volumes have been published [24, 25, 52, 53, 75].

Tribal histories in single volumes come under a variety of labels. Many writers have chosen to tell the story of a tribe in chronological form, traditionally with emphasis on events leading up to the close of the frontier. Within the past decade, individuals from Indian communities or the communities themselves have also started in increasing numbers to produce histories for public consumption. And there are other kinds of studies through which we may learn about this subject. Some may focus on a particular issue within tribal history, such as land use or politics. Many books consider the history of a state or region and the Indian peoples therein. Other works consider Indian policy but in the process tell us much about the tribe. Autobiographies and biographies yield additional perspectives. Through literature, Indians make important statements about identity—past, present, and future.

This essay is structured, then, upon these eight categories: tribal histories, tribal histories by Indian individuals or communities, issues within tribal history, state or regional Indian histories, histories of Indian policy, autobiographies, biographies, and Indian literature. Because of the wealth of material available, this survey is limited to works published after 1974 and to works that are published in book form. Dissertations are not included within this consideration as they are more difficult to obtain by most readers and they may be published eventually in revised form. The various bibliographies cited previously will assist readers in finding articles and other briefer analyses of tribal history. Even with these restrictions, many books have had to be omitted from the discussion here.

Tribal Histories

Edmund Jefferson Danziger, Jr., *The Chippewas of Lake Superior* [14] is one of the best examples of a modern tribal history. Four of his ten chapters consider the life of Chippewas in the twentieth century. Danziger uses oral history extensively. He discusses both the discouraging and the promising aspects of tribal existence. Another effective contribution to the University of Oklahoma Press's "Civilization of the American Indian Series" is David Baird's history of the Quapaws [2]. Three of his ten chapters chronicle the impact of land allotment, mineral leases and other forces upon the tribe. By contrast, a third well-received volume in this series, Martha Blaine's *The Ioway Indians* [5], centers almost exclusively on the eighteenth and nineteenth centuries, tracing the tribe's movement from the Midwest to Indian Territory, Kansas, and Nebraska.

Two books on the Potawatomis also have earned critical acclaim. James Clifton, *The Prairie People: Continuity and Change in Potawatomi Indian Culture, 1665-1965* [10], is a massive study emphasizing the Prairie Band of Potawatomis. The heart of the book concerns the days prior to the Treaty of 1846, with significant attention being paid to territorial expansion, leadership and governance, ideology, social organization, and religion. R. David Edmunds, *The Potawatomis: Keepers of the Fire* [16] nicely complements Clifton's book, with its concentration on the Old Northwest and its historian's viewpoint. Edmunds's book rests on thorough utilization of a great variety of manuscript sources.

Three other studies give detailed attention to the twentieth century. Roy W. Meyer, *The Village Indians of the Upper Missouri* [46], grew from his investigation of the Garrison Dam's impact upon the Fort Berthold Reservation of North Dakota. Thus the book has a natural focus on more recent events as well as consideration of earlier eras. My study, *The Navajo Nation* [35], analyzes the experience of the United States' largest tribe since World War II. Karen I. Blu, *The Lumbee Problem* [7], reviews the evolution of an Indian community in the South.

Three books that focus on the nineteenth century are Robert H. Ruby and John A. Brown, *The Chinook Indians: Traders of the Lower Columbia River* [62]; Donald Worcester, *The Apaches: Eagles of the Southwest* [86]; and, C. Gregory Crampton, *The Zunis of Cibola* [12]. Students interested in the Northwest and the period of initial American involvement in that region will find *The Chinook Indians* valuable. Worcester and Crampton give this century but a fleeting glance, yet present intriguing glimpses of Indian-White relations before the end of the Anglo-American frontier. Patricia K. Ourada's history of the Menominees [55] provides a detailed treatment of the earlier history of this Wisconsin people, but only a limited view of the controversy surrounding the termination and restoration of their reservation.

The two works that conclude this section are of a singular character. Peter John Powell has written an extraordinary two-volume saga of the Cheyenne: *People of the Sacred Mountain* [60]. It is an impressive rendering of the Cheyennes of a century and more ago by a man adopted into their midst, who tells their story as they see it, with the full drama of the age. Edward H. Spicer's cultural history of the Yaquis is a seminal study by one of the most eminent students of Indian life [71]. Published almost half a century after his initial field work with the Yaquis, the book includes tribal experiences in both Mexico and the United States. Spicer is concerned with "the uniqueness of the Yaqui spirit and those qualities which Yaquis share with others of their human type—the enduring peoples of the world." In this fine account, he underlines what most of the authors suggest or state directly: Indians will survive; Indians will endure.

Indian Tribal Histories

This theme of endurance is stressed naturally in the tribal histories written by individual Indians or Indian communities. Clearly one of the primary purposes of such studies is to testify to the ways in which identities may change yet continue. These histories also serve to teach both outsiders about the people, and the people themselves about their heritage.

Relatively few Indian individuals have attempted a formal history of their tribe. Several reasons may be given for the scarcity of such work, including the reluctance of people to write about their own relatives, the belief that certain topics should not be written about, and the unwillingness often to presume to speak for a larger community. Veronica E. Velarde Tiller, for example, is a member of the Jicarilla Apache tribe and holds a doctorate in history from the University of New Mexico. She has written *The Jicarilla Apache Tribe: A History, 1846-1970* [74]. Nonetheless, she cautions that her book is primarily about relations between the federal government and her people and that it is not written from an Indian viewpoint, since there can be no one composite view. It would seem that such disclaimers speak directly to the difficulty of a member of an Indian community writing such a history, even as it is evident that Tiller had full support of her tribal council and members of her family. Still, her book is a traditional history, relying almost exclusively upon the usual sources.

Perhaps the most successful of the individual tribal histories is Joe Sando's history of his own pueblo, Jemez. *Nee Hemish* [66] is more effective in its style and content than an earlier survey by Sando of New Mexico's Pueblos [65]. In the words of Alfonso Ortiz in the book's foreword, Sando "manages to impart a good sense of the seasonal round, of the flavor of everyday life at Jemez, proving it can be done without revealing things which Pueblo people feel have no place in print."

Carobeth Laird is not an Indian, but was married for many years to George Laird, a Chemehuevi. *The Chemehuevis* [41], she contends convincingly, is basically his book. Social organization, religion, and mythology are important concerns in the volume, one which teaches much about the tribal heritage.

Several tribal schools have produced histories of their communities. One of the most interesting is *Pute Tiyos'paye (Lip's Camp): The History and Culture of a Sioux Indian Village* [13], compiled and written by the students and faculty of Crazy Horse School on the Pine Ridge Reservation in Wanblee, South Dakota. The idea of principal Elijah Whirlwind Horse, the book includes community and personal history and topics range from religion to humor, the latter section admirably done by Maxine Standing Bear.

Navajo Community College Press began in the early 1970s to publish accounts of tribal history. Two of the more recent volumes are oral histories, both edited by Broderick Johnson: *Stories of Traditional Navajo Life* [38] and *Navajos and World War II* [37]. Each anthology contains the stories of individual Navajos and sheds light on cultural continuity and change during the twentieth century. The material on the Second World War may prove particularly fascinating to many readers.

Eve Ball's *Indeh: An Apache Odyssey* [3] is a marvelous collective view of Apache history. A resident of the Mescalero Apache country in New Mexico for four decades, Ball succeeded in encouraging many Apaches to record their understanding of the late nineteenth and twentieth century tribal experience. Daklugie, son of Juh (a contemporary of Geronimo and leader of the Nednhi Apaches), is the principal contributor.

Other small tribes or Indian peoples within different states are attempting to present brief chronicles of their history, sometimes aided by non-Indian scholars from universities. Examples of such collaboration include histories of the Walker River Paiutes [39] and Acoma Pueblo [48]. The Intertribal Council of Nevada has published four histories of the Western Shoshone, the Southern Paiute, the Northern Paiute, and the Washo [31, 32, 33, 34]. The Uintah-Ouray Ute Tribe a year later produced five books on their history and culture [77, 78, 79, 80, 81].

Aspects of Tribal History

Four exemplary works are used as examples here. Loretta Fowler's award-winning book dissects Northern Arapahoe political history and contemporary politics. In a sophisticated combination of fieldwork and ethnohistory, Fowler shows us how the Arapahoes, now residents of the Wind River Reservation in central Wyoming, have been able to "legitimize" "new authority relations." In so doing, she reveals how the past continues to influence centrally the Arapahoe present [19].

Michael D. Green, *The Politics of Indian Removal: Creek Government and Society in Crisis* [20], is the best of the recent studies on the Indian removal period. Green brings forth more of an internal view of a particular tribe than many earlier works which focused on federal policy. The book demonstrates that an area that has been examined frequently may still be reworked in a useful fashion.

W. W. Hill's ethnography of Santa Clara Pueblo, edited and annotated by Charles H. Lange, is a richly detailed study of one community's economy, material culture, life cycle and social organization, and political and ceremonial organization [26]. Finally, Richard White's analysis of the subsistence, environment and social change among the Choctaws, Pawnees and Navajos, is a provocative and searching examination of Indian land use by three Indian tribes in, respectively, the past three centuries [83].

Although these and other works rely on different kinds of sources and take different forms in their presentation, they demonstrate conclusively that they illuminate the histories of their various tribes. While less comprehensive, they may and indeed should tell us more about an important portion of the tribal experience.

State and Regional Indian Histories

Although more difficult to complete, more studies at the state and regional level are being attempted in American Indian history. Often the finished work will be the collective endeavor of many contributors, with the resulting product sometimes representing a cohesive anthology and other times a more disjointed set of essays. Surely these efforts in a comparative sense can bring forth some vital findings about tribal history.

Rennard Strickland, *The Indians in Oklahoma* [73], is a brief, well-illustrated introduction to Indian life in that state. The author, an Indian attorney, calls history "an act of remembrance," and labels this book a "pictorial, episodic" calendar of the Indian experience from the autumn of Indian nationhood before Oklahoma statehood to the modern summer of contemporary life, stressing survival and endurance. Strickland's account is impressionistic and sometimes emotional—qualities that will enhance its accessibility to many in its potential audience.

Three other state studies emphasize earlier times. Ronald N. Satz analyzes the historical experience of Tennessee's Indian peoples from white contact to removal [67]. Another brief overview is George H. Phillips, *The Enduring Struggle: Indians in California's History* [59]. Phillips is especially interested in Indian life during Hispanic and early United States administration of California, but he does bring the story up to the present day. His earlier book [58] focuses on Indian resistance and cooperation in Southern California during the Spanish mission period and fleshes out these important themes of tribal experiences.

William A. Haviland and Marjory W. Power's survey of Vermont Indians is an example of a book intended for the general reader that may be read profitably by specialists as well. *The Original Vermonters* [23] concentrates on the Indians of the state before European incursion, but also examines the impact of that incursion and reviews the status of Vermont Indians today. While there are no footnotes, there are extensive bibliographic notes and a complete bibliography.

Charles M. Hudson has contributed two books which have added to our knowledge of southeastern Indians. The more important is a synthesis, *The Southeastern Indians* [29], but he has also edited a volume of nine essays, *Four Centuries of Southern Indians* [30], which includes work by such scholars as Raymond D. Fogelson and James H. O'Donnell III.

Two other works on the Southeast have gained wide recognition: J. Leitch Wright, Jr., *The Only Land They Knew: The Tragic Story of the American Indians of the Old South* [87], and Walter L. Williams, editor, *Southeastern Indians since the Removal Era* [84]. Wright's study progresses into the colonial era, whereas Williams's volume, as its title indicates, extends into more recent times. In addition to members of the Five Civilized Tribes, other Indian communities, such as the Lumbee, Tunica, Houma, and Catawba are considered.

Theda Perdue has edited the oral histories collected during the 1930's in Oklahoma from members of the Cherokees, Choctaws, Chickasaws, Creeks, and Seminoles [57]. She has added helpful notes to allow the reader to gain maximum advantage of the assembled material. Robert H. Ruby and John A. Brown have continued their collaborative work in a history of the Indians of the Pacific Northwest [63]. Augmented by a great many photographs and other illustrations, the book surveys fruitfully the experience of many Indian peoples of the region, with almost exclusive emphasis on the nineteenth century.

Howard S. Russell has presented a detailed picture of Indian life up to the seventeeth century in Indian New England. Rather than using a chronological narrative, Russell has organized his findings topically. Housing, diet, farming, hunting, trade, social roles, health and religion are among the subjects covered [64].

Douglas H. Ubelaker and Herman J. Viola have edited a collection of essays in honor of John C. Ewers and Waldo R. Wedel that they entitle *Plains Indian Studies* [76]. The book is a richly deserved tribute to two of the region's most distinguished scholars. Moreover, though a festschrift, the volume is an important addition to Plains literature. The far-ranging essays include archaeological studies by such authorities as George C. Frison and Dennis J. Stanford and two first-rate examinations of tribal political life by Loretta Fowler and Thomas R. Wessel.

Indian Policy

Many books on federal Indian policy reveal something about tribal history. Increasingly, studies in this area have dealt more directly with Indian responses and initiatives. Five of the best of these works are included here.

Donald Berthrong, *The Cheyenne and Arapaho Ordeal: Reservation and Agency Life in the Indian Territory, 1875-1907* [4]; William T. Hagan, *United States-Comanche Relations: The Reservation Years* [21]; and Donald L. Parman, *The Navajos and the New Deal* [56], were all published in 1976. These solid studies by respected scholars quickly were recognized as valuable contributions to our understanding not only of Indians policies during their respective eras but to tribal history as well. The authors utilized traditional manuscript sources and focus more on policy than on Indian peoples, but their work demonstrates a good understanding of the people and their land.

In a similar vein, a more recent study by Clyde A. Milner II, of Quaker missionary work among the Pawnees, Otos, and Omahas in the 1870s shows how Quaker administration affected the lives of Indian people. There is also some sense here about how Indians reacted to the efforts to assimilate them [47].

Laurence M. Hauptman's study of the Iroquois and the New Deal is the most successful recent work in giving us a clear sense of tribal life while delineating policy at the federal level. Particularly with the Senecas, Hauptman presents a sharp image of tribal existence. This achievement is due in part to analysis of a period in the more immediate past. Hauptman has utilized oral history and other sources with great effectiveness [22].

The importance of such sources cannot be overemphasized. Oral history, for example, is not always reliable; traveling to the land of the people does not produce instant insight. But the current work in the field of Indian policy suggests that a new dimension may be brought by using carefully such techniques. With their employment, the historian has an enhanced opportunity to present a more complete picture of what happened. Written records are vital, but they may not reveal the full story.

Autobiographies

In many instances, Indian autobiographies have been filtered through the perspective of a non-Indian recorder and interpreter. The reluctance of Indian people to write tribal history is relevant to a similar hesitation in regard to telling one's own story. Indian autobiographies through the years have varied tremendously in their candor, their honesty, and their ability to reflect usefully upon the tribal existence.

The "as told to" format is still a prevalent one within Indian autobiographies, but more recent efforts seem more likely to be sensitive to the distortions that accompany such renditions. Michael S. Adams's work with the Papago leader Peter Blaine, Sr., is a good case in point. *Papagos and Politics* [6] is even labeled Blaine "as told to" Adams, but the latter has taken great care to preserve the essential syntax and diction of the former. The end result, as any fine autobiography or biography, tells us much about Blaine, but also about Papago life in his lifetime. There is special emphasis on the 1930s.

Another excellent autobiography—one that is still more ambitious in its scope—is *Navajo Blessingway Singer: The Autobiography of Frank Mitchell, 1881-1967*, edited by Charlotte J. Frisbie and David P. McAllester [49]. The product of a relationship developed through many years, the volume discloses much about Navajo ceremonial life. Frisbie and McAllester's familiarity with the Mitchell family and with Navajo history and culture are reflected throughout the book, along with the life of a remarkable man.

Most Indian autobiographies have been those of men. An exception is Irene Stewart's *A Voice in Her Tribe*, edited by Doris Ostrander Dawdy [72]. While simple in form and brief in length, the book is valuable for its recounting of Navajo women's roles, including Stewart's political participation.

Refugio Savala, *The Autobiography of a Yaqui Poet* [68], is another fascinating life story. Edited with background and interpretations by Kathleen M. Sands, this autobiography traces Yaqui life in this century in six parts, which Savala labels relocation, growth, extension, return, acceptance, and perseverance. Sands adds briefer chapters corresponding to each of these parts. The autobiography, in English, is the poet's own translation.

In *Big Falling Snow* [88], Albert Yava presents a version that is precise in its title as to its dual role: autobiography and tribal history. Edited by Harold Courlander, the book is subtitled "A Tewa-Hopi Indian's Life and Times and the History and Traditions of His People." As Courlander notes, Yava is more willing to talk about his village than himself.

N. Scott Momaday, *The Names* [50], is unique among these works. It is, as he says, a memoir and an act of the imagination. The Kiowas of the author's Oklahoma home and the southwestern Indians taught by his parents in the Indian Service figure in his stories. Particularly rewarding for those who have read *The Way to Rainy Mountain*, *The Names* is a beautifully written tribute to family and to tribe, evoked through what the author once termed the living racial memory.

Biographies

Until recently, most Indian biographies seemed to focus on warriors and thus on the days before the close of the frontier. While there remains a continuing fascination with the earlier period, some new efforts reveal something about Indian life during the past century. More contemporary biographies, as tribal histories, offer a better chance to use oral history and a wide variety of other tribal perspectives.

One of the first "non-warrior" biographies during recent years (despite its title) was William Armstrong's portrait of the Seneca leader Ely S. Parker [1]. Parker is shown as a man with ties to the tribal world who yet became very active in the larger society and who served as Commissioner of Indian Affairs. *Ohiyesa: Charles A. Eastman, Santee Sioux* [85] is a new biography by Raymond Wilson of the important Sioux writer, physician, and spokesman. My *Carlos Montezuma and the Changing World of American Indians* [36] examines the life of the controversial Yavapai physician and activist. Both *Ohiyesa* and *Carlos Montezuma* attempt to describe, in part, tribal life in the transitional world of the early twentieth century.

Again, as with autobiography, most studies have been of men. An exception is Gae Canfield's work on Sarah Winnemucca [9]. Of other figures whose lives largely or entirely came prior to this century, Angie Debo's biography of Geronimo [15] is perhaps the most compelling. Gary Moulton has written a straightforward study of the Cherokee leader, John Ross [51], while Margaret Coel has presented the story of Chief Left Hand of the Southern Arapahoes [11].

Three volumes introduce brief depictions of individual Indians. R. David Edmunds, *American Indian Leaders* [17], is subtitled "Studies in Diversity." The twelve men include Alexander McGillivray, Sitting Bull, and Washakie; the chapters show how different goals and strategies have been required in different situations. H. Glenn Jordan and Thomas M. Holm have edited a collection of essays on Oklahoma Indian leaders, such as Peter Pitchlynn, Black Kettle, and Claremore [40]. *American Indian Intellectuals* [43], edited by Margot Liberty, evolved from the 1976 meeting of the American Ethnological Society. Arthur C. Parker, Francis La Flesche, and John Joseph Mathews are among those sketched here.

Taken in sum these biographies reveal the potential that remains largely untapped by this approach. But they also indicate the kinds of choices that leaders and others have made, as individuals, as Indians, and often as representatives for their people. The best of the biographies inform us of not merely their immediate subject, but of the tribal world in which these people lived at least part of their lives.

Literature

Indian writers through the use of fiction may be more free to speak directly to tribal history. Through poems, short stories, novels, and other work, Indians may address not only contemporary situations, but a world of long ago. Often the past will be seen affecting the present. Frequently, but not always, Indian writers use the tribal world as a foundation for what they wish to say.

Simon Ortiz, from Acoma Pueblo, is a good example of a writer whose work reflects an awareness of the importance and power of history. *From Sand Creek* [54] is a case in point, where the tragedy of more than a century ago is interwoven with poems dealing with the present. Ortiz's poems often address the enduring nature of Indian life.

James Welch [82] and Leslie Marmon Silko [69] tend to set their stories in the more recent past, but the issues and problems confronted by main characters are affected sharply by historical developments in regard to the use of land, social custom, and tradition. These characters respond to current choices and problems within a context etched by history.

Within the past few years, there have been a number of anthologies published that bring together a variety of work by Indian authors. Two of the very best are Larry Evers, editor, *The South Corner of Time* [18], and Geary Hobson, editor, *The Remembered Earth* [27]. Evers's collection encompasses four southwestern tribes: Hopi, Navajo, Papago, and Yaqui. Hobson's book has strong representation from the Southwest, but is more national in scope. Together they introduce the reader to a great many fine writers, and in Evers's book, photographers as well. These people tell us about the land, about family, about community. Again and again one is struck by the themes that speak to resilience, or what Hobson terms continuance, strength, renewal, and remembering.

In all these forms, tribal histories say that the past and the present and the future are one. They say that there is continuity amidst change. They say that in the record of removal and loss, there may be rebirth and growth. They say that Indians will endure.

ALPHABETICAL LIST

[1] Armstrong, William H. 1978. *Warrior in Two Camps: Ely S. Parker, Union General and Seneca Chief*. Syracuse: Syracuse University Press.

[2] Baird, W. David. 1980. *The Quapaw Indians: A History of the Downstream People*. Norman: University of Oklahoma Press.

[3] Ball, Eve, ed., with Nora Henn and Lynda Sanchez. 1980. *Indeh: An Apache Odyssey*. Provo: Brigham Young University Press.

[4] Berthrong, Donald J. 1976. *The Cheyenne and Arapaho Ordeal: Reservation and Agency Life in the Indian Territory, 1875-1907*. Norman: University of Oklahoma Press.

[5] Blaine, Martha Royce. 1979. *The Ioway Indians*. Norman: University of Oklahoma Press.

[6] Blaine, Peter, Sr., with Michael S. Adams. 1981. *Papagos and Politics*. Tucson: Arizona Historical Society.

[7] Blu, Karen I. 1980. *The Lumbee Problem: The Making of an American Indian People*. Cambridge, England: Cambridge University Press.

[8] Brumble, H. David III. 1981. *An Annotated Bibliography of American Indian and Eskimo Autobiographies*. Lincoln: University of Nebraska Press.

[9] Canfield, Gae Whitney. 1983. *Sarah Winnemucca of the Northern Paiutes*. Norman: University of Oklahoma Press.

[10] Clifton, James A. 1977. *The Prairie People: Continuity and Change in Potawatomi Indian Culture, 1665-1965*. Lawrence: The Regents Press of Kansas.

[11] Coel, Margaret. 1981. *Chief Left Hand, Southern Arapaho*. Norman: University of Oklahoma Press.

[12] Crampton, C. Gregory. 1977. *The Zunis of Cibola*. Salt Lake City: University of Utah Press.

[13] Crazy Horse School. 1978. *Pute Tiyos'paye (Lip's Camp): The History*

and Culture of a Sioux Indian Village. Wanblee, South Dakota: Crazy Horse School.

[14] Danziger, Edmund Jefferson, Jr. 1978. *The Chippewas of Lake Superior*. Norman: University of Oklahoma Press.

[15] Debo, Angie. 1976. *Geronimo: The Man, His Time, His Place*. Norman: University of Oklahoma Press.

[16] Edmunds, R. David. 1978. *The Potawatomis: Keepers of the Fire*. Norman: University of Oklahoma Press.

[17] ———, ed. 1980. *American Indian Leaders: Studies in Diversity*. Lincoln: University of Nebraska Press.

[18] Evers, Larry, ed. 1980. *The South Corner of Time: Hopi-Navajo-Papago-Yaqui Tribal Literature*. Tucson: University of Arizona Press.

[19] Fowler, Loretta. 1982 *Arapahoe Politics, 1851-1978: Symbols in Crises of Authority*. Lincoln: University of Nebraska Press.

[20] Green, Michael D. 1982. *The Politics of Indian Removal: Creek Government and Society in Crisis*. Lincoln: University of Nebraska Press.

[21] Hagan, William T. 1976. *United States-Comanche Relations: The Reservation Years*. New Haven: Yale University Press.

[22] Hauptman, Laurence M. 1981. *The Iroquois and the New Deal*. Syracuse: Syracuse University Press.

[23] Haviland, William A., and Marjory W. Power. 1981. *The Original Vermonters: Native Inhabitants, Past and Present*. Hanover: University Press of New England.

[24] Heizer, Robert F., ed. 1978. *California*. Volume 8 of *Handbook of North American Indians*, gen. ed. William C. Sturtevant. Washington: Smithsonian Institution.

[25] Helm June, ed. 1978. *Subarctic*. Volume 6 of *Handbook of North American Indians*, gen. ed. William C. Sturtevant. Washington: Smithsonian Institution.

[26] Hill, W. W. 1982. *An Ethnography of Santa Clara Pueblo, New Mexico*, ed. Charles H. Lange. Albuquerque: University of New Mexico Press.

[27] Hobson, Geary, ed. 1981. *The Remembered Earth: An Anthology of Contemporary Native American Literature*. Albuquerque: University of New Mexico Press.

[28] Horsman, Reginald. 1982. "Well-Trodden Paths and Fresh Byways: Recent Writing on Native American History." *Reviews in American History* 10:234-44.

[29] Hudson, Charles M. 1976. *The Southeastern Indians*. Knoxville: University of Tennessee Press.

[30] ———, ed. 1975. *Four Centuries of Southern Indians*. Athens: University of Georgia Press.

[31] Intertribal Council of Nevada. 1976. *NEWW: A Western Shoshone History*. Reno: Intertribal Council of Nevada.

[32] ———. 1976. *NUMA: A Northern Paiute History*. Reno: Intertribal Council of Nevada.

[33] ———. 1976. *NUMA: A Southern Paiute History*. Reno: Intertribal Council of Nevada.

[34] ———. 1976. *WA SHE SHU: A Washo Tribal History*. Reno: Intertribal Council of Nevada.

[35] Iverson, Peter. 1981. *The Navajo Nation*. Westport, Conn.: Greenwood Press.

[36] ———. 1982. *Carlos Montezuma and the Changing World of American Indians*. Albuquerque: University of New Mexico Press.

[37] Johnson, Broderick, ed. 1977. *Navajos and World War II*. Tsaile: Navajo Community College Press.

[38] ———, ed. 1977. *Stories of Traditional Navajo Life and Culture*. Tsaile: Navajo Community College Press.

[39] Johnson, Edward C. 1975. *Walker-River Paiutes: A Tribal History*. Schurz, Nev.: Walker River Paiute Tribe.

[40] Jordan, H. Glenn, and Thomas M. Holm, eds. 1979. *Indian Leaders: Oklahoma's First Statesmen*. Oklahoma City: Oklahoma Historical Society.

[41] Laird, Carobeth. 1976. *The Chemehuevis*. Banning, Calif.: Malki Museum Press.

[42] Laird, W. David. 1977. *Hopi Bibliography: Comprehensive and Annotated*. Tucson: University of Arizona Press.

[43] Liberty, Margot, ed. 1978. *American Indian Intellectuals*. St. Paul: West Publishing Co.

[44] McGinnis, Dale K., and Floyd W. Sharrock. 1972. *The Crow People*. Phoenix: Indian Tribal Series.

[45] Marken, Jack W., and Herbert T. Hoover. 1980. *Bibliography of the Sioux*. Metuchen, N.J.: Scarecrow Press.

[46] Meyer, Roy W. 1977. *The Village Indians of the Upper Missouri: The Mandans, Hidatsas, and Arikaras*. Lincoln: University of Nebraska Press.

[47] Milner, Clyde A. II. 1982. *With Good Intentions: Quaker Work among the Pawnees, Otos, and Omahas in the 1870s*. Lincoln: University of Nebraska Press.

[48] Minge, Ward Alan. 1976. *Acoma: Pueblo in the Sky*. Albuquerque: University of New Mexico Press.

[49] Mitchell, Frank. 1978. *Navajo Blessingway Singer: The Autobiography of Frank Mitchell, 1881-1967*, ed. Charlotte J. Frisbie and David P. McAllester. Tucson: University of Arizona Press.

[50] Momaday, N. Scott. 1976. *The Names*. New York: Harper & Row.

[51] Moulton, Gary. 1978. *John Ross, Cherokee Chief*. Athens: University of Georgia Press.

[52] Ortiz, Alfonso, ed. 1979. *Southwest*. Volume 9 of *Handbook of North American Indians*, gen. ed. William C. Sturtevant. Washington: Smithsonian Institution.

[53] ———, ed. 1983. *Southwest*. Volume 10 of *Handbook of North Ameri-*

can Indians, gen. ed. William C. Sturtevant. Washington: Smithsonian Institution.

[54] Ortiz, Simon J. 1981. *From Sand Creek*. Oak Park, Illinois: Thunder's Mouth Press.

[55] Ourada, Patricia K. 1979. *The Menominee Indians: A History*. Norman: University of Oklahoma Press.

[56] Parman, Donald L. 1976. *The Navajos and the New Deal*. New Haven: Yale University Press.

[57] Perdue, Theda, ed. 1980. *Nations Remembered: An Oral History of the Five Civilized Tribes, 1865-1907*. Westport: Greenwood Press.

[58] Phillips, George Harwood. 1975. *Chiefs and Challengers: Indian Resistance and Cooperation in Southern California*. Berkeley and Los Angeles: University of California Press.

[59] ———. 1981. *The Enduring Struggle: Indians in California's History*. San Francisco: Boyd and Fraser Publishing Co.

[60] Powell, Peter John. 1981. *People of the Sacred Mountain: A History of the Northern Cheyenne Chiefs and Warrior Societies, 1830-1879, with an Epilogue, 1969-1974*. 2 volumes. New York: Harper & Row.

[61] Prucha, Francis Paul. 1982. *Indian-White Relations in the United States: A Bibliography of Works Published 1975-1980*. Lincoln: University of Nebraska Press.

[62] Ruby, Robert H., and John A. Brown. 1976. *The Chinook Indians: Traders of the Lower Columbia River*. Norman: University of Oklahoma Press.

[63] ———. 1981. *Indians of the Pacific Northwest*. Norman: University of Oklahoma Press.

[64] Russell, Howard S. 1980. *Indian New England before the Mayflower*. Hanover: University Press of New England.

[65] Sando, Joe S. 1976. *The Pueblo Indians*. San Francisco: Indian Historian Press.

[66] ———. 1982. *Nee Hemish: A History of Jemez Pueblo*. Albuquerque: University of New Mexico Press.

[67] Satz, Ronald N. 1979. *Tennessee's Indian Peoples: From White Contact to Removal, 1540-1840*. Knoxville: University of Tennessee Press.

[68] Savala, Refugio. 1980. *The Autobiography of a Yaqui Poet*, ed. Kathleen M. Sands. Tucson: University of Arizona Press.

[69] Silko, Leslie Marmon. 1977. *Ceremony*. New York: Viking Press.

[70] Smith, Dwight L. 1983. *Indians of the United States and Canada: A Bibliography*. Volume 2. Santa Barbara: ABC-Clio.

[71] Spicer, Edward H. 1980. *The Yaquis: A Cultural History*. Tucson: University of Arizona Press.

[72] Stewart, Irene. 1980. *A Voice in Her Tribe: A Navajo Woman's Own Story*, ed. Doris Ostrander Dawdy. Socorro: Ballena Press.

[73] Strickland, Rennard. 1980. *The Indians in Oklahoma*. Norman: University of Oklahoma Press.

[74] Tiller, Veronica E. Velarde. 1983. *The Jicarilla Apache Tribe: A History, 1846-1970*. Lincoln: University of Nebraska Press.

[75] Trigger, Bruce G., ed. 1978. *Northeast*. Volume 15 of *Handbook of North American Indians*, gen. ed. William C. Sturtevant. Washington: Smithsonian Institution.

[76] Ubelaker, Douglas H., and Herman J. Viola, eds. 1982. *Plains Indian Studies: A Collection of Essays in Honor of John C. Ewers and Waldo R. Wedel*. Smithsonian Contributions in Anthropology 30. Washington: Smithsonian Institution.

[77] Uintah-Ouray Tribe. 1977. *A Brief History of the Ute People*. Fort Duchesne, Utah: Uintah-Ouray Ute Tribe.

[78] ———. 1977. *The Ute People*. Fort Duchesne, Utah. Uintah-Ouray Ute Tribe.

[79] ———. 1977. *Ute Ways*. Fort Duchesne, Utah: Uintah-Ouray Ute Tribe.

[80] ———. 1977. *The Way It Was Told*. Fort Duchesne, Utah: Uintah-Ouray Ute Tribe.

[81] ———. 1977. *The Ute System of Government*. Fort Duchesne, Utah: Uintah Ouray Ute Tribe.

[82] Welch, James. 1979. *The Death of Jim Loney*. New York: Harper & Row.

[83] White, Richard. 1983. *The Roots of Dependency: Subsistence, Environment, and Social Change among the Choctaws, Pawnees, and Navajos*. Lincoln: University of Nebraska Press.

[84] Williams, Walter L., ed. 1979. *Southeastern Indians Since the Removal Era*. Athens: University of Georgia Press.

[85] Wilson, Raymond. 1983. *Ohiyesa: Charles A. Eastman, Santee Sioux*. Urbana: University of Illinois Press.

[86] Worcester, Donald E. 1979. *The Apaches: Eagles of the Southwest*. Norman: University of Oklahoma Press.

[87] Wright, J. Leitch, Jr. 1981. *The Only Land They Knew: The Tragic Story of the American Indians in the Old South*. New York: Free Press.

[88] Yava, Albert. 1978. *Big Falling Snow: A Tewa-Hopi Indian's Life and Times and the History and Traditions of His People*, ed. Harold Courlander. New York: Crown Publishers.

The Indian and the Fur Trade: A Review of Recent Literature

JACQUELINE PETERSON
Washington State University
and JOHN ANFINSON
University of Minnesota

Two SIGNIFICANT CONCLUSIONS are manifest in the proliferation of books and articles on the fur trade since 1970. First, as Daniel Francis and Toby Morantz in *Partners in Furs* [31] persuasively argue, the term itself is something of a misnomer. There were, in actuality, numerous fur trades, differing over time and across a vast cultural and ecological landscape. Secondly, with the possible exception of the much romanticized (albeit relatively brief) era of the Rocky Mountain trapper (circa 1820-46), the fur trade was far more than a first-stage colonial extractive industry forecasting the settlement and national development of the United States and Canada, views propounded by Frederick Jackson Turner in 1891 [100] and Harold A. Innis in 1930 [46] and still cherished by many historians of the West and North.

Rather, as Turner's flawed but remarkably durable thesis acknowledged, the fur trade, properly phrased, was an "Indian trade," a process of human interaction, in which the economic exchange of raw commodities for manufactured goods figured as vehicle and symbol for a much wider set of contacts between Indian and White. Although fur trade history continues to be written otherwise, a binding characteristic of much of the revisionist literature of the last fifteen years is the recognition of Indian centrality, or as Arthur J. Ray succinctly put it in 1978, of "Fur Trade History as an Aspect of Native History" [79].

Why so tardy a recognition? Considering the obvious involvement of Indians in the fur trade (at least half the social and economic equation), an enormous roster of monographs and articles on the subject by American and Canadian historians and anthropologists, and the perpetual public fascination with what Howard Lamar in *The Trader on the American Frontier: Myth's Victim* [58] termed "simply a variation of the eternal adventure story, American-style," the question is an important one.

Historians and anthropologists of North America long have had a vested interest in the study of American Indians, for reasons stemming at least in part from the discrete theoretical and methodological orientations of their respective disciplines. Historians, on the one hand, working primarily in documentary sources and often unfamiliar with living Indian cultures, have found the Indian a convenient foil, a backdrop against which the unfolding saga of westering Euroamericans has been set. It thus is not surprising that until recently fur trade history tended to be viewed, ethnocentrically, as an aspect of the histories of national exploration and expansion, as in Bernard De Voto, *Across the Wide Missouri* (1947); Robert Glass Cleland, *This Reckless Breed of Men: The Trappers and Fur Traders of the Southwest* (1950); and E. E. Rich, *The Fur Trade and the Northwest to 1857* (1967). Alternatively, the fur trade has been cast as part of world-wide capitalist development or of economic history, as in Paul Chrisler Phillips, *The Fur Trade* (1961); Harold Innis's still important *The Fur Trade in Canada: An Introduction to Canadian Economic History* [46]; and Glyndwr Williams, "Highlights of the First 200 Years of the Hudson's Bay Company," published in *The Beaver* in 1970 [110].

Viewed from these perspectives, white fur traders and adventurers, rather than their Indian clients and partners, understandably have garnered the bulk of the attention. A staggering array of biographies, autobiographies, memoirs, and the correspondence of mountain men, company founders and officers, and trader-explorers have been published over the last century, and the trend shows no evidence of diminishing. In addition to book-length biographies of major fur trade innovators, such as Gloria Griffen Cline's *Peter Skene Ogden and the Hudson's Bay Company* [20] and Richard M.

Clokey's *William H. Ashley: Enterprise and Politics in the Trans-Mississippi West* [21], and regional group biographies such as David J. Weber, *The Taos Trappers: The Fur Trade in the Far Southwest, 1540-1846* [106], lesser luminaries, all of them Hudson's Bay Company men, are the subject of Theodore J. Karamanski's *Fur Trade and Exploration: Opening the Far Northwest, 1821-1852* [52], Elaine Allan Mitchell's *Fort Timiskaming and the Fur Trade* [67], and Lois Halliday McDonald's capably annotated, *Fur Trade Letters of Francis Ermatinger, Written to His Brother Edward during his Service with the Hudson's Bay Company 1818-1853* [62].

The most impressive biographical effort of the last fifteen years has unquestionably been LeRoy R. Hafen, ed., *The Mountain Men and the Fur Trade of the Far West* [39], a ten-volume collaborative collection of the lives of 292 trappers and traders, with an introductory essay by Hafen. Like most biographical dictionaries, this "who's who" of the western fur trade weighs heavily in favor of men of notoriety and influence. However, it also focuses disproportionately on mountain men operating out of St. Louis and Santa Fe-Taos, providing only random sketches of traders affiliated with major companies such as the American Fur Company, the Columbia Fur Company and the North West Company active in the West. Employees at the lower echelons of the trade are underrepresented and only a few Indian trappers and traders are included, an omission which Theodore Karamanski's brief "The Iroquois and the Fur Trade of the Far West" [51] begins to correct. While the collection provides a wealth of useful detail, unmatched in other regions, taken as whole it tends to substantiate the mythic stature of a fraternity of adventurers better known to the American reading public than any other occupational group, with the possible exception of cowboys.

The memorializing of fur traders and trappers as quasi-national folk heroes has had an unfortunate side effect. Within the United States, especially, works on the fur trade by historians prior to the 1970s often carried with them a subtle determinism. Indian fur gatherers, processors, middlemen and traders were not active participants or agents of change but destiny's unwitting victims, pawns in a game played out by shrewd and enterprising Whites. Thus, whether American historians cast the fur trade as a daring adventure, a hard-headed business venture, the cutting edge of frontier settlement, a primitive playground for degenerate and rapacious Whites, or the rapid corrupter and despoiler of Indian societies—all interpretations were, and are, present—the Indian was a bit player, since his demise was never doubted. Notable exceptions were George T. Hunt's 1940 *The Wars of the Iroquois* [43], whose thesis that economic competition underlay seventeenth century Huron-Iroquois warfare was to launch a debate over Indian economic behavior; and Lewis O. Saum's 1965 *The Fur Trader and the Indian* [86] which, while focusing primarily upon white attitudes, revealed a social dimension to the fur trade hitherto unexplored.

Early twentieth century anthropologists, on the other hand, especially those living among and studying Subarctic and Northeastern Indian hunters, were struck by what appeared to them to be the survival of aboriginal beliefs, traditions, and subsistence strategies within groups whose involvement in the fur trade could be traced to the seventeenth century. The discovery and study of American Indian cultural persistence has been to American anthropology what the description of change over time has been to history, but in this case anthropologists themselves began and yet dominate an argument over whether certain forms of land tenure and property rights were aboriginal or were adapted from European models during the fur trade era. This argument is outlined by Richard White elsewhere in this volume and will not be repeated here.

Although, ultimately, anthropologists' first-hand experiences with contemporary hunting bands were to contribute far more to the development of an intercultural fur trade history than the exclusively archival approach of traditional historians, inattention to historical process and uncritical use of documents flawed much of the early work published. Here, too, there were notable exceptions. John C. Ewers has been a prolific and insightful commentator on Indian participation in the fur and hide trade of the American plains. His classic ethnohistorical study, *The Blackfeet: Raiders on the Northwestern Plains* (1958) still deserves a careful reading, as does Oscar Lewis, *The Effects of White Contact upon Blackfeet Culture, with Special Reference to the Role of the Fur Trade* (1942), and Preston Holder, "The Fur Trade as Seen from the Indian Point of View," in John Francis McDermott, ed., *The Frontier Re-examined* (1967). These works demonstrated the influence of long-established intertribal trade networks and centers as well as traditional exchange concepts and social institutions on the post-contact fur trade, a theme reiterated by John Ewers in his "The Influence of the Fur Trade Upon the Indians of the Northern Plains" [26] and by Howard Lamar [58].

Until the 1960s, historians and anthropologists interested in the fur trade and its impact upon native peoples tracked parallel courses, rarely intersecting so as to shape a debate. During the past twenty years, however, a number of trends — the new historic archaeology; the new social and economic histories; the maturation of a new subdiscipline, ethnohistory; the rise of Indian Studies; and, most recently, neo-Marxist approaches to the colonization process — have combined so as to make of the fur trade a testing ground for a more sophisticated analysis of Indian-White contact and of Indian motivation and behavior in the trade. The appearance in 1974 of two major works, Charles A. Bishop's *The Northern Ojibway and the Fur Trade: An Historical and Ecological Study* [6] which employed a technique called "upstreaming" to reveal the incremental processes of cultural and social change unleashed by contact and intensifying Ojibway involvement in the fur trade, and Arthur J. Ray's *Indians in The Fur Trade: Their Role as Hunters, Trappers and Middlemen in the Lands Southwest of Hudson Bay, 1660-1870* [77], a path-breaking geographical and ecological analysis of the numerous roles, motivations, and decision-making strategies of Assiniboine and Cree hunters, signalled by their titles alone the emphasis now to be accorded to Indian peoples in any significant revision of fur trade history.

It is noteworthy, perhaps, that in addition to historians and anthropologists, fur trade studies have recently engaged the attentions of economists, political scientists and, especially, geographers. Whatever the immediate concerns and foci of these diverse authors, however, all attempt to answer several fundamental questions: Why, in what fashion, and to what degree did native peoples across northern North America engage in the fur trade? How was the trade shaped and what did it signify? How rapidly and in what ways did native involvement alter precontact patterns?

Not unexpectedly, the earliest and still most vital debate concerning Indian participation in the trade rose out of the older treatment of fur trade history as an aspect of business or economic history. Prior to the 1960s, it had not occurred to scholars such as

Harold A. Innis and George T. Hunt, writing from an unqualified neoclassical perspective, to question the "why" of Indian involvement. It was self-evident. Indian hunters, like their white trader counterparts, were rational economic men driven by the profit motive and susceptible to the forces of the marketplace. While tacitly recognizing that most tribal economies were subsistence-oriented and that Indian tribes placed a peculiarly high value upon generosity and gift-giving, this view assumed that any original differences in tribal economic beliefs or practices were quickly subordinated by the desire for new sources of wealth and superior European commodities.

Beginning in the 1960s, these assumptions increasingly came under fire as scholars took a closer look at the actual behavior of Indian hunters and traders over time. E. E. Rich, the first scholar to delve deeply into the riches of the Hudson's Bay Company archives, took a major step away from Innis and Hunt in his 1960 essay, "Trade Habits and Economic Motivation Among the Indians of North America" [84] by acknowledging that Subarctic people did not maximize, accumulate, or take profit as theory predicted, but rather had "limited consumer demands." Rich noted moreover that Indian attitudes about reciprocity and gift-giving helped to shape and define the trade in ways which were formal and social rather than purely economic. While recognizing that Indians responded differently to exchange opportunities than Europeans, however, Rich was unable to explain why or to question the assumption that the irresistable superiority of European trade goods rendered Indians economically dependent.

The suggestion that classical economic theory did not fit precisely Indian trade behavior led Iroquoian scholars to reevaluate Hunt's thesis. In "The Iroquois and the Western Fur Trade: A Problem of Interpretation," [97] Alan W. Trelease argued that social institutions such as the blood feud and the traditional pursuit of male prestige explained Iroquois activity in the fur trade wars as much if not more than economic opportunism. Bruce G. Trigger, in a series of articles and, finally, in his two-volume *The Children of Aataentsic* [99] similarly denied that the Huron were motivated exclusively by economic opportunities presented and controlled by white outsiders, or that they were pawns quickly rendered dependent and stripped of their aboriginal beliefs. Rather, in a model and painstaking portrait, Trigger recreated the intricate web of institutions, values and relationships which informed the actions of various groups and individuals within a society long attached to trade.

Trelease and Trigger, while breaking with Hunt in an effort to emphasize the interplay and importance of social and cultural institutions, did not deny that economic motivations were present in tribal societies, however different they might appear from European motivations. Their works represent a transition from the blunt economic determinism of the 1930s to a period beginning in the early 1970s in which a number of scholars rejected outright the application of classical economic theory to American Indian societies' involvement in the trade. In opposition to neoclassicists or formalists, who have sought to temper economic explanations with cultural ingredients, a new group, representing the "substantivist" position of Karl Polanyi, would argue that North American Indian peoples neither believed nor behaved as Europeans and that what appeared to be economically motivated activity may have had other causes and meanings. This position was first advanced in Abraham Rotstein's 1972 article, "Trade and Politics: An Institutional Approach" [85], which maintained that from a tribal perspective the fur trade was subordinate to the politics of security, i.e., that economy was embedded in the institution of politics. Bruce M. White subsequently attempted to enlarge this approach by linking trade to the institutions of gift-giving and kinship in "'Give Us a Little Milk'" [108].

The most engaging substantivist approach has come from the pen of Calvin Martin. In *Keepers of the Game: Indian-Animal Relationships and the Fur Trade* [65] and a supporting article, "Subarctic Indians and Wildlife" [66], Martin suggests that rather than conceiving of animals as potential commodities, northern hunters regarded game animals as close spiritual relatives. Animals allowed themselves to be caught upon the condition that they be treated with reverence before, during, and after the kill. As long as Indians in northeastern North America held to these beliefs they could not have participated in a commercial enterprise predicated upon the slaughter of animals for personal gain. As post-contact Indian hunters did just this, in Martin's view, aboriginal Indian religion must have suffered a catastrophic blow.

Virgin soil epidemics, racing far in advance of European traders, left Indian hunters questioning their belief systems for a cause. The most convincing answer they found, according to Martin, was that the animals had launched a war to eliminate the human beings and the humans, in self-defense, had to exterminate them first. With their traditional world view in disarray, Indian hunters were susceptible to the economic lures of the fur trade. Economy was by this process disembedded from religion resulting in a different kind of Indian, one who practiced overkill rather than conservation.

Unfortunately, documentary support for this intriguing and elegantly crafted theory is thin and, in fact, the impressive work of Adrian Tanner and Harvey Feit, from which much of Martin's understanding of the spiritual relationship between animals and northern hunters is derived, points to a contrary conclusion. Harvey A. Feit's "The Ethno-Ecology of the Waswanipi Cree; or How Hunters Can Manage Their Resources" [27], and Adrian Tanner's "The Significance of Hunting Territories Today" [92], as well as Tanner's signally important thesis, *Bringing Home Animals: Religious Ideology and Mode of Production of the Mistassini Cree Hunters* [93], demonstrate both the persistence and vitality of a world view Martin pronounced dead, and the ability of the Cree to "manage" rather than wantonly slaughter their animal resources. Further proof of forest hunters' sensitivity to fluctuating animal populations is provided in Jeanne Kay, "Wisconsin Indian Hunting Patterns, 1634-1836" [53] which portrays the Menomini and Winnebago as rotating their trade-related hunting activities in tune with species availability.

Paralleling the growing appreciation of the importance of world view and religious ideology to the hunting practices of native bands engaged in the fur trade has been a more persuasive and inclusive neoclassicism in reaction to Rotstein's and Martin's nonmaterialist interpretations. Since neoclassicists believe that the same economic rationality underlies all human actions, regardless of time or space, no catastrophic explanations are necessary to account for readjustments in Indian decision-making as a result of the fur trade. If Indian behavior appears irrational or inefficient, they would argue, scholars have not yet identified the correct neoclassical method of analysis or they have been misled by the historical record.

John McManus's 1972 article, "An Economic Analysis of Indian Behavior in the North American Fur Trade" [63] apparently failed to find the right neoclassical constraint in its unpersuasive attempt to explain the underlying rationale of the Montagnais-Naskapi economy. Far more successful in reinvigorating the formalist approach has been Canadian geographer Arthur J. Ray. In "Indians as Consumers in the Eighteenth Century" [80], Ray depicts the Cree and Assiniboine as shrewd buyers, fully the equals of their European trading partners, who knew how to take advantage of Anglo-French competition in order to obtain the highest quality at the best price possible, and whose precise demands stimulated technological innovation among European manufacturers of Indian trade goods.

In "Competition and Conservation in the Early Subarctic Fur Trade" [78], as in his *Indians in the Fur Trade* [77], Ray focused on western Cree middlemen who manipulated the fur trade to meet their own needs to the frustration of the English at the Bay and of interior tribes forced to accept used goods at high mark-ups. This vigorous portrait of Subarctic middlemen traders keenly aware of profit has not gone unchallenged. Bruce Cox offers a reassessment in his "Indian Middlemen and the Early Fur Trade: Reconsidering the Position of the Hudson's Bay Company's 'Trading Indians'" [22]. On the other hand, clear evidence of entrepreneurial activity drawn from a later period and the Northwest Coast, is presented in Robert L. Whitner's interesting "Makah Commercial Sealing, 1860-1897" [109].

Ray's most persuasive critique of the substantivist school and particularly of Rotstein's notion of politically motivated or "treaty" trade appeared in *"Give Us Good Measure": An Economic Analysis of Relations Between the Indians and the Hudson's Bay Company before 1763*, coauthored with Donald B. Freeman [82]. Subarctic Indians were not organized into sufficiently large or cohesive political units to carry on treaty trade, they maintain, and a far more accurate rendering of Indian behavior in the fur trade results from applying marketplace theory. Ray's and Freeman's conclusions are based upon an inventive statistical analysis of Hudson's Bay Company post documents which they believe should lay to rest several persistent misconceptions about Indian attitudes toward price and profit. For example, scholars formerly believed that fixed prices did not vary over long periods, from which they deduced that Indians were not profit-oriented. Ray and Freeman demonstrate, however, that earlier researchers were misled by the complex method developed by

HBC post officials to exact a profit from the trade. Once the "overplus" system is understood, they argue, significant fluctuations in price over time are revealed, as are concerted native attempts to secure "full measure" for their furs.

Calvin Martin's *Keepers of the Game* [65] has also drawn well-aimed criticism. *Indians, Animals, and the Fur Trade: A Critique of Keepers of the Game*, edited by Shepard Krech [57], contains a series of articles which confront Martin's analysis in two respects. First, most of the articles question Martin's analysis of the meaning of the relationship between animals and Cree and Ojibway hunters and reject the idea that his thesis is likely to apply to other Indian groups. Secondly, most of the articles argue that Indian hunters made economic decisions based upon material rather than ideational premises. Although both criticisms are revealing of Martin's inadequate empirical foundation, Krech's slim volume provides little new information and does not challenge the theoretical potential of the substantivist position, as Martin's final comment suggests.

Because most of the debate over Indian participation in the fur trade has raged between economic neoclassicists and the substantivists, discussion has centered on exchange behavior. While representatives of the two schools disagree over the influence of Indian culture and belief in the economic sphere, they agree that it is in the exchange process that Indian motivations and activities in the fur trade are best understood. Production aspects of the trade, as a result, have been largely ignored.

The importance of the production sphere has recently gained recognition and neo-Marxist interpretations of the fur trade should prove a stimulating alternative to substantivism and neoclassicism in the 1980s. Representative of early forays in this direction, Harold Hickerson's "Fur Trade Colonialism and the North American Indian" [42] recast the image of the Indian as pawn in the garb of wilderness proletariat. Like colonized peoples elsewhere, Hickerson argued, Indians who linked their economies to the fur trade lost control of the means of production and, as a result, became dependent upon their colonizers, even to the point of warring over available resources (Hunt, upside-down). Hickerson's article, while provocative, provided little substantial evidence of the historical process of colonization and obscured tribal variations.

The subjugation of an Indian production system to outside forces is more revealingly outlined by Patricia A. McCormack in her "The Transformation to a Fur Trade Mode of Production at Fort Chipewyan" [61]. Presented at the Fourth North American Fur Trade Conference in 1981, this essay describes the shift from an aboriginal mode of production (in which Indians controlled the means and produced food and domestic manufactures for their use value only) to a "fur trade" or capitalist mode (in which Europeans controlled the means of production and Indians were forced to produce goods for their market value).

The devastating impact of colonization and the shift to a market economy upon the status and productive roles of tribal women, in particular, has recently been explored by Eleanor Leacock in the introduction to Mona Etienne and Eleanor Leacock, eds., *Women and Colonization: Anthropological Perspectives* [25] and in "Women's Status in Egalitarian Society: Implications for Social Evolution" [59]; Patricia C. Albers, "Sioux Women in Transition: A Study of Their Changing Status in Domestic and Capitalist Sectors of Production" [1]; and Alan Klein in "The Political Economy of Gender: A 19th Century Plains Indian Case Study" [55]. Klein's article, although lean in documentation, makes a compelling case for the analysis of gender-specific and group-specific responses to the fur trade. On the Plains, he argues, men grew in wealth, status, warlike proclivities, and political dominance at the expense of their women after the horse and hide trades replaced domestic production for use as the primary subsistence strategies.

Etienne and Leacock [25] and Albers [1] have noted that women were not, any more than men, passive victims of colonization in the guise of the fur trade. Some resisted; others adapted to new opportunities by enlarging upon precontact leadership roles, as shown in Robert Steven Grumet, "Sunksquaws, Shamans and Tradeswomen: Middle Atlantic Coastal Algonkian Women During the 17th and 18th Centuries" [37], and in Sylvia Van Kirk, *"Many Tender Ties": Women in Fur-Trade Society in Western Canada, 1670-1870* [102]. Van Kirk's pathbreaking volume argues, moreover, that at least for the first century of fur trade expansion, tribal women were essential economic contributors, depended upon and valued for their skills as provisioners of small game, fish and cultigens, as well as snowshoe and moccasin makers, house-builders, transporters, guides, interpreters, and, occasionally, as traders. Van Kirk pays insufficient attention to the tribal backgrounds and varying cultures of the native women she describes; however, "*Many Tender Ties*" remains the most comprehensive treatment of Indian women's roles in the fur trade.

The most sophisticated analysis to date of the influence of a market economy upon the mode of production of northern hunters is Adrian Tanner's *Bringing Home Animals* [93]. Tanner combines religious ideology with material and ecological constraints to explain the nature and extent of Mistassini Cree involvement in the fur trade. Contrary to scholars still inclined to paint Indian involvement in absolute terms, Tanner was impressed, as was Toby Morantz in "The Fur Trade and the Cree of James Bay" [69], by the degree of flexibility the Cree still exhibited in the 1970s in their subsistence pursuits. The Mistassini, Tanner observed, practiced two modes of production simultaneously: hunting for furs for the external world and hunting for subsistence to sustain the interior traditional world. Of the two modes, hunting for subsistence with all of its spiritual prescriptions intact was clearly dominant.

Other researchers, such as David V. Burley in his "Proto-Historic Ecological Effects of the Fur Trade on Micmac Culture in Northeastern New Brunswick" [16] have argued that the opportunity to trade furs for manufactured goods and foodstuffs added to the store of available subsistence strategies, particularly among marginal northeastern horticulturists. Contrariwise, D. W. Moodie, in "Agriculture and the Fur Trade" [68] noted that the opportunity to trade did not wean tribes like the Ottawa and Sauk from their corn fields, but rather that fur trade expansion depended upon provisionment by Indians. Herman G. Sprenger made a similar point in his "The Metis Nation: Buffalo Hunting vs. Agriculture in the Red River Settlement (Circa 1810-1870)" [88] demonstrating that the Métis rejected agriculture in favor of pemmican provisioning for sound economic and ecological reasons prior to 1870.

The dependence of white fur trade personnel upon native provisioners was most keenly felt in the Subarctic and Arctic regions. The problem of supply plagued the Russian fur trade, in particular, and is the subject of an important book-length work by geographer James R. Gibson, *Imperial Russia in Frontier America: The Changing*

Geography of Supply of Russian America, 1784-1867 [32]. In two subsequent articles, "The Russian Fur Trade" [34] and "European Dependence Upon American Natives: The Case of Russian America" [33], Gibson elaborated upon the significant economic role played by native provisioners, as did Donald A. Harris and George C. Ingram in "New Caledonia and the Fur Trade: A Status Report" [40]; Shepard Krech, "The Eastern Kutchin and the Fur Trade, 1800-1860" [56]; and Carol M. Judd, "Mixed Bloods of Moose Factory, 1730-1981: A Socio-Economic Study" [49], which focuses on the "Home Guard" Cree goose hunters of southern James Bay.

That provisioning could serve as an alternative tribal strategy is revealed in Lynn Ceci's interesting dissertation, "The Effect of European Contact and Trade on the Settlement Patterns of Indians in Colonial New York, 1524-1665: The Archeological and Documentary Evidence" [18]. Ceci contends that semi-sedentary coastal tribes turned to sedentary agricultural production and wampum manufacture once animal resources dwindled in an effort to reap the benefits of a triangular trade with Europeans and inland hunters, as well as to defend their remaining lands and autonomy from European encroachment.

The idea that Indians may have overhunted in a short-lived fur and hide trade to forestall the outbreak of war with Europeans is explored in Richard L. Haan, "The 'Trade Do's Not Flourish as Formerly': The Ecological Origins of the Yamassee War of 1715" [38] and by Charles Hudson in Shepard Krech, ed., *Indians, Animals, and the Fur Trade* [57]. That such action often weakened the subsistence base of participating tribal societies did not indicate shortsightedness, however, as Peter A. Thomas has recently argued in his "The Fur Trade, Indian Land and the Need to Define Adequate Environmental Parameters" [94]. Indians of the seventeenth and eighteenth centuries lacked the benefit of hindsight bequeathed to modern scholars and should not be judged today for adopting what appeared to them to be sensible strategies of survival, accommodation, and, even, material enrichment.

Since the early 1970s, works focusing on the economic aspects of the fur trade have become increasingly detailed and complex; however, all point to the inescapable conclusion that there were many fur trades, both within the same tribal and linguistic group as

Francis and Morantz [31] and Morantz [69] show for the Cree, and within the same ecological zone as Arthur J. Ray revealed in *Indians in the Fur Trade* [77]. Unfortunately, with the exception of book-length works by Francis and Morantz, and Tanner on the Cree, Ray on the Western Cree and the Assiniboine, and Charles Bishop on the Northern Ojibway; and, articles by Shepard Krech on "The Eastern Kutchin and the Fur Trade, 1800-1860" [56] and James W. VanStone on "The Yukon River Ingalik: Subsistence, the Fur Trade, and a Changing Resource Base" [104], detailed treatments of the historic involvement of individual tribes in the fur trade are still lacking.

What we have, instead, are a number of regional studies, written primarily by historians, which seek to describe the differing aims and methods devised by competing European nations, individual fur companies, and, in some cases, by influential individuals and particular groups of personnel. Only a few of these works, such as Robin Fisher, *Contact and Conflict: Indian-European Relations in British Columbia, 1774-1890* [28]; Conrad E. Heidenreich and Arthur J. Ray, *The Early Fur Trades: A Study in Cultural Interaction* [41]; Cornelius J. Jaenen, *Friend and Foe: Aspects of French-Amerindian Cultural Contact in the Sixteenth and Seventeenth Centuries* [47]; and, to a lesser extent, Patricia Dillon Woods, *French-Indian Relations on the Southern Frontier, 1699-1762* [112] concern themselves directly with Indian influences on the shape of the trade and the developing content of Indian-White relations. Taken together, however, these studies substantiate the growing belief that the fur trade was a highly variable institution.

The northern Pacific maritime trade in fur seals and sea otters, especially under Russian auspices, is perhaps the least understood of the regional fur trades. Limited access to Russian repositories, the loss of most of the Russian-American Company papers, and the paucity of English-language sources have inhibited research. Beyond the pathbreaking work of James R. Gibson [32, 33, 34], a chapter in Robin Fisher's *Contact and Conflict* [28], and Natalie B. Stoddard's "Some Ethnological Aspects of the Russian Fur Trade" [89], which like Gibson's "The Russian Fur Trade" [34], contrasted Aleut subjugation and decimation with Tlingit resistance and autonomy, the interested reader must turn to Russian works, recently published in English. The most important of these is P. A. Tikhmenev, *A History of the Russian-American Company* [96] which although dated (1861-63), is based upon documents no longer extant. Raisa V. Makarova's *Russians on the Pacific, 1743-1799* [64], also based in Russian sources and carefully documented, is an intriguing example of post-Stalinist party history. Makarova views the fur trade as a form of merchant capitalism, but belittles the impact of Russian rule on Aleut society. Contra Gibson and Stoddard, who portray the post-contact Aleuts as virtual "serfs," Makarova finds evidence of Aleut classes and contends that Russian influences turned former native rulers into "rank and file" working alongside their former slaves.

In the eastern portions of North America, where French, British, Dutch and, later, American trading systems competed for Indian furs and alliances, the picture is somewhat more complete. The differing approaches to the fur trade developed by the English out of Hudson Bay and the French on the St. Lawrence have been described by Innis and others. Only recently, however, have the spatial organizations and institutional structures of the two systems been schematized by Heidenreich and Ray in *The Early Fur Trades* [41], an appealing introductory text aimed at undergraduates.

Heidenreich and Ray's comparison of seventeenth century French-Huron trade and the eighteenth century English-Cree trade west of Hudson Bay revealed "strikingly similar patterns of spatial interaction" in which Indian middlemen played a pivotal role. It might be questioned, however, whether a comparison of two trading systems so widely separated in time and space is not overdrawn. In fact, after 1700, the influence of Indian middlemen within the French system declined dramatically as a home-grown cadre of voyageurs and engages from the St. Lawrence and the Great Lakes posts took to the field. Moreover, after the British conquest, the new trading partnerships formed by the British out of Montreal, as well as the Hudson's Bay Company itself, were of necessity obliged to adopt French trading practices and seasoned personnel from the St. Lawrence. Interestingly, this group included a number of mission Iroquois, whose roles as trappers, traders and immigrant settlers of the Canadian West have been ably described by Trudy Nicks in "The Iroquois and the Fur Trade in Western Canada" [71].

Heidenreich and Ray did not attempt to minimize French-English differences in the early colonial period or to deny that French fur trade policies, intertwined as they were with the goals of colonization and Christianization, bred greater familiarity between Indian and White than was the case by the Bay. However, the belief, reiterated by Howard Lamar [58] and Jacqueline Peterson in "Prelude to Red River" [73] that the French were less ethnocentric than the British in their contacts with tribal peoples has lately been qualified by Cornelius J. Jaenen in *Friend and Foe* [47] and Olive Patricia Dickason in "From 'One Nation' in the Northeast to 'New Nation' in the Northwest" [24], and disputed by Patricia Dillon Woods for the Gulf region in *French-Indian Relations on the Southern Frontier, 1699-1762* [112]. Among the Iroquois, the French "embrace" was persistently refused, ultimately securing New York for the English after 1761. However, as Thomas Elliot Norton has argued in *The Fur Trade in Colonial New York* [72], Iroquois neutrality had less to do with the appeal of the English than with the influence of the Albany Dutch traders, with whom they shared common interests and a concern for military security.

At least at the policy level, French and English interests and goals vis-à-vis the fur trade had diverged. Yet, as Jennifer S. H. Brown's seminal study of the institutional structures and officer ranks of the Hudson's Bay Company and North West Company demonstrates, the trading systems devised by the British were by no means monolithic. In *Strangers in Blood: Fur Trade Company Families in Indian Country* [12], Brown persuasively argues that it was not French influence, clearly more apparent within the North West Company, but rather strong kinship linkages among the predominantly Scots officer class of this company which distinguished it from the disciplined and hierarchically ordered Hudson's Bay Company, where ties developed vertically among unrelated employees at various ranks.

A comparative approach, focusing upon successive or competing regional fur trade systems has also been applied to the American Midwest. Lyle M. Stone, in *Fort Michilimackinac, 1715-1781: An Archaeological Perspective on the Revolutionary Frontier* [90], provides solid material evidence of differing values, residential patterns and lifeways under French and British trading systems in the upper Great Lakes. Jacqueline Peterson in "The People in Between: Indian-White Marriage and the Genesis of a Metis Society and Culture in the Great Lakes Region, 1690-1830" [74] has built upon these findings and the earlier theoretical contributions of George Irving Quimby, in his *Indian Culture and European Trade Goods* [76], in an effort to document the spread and persistence of a French-inspired fur trade complex well beyond the British conquest.

Works on the American West have generally cut less wide a swath. While, as Howard Lamar has pointed out, the fur trade in the trans-Mississippi West lasted from 1600 to 1900, cutting across successive Spanish, French, Mexican and American regimes and involving dozens of Indian nations, few recent studies have approached the western trade from a comparative perspective. David J. Weber's *The Taos Trappers: The Fur Trade in the Far Southwest, 1540-1846* [106], which includes an illuminating analysis of the little-studied Spanish trade in the Southwest derived from Mexican archival sources, is an important exception, as is David J. Wishart, *The Fur Trade of the American West 1807-1840: A Geographical Synthesis* [111].

Wishart, like Heidenreich and Ray, has effectively charted the spatial organizations and production systems of two competing regional fur trade systems, and the roles of Indian hunters and processors within them. In comparing the Rocky Mountain rendezvous with the Upper Missouri River trade in buffalo hides, however, Wishart pays scant attention to the fur trade as a system of human or cultural interaction, emphasizing instead the devastation wrought upon the physical environment by short-sighted trappers and traders.

Wishart's account represents a major advance in a regional literature still devoted to colorful accounts of legendary characters, as in Fred R. Gowans's uncritical pastiche, *Rocky Mountain Rendezvous: A History of the Fur Trade Rendezvous, 1825-1840* [36]. Nonetheless, Wishart's uncomplimentary portrait of western American trappers and traders falls neatly within the parameters of the debate which has captivated historians of the western fur trade for decades. Because it has been assumed that the Rocky Mountain trade was a special case in which white trappers replaced Indian hunters as the primary fur gatherers, attention has focused on the character, motivation, and behavior of white fur trade personnel rather than their Indian clients, partners, wives and allies. Was the American trapper primarily a daring but degraded nonconformist, an expectant capitalist, or a heroic adventurer? Harvey Lewis Carter and Marcia Carpenter Spencer, in "Stereotypes of the Mountain Man" [17] conclude from a review of the life histories published in Hafen's *The Mountain Men and the Fur Trade of the Far West* [39] that overall "heroic adventurer" represents the best fit. Richard M. Clokey's *William H. Ashley: Enterprise and Politics in the Trans-Mississippi West* [21], on the other hand, offers a clear example of the Jacksonian entrepreneurial spirit at work, crediting Ashley with the invention of the rendezvous system.

The most forceful and convincing portrait of the American trader as expectant capitalist has been drawn by Robert A. Trennert in *Indian Traders of the Middle Border: The House of Ewing, 1827-1854* [98]. Trennert's study sheds considerable light not only on a neglected region in transition from a trading to a settlement frontier, but on the manner by which a little-known firm like the House of Ewing could influence the direction of U. S. Indian policy. His thesis that the nineteenth century western American trade drew into its ranks a new breed of businessman, eyeing the quick profits of venture capitalism rather than a long-term relationship with tribal hunters and clients, deserves elaboration.

The attempt to generalize about the character of the American trader has come full circle in Howard Lamar's *The Trader on the American Frontier: Myth's Victim* [58]. Lamar's dismantling of stereotypical images is weakened by the resort to generalization through combination: the trader was *both* a scavenger-hunter and an expectant capitalist. However, his appeal for a reappraisal of the trader from within the normative context of the trading sphere and from an Indian perspective is a welcome one.

Increasingly, scholars have recognized that, like the fur trade itself, the personnel of the trade were a highly diverse lot. However, dependence upon sources skewed in favor of literate and white or high-ranking employees has limited investigation and understanding of lower-ranking personnel and particularly of large numbers of seasonally or irregularly employed freemen and native and Métis transporters, middlemen, provisioners, guides and servants. While as Jennifer S. H. Brown's "'Man in His Natural State': The Indian Worlds of George Nelson" [14] suggests, literate traders occasionally overcame their ethnocentric biases, opening a window into the views and activities of Indian participants and low-status employees, the human underside of the fur trade hierarchy has yet to be fully revealed.

Recently, scholars have begun to apply statistical techniques to the study of largely unlettered groups of personnel, with promising results. The most sophisticated of these efforts are two important demographic analyses of French-Canadian voyageurs during the French regime: Gratien Allaire's "Fur Trade Engagés, 1701-1745" [2], and Herbert Charbonneau, Bertrand Desjardins, and Pierre Beauchamps, "Les Comportement démographique des voyageurs sous le régime français" [19]. Others have focused on ethnicity rather than rank as the organizing principle, as in John Nicks, "Orkneymen in the HBC, 1780-1821" [70], and Trudy Nicks, "The Iroquois and the Fur Trade in Western Canada" [71].

The increasing heterogeneity of Hudson's Bay Company personnel after the 1821 merger with the North West Company, and the downward mobility of employees of French-Canadian, mixed or native descent, is the subject of Carol M. Judd's "'Mixed Bands of Many Nations': 1821-70" [48]. Judd explores the link between ethnicity and rank, a relationship demonstrated for the upper Great Lakes region in Jacqueline Peterson, "The People in Between" [74]; for the American West in William R. Swagerty's statistical analysis of the men listed in the Hafen series, "Marriage and Settlement Patterns of Rocky Mountain Trappers and Traders" [91]; and for Western Canada in Jennifer S. H. Brown's *Strangers in Blood* [12].

These studies reveal that French-speakers and those of native descent had been pushed to the bottom rungs of the occupational ladder by the early nineteenth century, as a rigidifying classification system based on race gained ascendancy. The precise mechanisms fueling the growth of race consciousness and race prejudice within the fur trade are as yet imperfectly understood. However, Jennifer S. H. Brown's "Linguistic Solitudes and Changing Social Categories" [11] is a significant beginning.

Taken as a whole, works which have approached the study of the fur trade from a regional, company, personnel group, or individual perspective have only inferentially cast light on the motivations and roles of tribal participants. They have, however, contributed to an understanding of the nature and chronology of change within the oldest and most durable industry involving the cooperation of Indian and White in North America. At least implicit in these studies and in most other recent writing on the fur trade has been the question: what were the effects of this partnership?

Few scholars would argue that tribal societies in the United States and Canada were not modified by their involvement in the trade, or that the trade itself did not spawn a new complex of behaviors and materiél adopted by both Indians and Whites. Changes in material culture alone have been amply illustrated by a number of well-conceived and beautifully produced fur trade exhibit catalogs, such as Carolyn Gilman, *Where Two Worlds Meet: The Great Lakes Fur Trade* [35], and Thomas Vaughan and Bill Holm, eds., *Soft Gold: The Fur Trade and Cultural Exchange on the Northwest Coast of America* [105], and by archaeological site reports of fur trade post excavations.

In addition to Lyle M. Stone's comprehensive *Fort Michilimackinac, 1715-1781* [90], studies which shed light on the material aspects of fur trade culture in a variety of regional, temporal, and company contexts include Robert C. Wheeler, Walter A. Kenyon, Alan R. Woolworth and Douglas A. Birk, *Voices From the Rapids: An Underwater Search for Fur Trade Artifacts, 1960-73* [107]; John A. Hussey's two-volume, *Fort Vancouver Historic Structure Report* [44, 45]; and C. S. "Paddy" Reid, ed., *Northern Ontario Fur Trade Archaeology: Recent Research* [83]. Of additional interest is Alice B. Kehoe's brief "Ethnicity at a Pedlar's Post in Saskatchewan" [54], which applies a gender analysis to the artifacts of fur trade post life, and the careful and detailed studies of culture change among the Huron by Bruce G. Trigger [99] and among the Northern Ojibway by Charles A. Bishop [6]. George Irving Quimby's *Indian Culture and European Trade Goods* [76] still commands attention, particularly for its insight into the development of a Pan-Indian fur trade culture.

By and large, historic archaeologists have made few value judgments about the impact of European trade goods upon tribal societies; however, Trigger and Bishop have engaged directly the larger question of Indian dependency and loss of autonomy, which scholars such as E. E. Rich claimed were the immediate consequences of fur trade involvement. Bishop, while not denying that the Northern Ojibway were substantially changed by participation in the trade, has pushed the timetable forward, dating accelerating dependency and loss of autonomy from the 1821 merger of the two major British companies. In this context, Donald F. Bibeau's claim in "Fur Trade Literature from a Tribal Point of View: A Critique" [5] that Bishop is an advocate of the dependency school does not seem wholly fair. However, a number of scholars have been quick to challenge or modify Bishop's interpretations and time-frame, when applied to other groups.

Howard Lamar, perhaps in reaction to a vocal minority of western American historians who would argue that the fur trade had a devastating and demoralizing impact upon tribal societies of the Plains, has noted that, in contrast to other frontiers, the fur trade was marked by peaceful communication and that Plains tribes traded with Whites for seven generations without losing their cultural or tribal integrity. Similarly, James R. Gibson in "European Dependence Upon American Natives: The Case of Russian America" [33] has hung the dependency tag on the Russians not the Aleuts. The rapid decimation of the Aleut population under Russian rule would seem to contradict Gibson's assertions; however, the persistence of Tlingit autonomy and cultural integrity is demonstrated by Natalie B. Stoddard [89] and enlarged to encompass the native peoples of British Columbia in Robin Fisher's *Contact and Conflict* [28]. Fisher's work, which traces the history of Indian-White relations in British Columbia to 1890, concludes that white settlement and missionization were far more injurious to tribal autonomy than the fur trade and that dependency and cultural disruption did not set in until after the trade's decline. This conclusion has recently been extended to the Cree by Daniel Francis and Toby Morantz in *Partners in Furs* [31] and by Morantz in "The Fur Trade and the Cree of James Bay" [69].

Mutual dependency is the theme of Donald A. Harris and George C. Ingram, "New Caledonia and the Fur Trade" [40]. In the forbidding isolation of interior British Columbia—the "Siberia" of Canada—transportation and provisioning problems mitigated against full involvement in and dependency upon the trade by the Carrier Indians. As Charles A. Bishop's rare biography of a native trading captain, "Kwah: A Carrier Chief" [7] illuminates, the fur trade in New Caledonia posed opportunities rather than limitations upon the expression of traditional Carrier values and leadership roles.

Michael I. Asch, like Harris and Ingram, views technology, transport, and isolation as important variables in the timing and extent of Indian involvement in the trade. In "Some Effects of the Late

Nineteenth Century Modernization of the Fur Trade on the Economy of the Slavey Indians" [4], Asch maintains that the Slavey remained virtually independent of the trade until 1870 when steam and rail transport, steel traps, higher prices for furs, and a better assortment of trade goods motivated them to work for HBC traders. Cultural transformation and dependency followed swiftly thereafter however. In contrast to Asch, James W. VanStone [104] has argued that the Yukon River Ingalik altered their traditional subsistence patterns in order to hunt fur bearers almost immediately after the introduction of trade goods.

Arthur J. Ray's *Indians in the Fur Trade* [77] and Francis and Morantz, *Partners in Furs* [31] have been particularly successful in depicting Native American peoples as active and intelligent decision-makers in matters affecting the rate and extent of change within their own cultures. Dependency, loss of autonomy, and even participation in the trade itself, were not foregone conclusions. On the plains, the Assiniboine and numerous other tribes rejected the siren call of the fur trade in favor of an economy and material culture revolving around the bison hunt. Among the Cree of Eastern James Bay, Francis and Morantz point out, different groups—Coasters, mixed-bloods and inlanders—chose to participate in varying degrees and thus were affected differentially. Even the main producers among the Cree did not depend entirely upon their "earnings" from the trade and maintained a level of autonomy not usually accorded to them by historians.

In addition to the larger concern with dependency versus autonomy, scholars have begun to look at the impact of the fur trade upon the political organizations of tribes involved, as well as upon intertribal relations. Charles A. Bishop, Arthur J. Ray, Carol Judd and Daniel Francis with Toby Morantz have all noted the emergence of a new leadership role, the "trading captain," whose influence, while dependent upon traditional skills, also was derived from Euroamerican support and acknowledgment. These authors, following John Elgin Foster, in "The Origins of the Mixed-Bloods in the Canadian West" [29], have also described the evolution of a new band structure among the Cree, the "Homeguard," whose activities as provisioners and employees for the Hudson's Bay Company and intermarriages with Hudson's Bay Company personnel set them apart from their migratory hunter-cousins in the interior. Such patterns, while perhaps unique to the Subarctic, deserve testing in other regions of fur trade activity.

The relationship between an expanding fur trade and intertribal warfare continues to be probed, particularly by Iroquoian scholars such as Bruce G. Trigger. In an interesting reversal, however, James G. E. Smith has argued in his "Chipewyan, Cree and Inuit Relations West of Hudson Bay, 1714-1855" [87] that the endemic warfare between autonomous bands west of Hudson Bay diminished as the fur trade enlisted their cooperation, transforming ethnocentric bands into tribes.

The most significant new development in fur trade studies during the last decade falls under the rubric "fur trade social history." Whatever the fur trade may have meant, and whatever changes were wrought, in the economic, political and cultural spheres, it was at base a complex web of social interactions and compacts between Indian and white men, and, as is now recognized, between Indian women and white men. In the aggregate, and over time, such compacts were to generate what Sylvia Van Kirk in "*Many Tender Ties*" [102] termed a "fur trade society."

The native demand for rituals of reciprocity such as gift-giving as a prelude to trading was deemed important by E. E. Rich in "Trade Habits and Economic Motivation Among the Indians of North America" [84]. Only recently, however, have scholars such as Bruce M. White in "'Give Us a Little Milk': The Social and Cultural Significance of Gift Giving in the Lake Superior Fur Trade" [108] interpreted such rituals as a metaphor for the creation of a kinship relationship between trader and Indian. The importance of kinship ties has lately been recognized by a number of scholars, including Arthur J. Ray in his "Reflections on Fur Trade Social History and Métis History in Canada" [81]. However, other than Jennifer S. H. Brown's "'Man in His Natural State'" [14], little attention has focused upon the mechanisms by which white traders were made kin, or on the actual relationships between white and tribal males.

Instead, most of the recent literature concerning social relations, which has been summarized and interpreted by Sylvia Van Kirk in "Fur Trade Social History: Some Recent Trends" [101] and by Arthur J. Ray in "Reflections on Fur Trade Social History" [81], looks at marriages between native women and white men of the trade, at the roles of such "women in between," and at the families which such unions produced. In addition to the seminal book-length works by Jennifer S. H. Brown and Sylvia Van Kirk, intermarriage is the subject of Harry H. Anderson, "Fur Traders as Fathers: The Origins of the Mixed-Blooded Community Among the Rosebud Sioux" [3]; John Elgin Foster, "The Origins of the Mixed Bloods in the Canadian West" [29]; Jacqueline Peterson, "The People in Between" [74] and "Ethnogenesis: The Settlement and Growth of a 'New People' in the Great Lakes Region, 1702-1815" [75]; Tanis Chapman Thorne, "The Chouteau Family and the Osage Trade: A Generational Study" [95]; and William R. Swagerty, "Marriage and Settlement Patterns of Rocky Mountain Trappers and Traders" [91].

These writers generally concur that white traders were motivated by the desire for economic and diplomatic alliances with a woman's male kin, as well as by the skills and companionship of a native woman herself. The motivations of Indian women are less clearly understood, particularly since as Jennifer S. H. Brown points out in "A Demographic Transition in the Fur Trade Country" [10], native wives of white traders exposed themselves to the rigors of more frequent childbirth and the risks of infectious European diseases. Van Kirk, in "*Many Tender Ties*" [102] emphasizes material comfort and role enlargement, while Jacqueline Peterson in "The People in Between" [74] cautions against generalizing about native wives, suggesting that outmarriage must be viewed from within a tribal context. Women who married Whites took on exceptional roles, sanctioned perhaps by visions or dreams.

During the early years of fur trade expansion, marriages occurred largely between white men and native women reared in a tribal setting. This was as true of the Great Lakes region and western Canada in the seventeenth and eighteenth centuries as it was in the American West in the early nineteenth century. Increasingly, however, as fur trade personnel took their native wives to live in a trading post or fort, stable family relationships developed. Such marriages did not occur in the presence of priest or justice, but where they acquired stability, customary marriage or "marriage à la façon du pays" took on the force of law. This institution, as Van Kirk in "*Many Tender Ties*" perceptively argues, was the sign of an emergent fur trade society, composed of fur trade personnel, their native wives and mixed blood children, and marked by a set of norms and values unique to the fur trade country.

Van Kirk, Brown in *Strangers in Blood* [12] and "A Demographic Transition in the Fur Trade Country" [10], Peterson [73, 74, 75], Swagerty [91], Foster in "The Origins of the Mixed Bloods in the Canadian West" [29], Carol M. Judd in "Mixed Bloods of Moose Factory" [49], and Harry H. Anderson [3] have all detailed the rising numbers of children of mixed-descent as a result of fur trade intermarriages. The phenomenon, as these diverse studies suggest, was by no means limited to the Canadian fur trade or to French-speaking personnel, although, as Lamar points out, the French voyageurs were the prototypes and master teachers of biculturalism on the frontier.

Van Kirk in "*Many Tender Ties*" and Peterson in "The People in Between" have attempted to establish a chronology for the development of a fur trade society in the Canadian West and the American Great Lakes region, respectively, and Peterson has looked at material culture and language as indicators of group identity. Jennifer S. H. Brown, in *Strangers in Blood*, alternatively, has pointed to two lines of social development, growing out of the separate traditions and behavioral patterns of Hudson's Bay Company and North West Company personnel. These authors agree that by 1800 daughters of mixed-descent, the product of two cultures, had replaced native women as the preferred mates of fur trade personnel and that fur trade society was becoming increasingly endogamous.

The growth of residential communities inhabited by fur trade families has been noted by Peterson in "Prelude to Red River" [73] and "Ethnogenesis" [75] for the Great Lakes region. Similar communities were established by Rocky Mountain trappers and traders in the Southwest, Pacific Northwest and the northern Plains, as W. R. Swagerty [91] and Harry H. Anderson [3] revealed. In the Southwest, fur trade personnel took Mexican as well as native wives, so that communities spawned by the trade were truly multicultural. A model study of three such Southwestern communities is Janet LeCompte's *Pueblo, Hardscrabble, Greenhorn: The Upper Arkansas, 1832-1856* [60].

The ultimate consequences of wide-spread intermarriage accompanying the fur trade are to be seen in the persistence and vitality of a native population and identity termed "Métis." Métis history has recently established itself as a separate field of study and is perforce beyond the scope of this essay. However, to the degree that the Métis are in a very real sense the human legacy of the fur trade, several articles deserve mention. As a beginning, particularly for American readers, John Elgin Foster in "The Métis: The People and the Term" [30] provides a useful introduction to a group identity, formerly reserved for those of mixed tribal and French descent and linked historically to the Red River colony, but now being extended to those of mixed ancestry generally. The roots of Métis identity and nationality, evident by the 1820s, are still poorly understood. Jennifer S. H. Brown in "Linguistic Solitudes and Changing Social Categories" [11] examines the impact of a racial classification system imposed by Hudson's Bay Company officials which cast children of mixed-descent as a separate group within western Canadian fur trade society. Olive P. Dickason, in a supporting article, "From 'One Nation' in the Northeast to 'New Nation' in the Northwest: A Look at the Emergence of the Métis" [24] argues that despite significant French-native intermarriage in the Northeast during the French regime, Métis group consciousness did not coalesce until the British period and then on the western Canadian prairies.

Jacqueline Peterson [74, 75] suggests, alternatively, that Métis identity was not merely a reaction to Anglo-American pressures, but was the culmination of nearly a century of community-building in the Great Lakes region. However, even where substantial intermarriage occurred and residential communities were established, Métis identity did not necessarily follow. As Jennifer S. H. Brown in *Strangers in Blood* [12], John Elgin Foster in "The Origins of the Mixed Bloods in the Canadian West" [29], and Carol M. Judd in "Mixed Bloods of Moose Factory, 1730-1981" [49] demonstrate, neither the "Home Guard" Cree nor the "country born," both the result of English-native intermarriage, identified themselves as Métis, but rather as native or English-Canadian.

That there were children of many fur trades, following divergent paths and adopting different identities is amply illustrated in Jennifer S. H. Brown's "Children of the Early Fur Trades" [13]. Elsewhere, in "Woman as Centre and Symbol in the Emergence of Métis Communities" [15] Brown suggests that Métis identity stemmed from the orientation of children of French-speaking fathers toward their native mothers' sphere, whereas children of

British fathers were actively pushed toward integration within the larger Anglo community. That such children were, in the racist climate of mid-nineteenth century North America, caught between two worlds, unable both to view themselves as Métis or to identify with Métis national aspirations and to gain acceptance as white is the subject of Sylvia Van Kirk's poignant, "'What if Mama is an Indian?': The Cultural Ambivalence of the Alexander Ross Family" [103].

Fur trade history as an aspect of native history continues to attract scholars from many disciplines and is perhaps unique among approaches to North American Indian history generally in that four international conferences have been devoted to the subject. Interested readers may turn to the published proceedings of these conferences: Malvina Bolus, ed., *People and Pelts: Selected Papers of the Second North American Fur Trade Conference* [8], Carol M. Judd and Arthur J. Ray, eds., *Old Trails and New Directions: Papers of the Third North American Fur Trade Conference* [50], and Thomas C. Buckley, ed., *Rendezvous: Selected Papers of the Fourth North American Fur Trade Conference, 1981* [9], as well as to *Cultural Ecology: Readings on the Canadian Indians and Eskimos*, edited by Bruce Cox [23] for additional perspectives. In future, one hopes that the scholarly chorus will be joined by more native voices. Donald F. Bibeau, in "Fur Trade Literature from a Tribal Point of View: A Critique" [5] has shared an Indian perspective on a history still not owned by Indians themselves.

ALPHABETICAL LIST

[1] Albers, Patricia C. 1983. "Sioux Women in Transition: A Study of Their Changing Status in Domestic and Capitalist Sectors of Production." In *The Hidden Half: Studies of Plains Indian Women*, eds. Patricia Albers and Beatrice Medicine, pp. 175-223. Washington, D.C.: University Press of America, Inc.

[2] Allaire, Gratien. 1983. "Fur Trade Engages, 1701-1745." In *Rendezvous: Selected Papers of the Fourth North American Fur Trade Conference, 1981*, ed. Thomas C. Buckley, pp. 15-26. See [9].

[3] Anderson, Harry H. 1973. "Fur Traders as Fathers: The Origins of the Mixed-Blooded Community Among the Rosebud Sioux." *South Dakota History* 3:233-70.

[4] Asch, Michael I. 1976. "Some Effects of the Late Nineteenth Cen-

tury Modernization of the Fur Trade on the Economy of the Slavey Indians." *Western Canadian Journal of Anthropology* 6:7-15.

[5] Bibeau, Donald F. 1983. "Fur Trade Literature from a Tribal Point of View: A Critique." In *Rendezvous: Selected Papers of the Fourth North American Fur Trade Conference, 1981*, ed. Thomas C. Buckley, pp. 83-92. See [9].

[6] Bishop, Charles A. 1974. *The Northern Ojibway and the Fur Trade: An Historical and Ecological Study*. Toronto and Montreal: Holt, Rinehart and Winston of Canada, Limited.

[7] ———. 1980. "Kwah: A Carrier Chief." In *Old Trails and New Directions: Papers of the Third North American Fur Trade Conference*, eds. Carol M. Judd and Arthur J. Ray, pp. 191-204. See [50].

[8] Bolus, Malvina, ed. 1972. *People and Pelts: Selected Papers of the Second North American Fur Trade Conference*. Winnipeg, Manitoba: Peguis Publishers.

[9] Buckley, Thomas C., ed. 1983. *Rendezvous: Selected Papers of the Fourth North American Fur Trade Conference, 1981*. St. Paul, Minnesota: North American Fur Trade Conference.

[10] Brown, Jennifer S. H. 1976. "A Demographic Transition in the Fur Trade Country: Family Sizes and Fertility of Company Officers and Country Wives, ca. 1750-1850." *Western Canadian Journal of Anthropology* 6:61-71.

[11] ———. 1980. "Linguistic Solitudes and Changing Social Categories." In *Old Trails and New Directions: Papers of the Third North American Fur Trade Conference*, eds. Carol M. Judd and Arthur J. Ray, pp. 147-59. See [50].

[12] ———. 1980. *Strangers in Blood: Fur Trade Company Families in Indian Country*. Vancouver and London: University of British Columbia Press.

[13] ———. 1982. "Children of the Early Fur Trades." In *Childhood and Family in Canadian History*, ed. Joy Parr, pp. 44-68. Toronto: McClelland and Stewart.

[14] ———. 1983. "'Man in His Natural State': The Indian Worlds of George Nelson." In *Rendezvous: Selected Papers of the Fourth North American Fur Trade Conference, 1981*, ed. Thomas C. Buckley, pp. 199-206. See [9].

[15] ———. 1983. "Woman as Centre and Symbol in the Emergence of Métis Communities." *Canadian Journal of Native Studies* 3:39-46.

[16] Burley, David V. 1981. "Proto-Historic Ecological Effects of the Fur Trade on Micmac Culture in Northeastern New Brunswick." *Ethnohistory* 28:203-16.

[17] Carter, Harvey Lewis, and Marcia Carpenter Spencer. 1975. "Stereotypes of the Mountain Man." *Western Historical Quarterly* 6:17-32.

[18] Ceci, Lynn. 1977. "The Effect of European Contact and Trade on

the Settlement Patterns of Indians in Colonial New York, 1524-1665: The Archeological and Documentary Evidence." Ph.D. dissertation, City University of New York.

[19] Charbonneau, Herbert, Bertrand Desjardins, and Pierre Beauchamps. 1978. "Les Comportement démographique des voyageurs sous le régime français." *Histoire Social/Social History* 11:120-33.

[20] Cline, Gloria Griffen. 1974. *Peter Skene Ogden and the Hudson's Bay Company*. Norman: University of Oklahoma Press.

[21] Clokey, Richard M. 1980. *William H. Ashley: Enterprise and Politics in the Trans-Mississippi West*. Norman: University of Oklahoma Press.

[22] Cox, Bruce. 1983. "Indian Middlemen and the Early Fur Trade: Reconsidering the Position of the Hudson's Bay Company's 'Trading Indians'." In *Rendezvous: Selected Papers of the Fourth North American Fur Trade Conference, 1981*, ed. Thomas C. Buckley, pp. 93-100. See [9].

[23] ———, ed. 1973. *Cultural Ecology: Readings on the Canadian Indians and Eskimos*. Toronto: McClelland and Stewart Limited.

[24] Dickason, Olive Patricia. 1982. "From 'One Nation' in the Northeast to 'New Nation' in the Northwest: A Look at the Emergence of the Métis." *American Indian Culture and Research Journal* 6:1-21.

[25] Etienne, Mona, and Eleanor Leacock, eds. 1980. *Women and Colonization: Anthropological Perspectives*. New York: Praeger Publishers and J. F. Bergin Publishers, Inc.

[26] Ewers, John C. 1972. "The Influence of the Fur Trade Upon the Indians of the Northern Plains." In *People and Pelts: Selected Papers of the Second North American Fur Trade Conference*, ed. Malvina Bolus, pp. 1-26. See [8].

[27] Feit, Harvey A. 1973. "The Ethno-Ecology of the Waswanipi Cree; or How Hunters Can Manage Their Resources." In *Cultural Ecology: Readings on the Canadian Indians and Eskimos*, ed. Bruce Cox, pp. 115-25. See [23].

[28] Fisher, Robin. 1977. *Contact and Conflict: Indian-European Relations in British Columbia, 1774-1890*. Vancouver: University of British Columbia Press.

[29] Foster, John Elgin. 1976. "The Origins of the Mixed Bloods in the Canadian West." In *Essays on Western History*, ed. Lewis H. Thomas, pp. 71-82. Edmonton: University of Alberta Press.

[30] ———. 1978. "The Metis: The People and the Term." *Prairie Forum* 3:79-90.

[31] Francis, Daniel, and Toby Morantz, 1983. *Partners in Furs: A History of the Fur Trade in Eastern James Bay 1600-1870*. Kingston and Montreal: McGill-Queens.

[32] Gibson, James R. 1976. *Imperial Russia in Frontier America: The Changing Geography of Supply of Russian America, 1784-1867*. New York: Oxford University Press.

[33] ———. 1978. "European Dependence Upon American Natives: The Case of Russian America." *Ethnohistory* 25:359-85.

[34] ———. 1980. "The Russian Fur Trade." In *Old Trails and New Directions: Papers of the Third North American Fur Trade Conference*, eds. Carol M. Judd and Arthur J. Ray, pp. 217-30. See [50].

[35] Gilman, Carolyn. 1982. *Where Two Worlds Meet: The Great Lakes Fur Trade*, with essays by Alan R. Woolworth, Douglas A. Birk and Bruce M. White. St. Paul: Minnesota Historical Society.

[36] Gowans, Fred R. 1977. *Rocky Mountain Rendezvous: A History of the Fur Trade Rendezvous, 1825-1840*. Provo, Utah: Brigham Young University Press.

[37] Grumet, Robert Steven. 1980. "Sunksquaws, Shamans and Tradeswomen: Middle Atlantic Coastal Algonkian Women During the 17th and 18th Centuries." In *Women and Colonization: Anthropological Perspectives*, eds. Mona Etienne and Eleanor Leacock, pp. 43-62. See [25].

[38] Haan, Richard L. 1981. "The 'Trade Do's not Flourish as Formerly': The Ecological Origins of the Yamassee War of 1715." *Ethnohistory* 28:341-58.

[39] Hafen, LeRoy R., ed. 1965-1972. *The Mountain Men and the Fur Trade of the Far West*. 10 vols. Glendale, California: The Arthur H. Clark Company.

[40] Harris, Donald A., and George C. Ingram. 1972. "New Caledonia and the Fur Trade: A Status Report." *Western Canadian Journal of Anthropology* 3:179-94.

[41] Heidenreich, Conrad E., and Arthur J. Ray. 1976. *The Early Fur Trades: A Study in Cultural Interaction*. Toronto: McClelland and Stewart Limited.

[42] Hickerson, Harold. 1973. "Fur Trade Colonialism and the North American Indian." *Journal of Ethnic Studies* 1:15-44.

[43] Hunt, George T. 1940. *The Wars of the Iroquois, A Study in Intertribal Relations*. Madison: University of Wisconsin Press. New ed., 1967.

[44] Hussey, John A. 1972. *Fort Vancouver Historic Structure Report–Historical Data, Volume I*. Denver, Colorado: National Park Service.

[45] ———. 1976. *Fort Vancouver Historic Structure Report–Historical Data, Volume II*. Denver, Colorado: National Park Service.

[46] Innis, Harold A. 1930. *The Fur Trade in Canada: An Introduction to Canadian Economic History*. New Haven: Yale University Press. Revised eds. Toronto: University of Toronto Press, 1956, 1970.

[47] Jaenen, Cornelius J. 1976. *Friend and Foe: Aspects of French-Amerindian Cultural Contact in the Sixteenth and Seventeenth Centuries*. Toronto: University of Toronto Press.

[48] Judd, Carol M. 1980. "'Mixed Bands of Many Nations': 1821-70." In *Old Trails and New Directions: Papers of the Third North American*

Fur Trade Conference, eds. Carol M. Judd and Arthur J. Ray, pp. 127-46. See [50].

[49] ———. 1982. "Mixed Bloods of Moose Factory, 1730-1981: A Socio-Economic Study." *American Indian Culture and Research Journal* 6:65-88.

[50] Judd, Carol M., and Arthur J. Ray, eds. 1980. *Old Trails and New Directions: Papers of the Third North American Fur Trade Conference*. Toronto, Buffalo and London: University of Toronto Press.

[51] Karamanski, Theodore J. 1982. "The Iroquois and the Fur Trade of the Far West." *The Beaver* (Spring):5-13.

[52] ———. 1983. *Fur Trade and Exploration: Opening the Far Northwest, 1821-1852*. Norman: University of Oklahoma Press. Canadian ed., Vancouver: University of British Columbia Press.

[53] Kay, Jeanne. 1979. "Wisconsin Indian Hunting Patterns, 1634-1836." *Annals of the Association of American Geographers* 69:402-18.

[54] Kehoe, Alice B. 1976. "Ethnicity at a Pedlar's Post in Saskatchewan." *Western Canadian Journal of Anthropology* 6:52-60.

[55] Klein, Alan. 1983. "The Political Economy of Gender: A 19th Century Plains Indian Case Study." In *The Hidden Half: Studies of Plains Indian Women*, eds. Patricia Albers and Beatrice Medicine, pp. 143-73. Washington, D.C.: University Press of America.

[56] Krech, Shepard. 1976. "The Eastern Kutchin and the Fur Trade, 1800-1860." *Ethnohistory* 23:213-35.

[57] ———, ed. 1981. *Indians, Animals, and the Fur Trade: A Critique of Keepers of the Game*. Athens: University of Georgia Press.

[58] Lamar, Howard R. 1977. *The Trader on the American Frontier: Myth's Victim*. College Station and London: Texas A&M University Press.

[59] Leacock, Eleanor. 1978. "Women's Status in Egalitarian Society: Implication for Social Evolution." *Current Anthropology* 19:247-55.

[60] LeCompte, Janet. 1978. *Pueblo, Hardscrabble, Greenhorn: The Upper Arkansas, 1832-1856*. Norman: University of Oklahoma Press.

[61] McCormack, Patricia A. 1983. "The Transformation to a Fur Trade Mode of Production at Fort Chipewyan." In *Rendezvous: Selected Papers of the Fourth North American Fur Trade Conference, 1981*, ed. Thomas C. Buckley, pp. 155-76. See [9].

[62] McDonald, Lois Halliday. 1980. *Fur Trade Letters of Francis Ermatinger, Written to His Brother Edward during his Service with the Hudson's Bay Company 1818-1853*. Glendale, California: The Arthur H. Clark Company.

[63] McManus, John. 1972. "An Economic Analysis of Indian Behavior in the North American Fur Trade." *Journal of Economic History* 32:36-53.

[64] Makarova, Raisa V. 1975. *Russians on the Pacific, 1743-1799*. Trans. and eds. Richard A. Pierce and Alton S. Donnelly. Kingston, On-

tario: The Limestone Press. Original Russian edition, U.S.S.R.: Nauka, 1968.

[65] Martin, Calvin. 1978. *Keepers of the Game: Indian-Animal Relationships and the Fur Trade*. Berkeley, Los Angeles and London: University of California Press.

[66] ———. 1980. "Subarctic Indians and Wildlife." In *Old Trails and New Directions: Papers of the Third North American Fur Trade Conference*, eds. Carol M. Judd and Arthur J. Ray, pp. 73-81. See [50]. Reprinted in *American Indian Environments: Ecological Issues in Native American History*, eds. Christopher Vecsey and Robert W. Venables, pp. 38-45. Syracuse, New York: Syracuse University Press.

[67] Mitchell, Elaine Allan. 1977. *Fort Timiskaming and the Fur Trade*. Toronto: University of Toronto Press.

[68] Moodie, D. W. 1980. "Agriculture and the Fur Trade." In *Old Trails and New Directions: Papers of the Third North American Fur Trade Conference*, eds. Carol M. Judd and Arthur J. Ray, pp. 272-90. See [50].

[69] Morantz, Toby. 1980. "The Fur Trade and the Cree of James Bay." In *Old Trails and New Directions: Papers of the Third North American Fur Trade Conference*, eds. Carol M. Judd and Arthur J. Ray, pp. 39-58. See [50].

[70] Nicks, John. 1980. "Orkneymen in the HBC, 1780-1821." In *Old Trails and New Directions: Papers of the Third North American Fur Trade Conference*, eds. Carol M. Judd and Arthur J. Ray, pp. 102-26. See [50].

[71] Nicks, Trudy. 1980. "The Iroquois and the Fur Trade in Western Canada." In *Old Trails and New Directions: Papers of the Third North American Fur Trade Conference*, eds. Carol M. Judd and Arthur J. Ray, pp. 85-101. See [50].

[72] Norton, Thomas Elliot. 1974. *The Fur Trade in Colonial New York, 1686-1776*. Madison: University of Wisconsin Press.

[73] Peterson, Jacqueline. 1978. "Prelude to Red River: A Social Portrait of the Great Lakes Metis." *Ethnohistory* 25:41-67.

[74] ———. 1981. "The People in Between: Indian-White Marriage and the Genesis of a Metis Society and Culture in the Great Lakes Region, 1680-1830." Ph.D. dissertation, University of Illinois at Chicago. Ann Arbor: University Microfilms.

[75] ———. 1982. "Ethnogenesis: The Settlement and Growth of a 'New People' in the Great Lakes Region, 1702-1815." *American Indian Culture and Research Journal* 6(2):23-64.

[76] Quimby, George Irving. 1966. *Indian Culture and European Trade Goods: The Archaeology of the Historic Period in the Western Great Lakes Region*. Madison: University of Wisconsin Press.

[77] Ray, Arthur J. 1974. *Indians in the Fur Trade: Their Role as Hunters, Trappers and Middlemen in the Lands Southwest of Hudson Bay, 1660-1870*. Toronto and Buffalo: University of Toronto Press.

[78] ———. 1978. "Competition and Conservation in the Early Subarctic Fur Trade." *Ethnohistory* 25:347-57.

[79] ———. 1978. "Fur Trade History as an Aspect of Native History." In *One Century Later: Western Canadian Reserve Indians Since Treaty 7*, eds. Ian A. L. Getty and Donald B. Smith, pp. 7-19. Vancouver: University of British Columbia Press.

[80] ———. 1980. "Indians as Consumers in the Eighteenth Century." In *Old Trails and New Directions: Papers of the Third North American Fur Trade Conference*, eds. Carol M. Judd and Arthur J. Ray, pp. 255-71. See [50].

[81] ———. 1982. "Reflections on Fur Trade Social History and Métis History in Canada." *American Indian Culture and Research Journal* 6(2):91-107.

[82] Ray, Arthur J., and Donald B. Freeman. 1978. *"Give Us Good Measure": An Economic Analysis of Relations Between the Indians and the Hudson's Bay Company before 1763*. Toronto, Buffalo and London: University of Toronto Press.

[83] Reid, C. S. "Paddy," ed. 1980. *Northern Ontario Fur Trade Archaeology: Recent Research*. Archaeological Research Report No. 12. Toronto: Historical Planning and Research Branch, Ontario Ministry of Culture and Culture Recreation.

[84] Rich, E. E. 1960. "Trade Habits and Economic Motivation Among the Indians of North America." *Canadian Journal of Economics and Political Science* 26:35-53.

[85] Rotstein, Abraham. 1972. "Trade and Politics: An Institutional Approach." *Western Canadian Journal of Anthropology* 3:1-28.

[86] Saum, Lewis O. 1965. *The Fur Trader and the Indian*. Seattle: University of Washington Press.

[87] Smith, James G. E. 1981. "Chipewyan, Cree and Inuit Relations West of Hudson Bay, 1714-1855." *Ethnohistory* 28:133-55.

[88] Sprenger, Herman G. 1972. "The Metis Nation: Buffalo Hunting vs. Agriculture in the Red River Settlement (Circa 1810-1870)." *Western Canadian Journal of Anthropology* 3:158-78.

[89] Stoddard, Natalie B. 1972. "Some Ethnological Aspects of the Russian Fur Trade." In *People and Pelts: Selected Papers of the Second North American Fur Trade Conference*, ed. Malvina Bolus, pp. 39-58. See [8].

[90] Stone, Lyle M. 1974. *Fort Michilimackinac, 1715-1781: An Archaeological Perspective on the Revolutionary Frontier*. Publications of the Museum. Michigan State University Anthropological Series, in cooperation with the Mackinac Island State Park Commission, Mackinac Island, Michigan. East Lansing: The Museum.

[91] Swagerty, William R. 1980. "Marriage and Settlement Patterns of Rocky Mountain Trappers and Traders." *Western Historical Quarterly* 11:159-80.

[92] Tanner, Adrian. 1973. "The Significance of Hunting Territories Today." In *Cultural Ecology: Readings on the Canadian Indians and Eskimos*, ed. Bruce Cox, pp. 101-14. See [23].

[93] ———. 1979. *Bringing Home Animals: Religious Ideology and Mode of Production of the Mistassini Cree Hunters*. New York: St. Martin's Press.

[94] Thomas, Peter A. 1981. "The Fur Trade, Indian Land and the Need to Define Adequate Environmental Parameters." *Ethnohistory* 28:359-79.

[95] Thorne, Tanis Chapman. 1983. "The Chouteau Family and the Osage Trade: A Generational Study." In *Rendezvous: Selected Papers of the Fourth North American Fur Trade Conference, 1981*, ed. Thomas C. Buckley, pp. 109-20. See [9].

[96] Tikhmenev, P. A. 1978. *A History of the Russian-American Company*. Trans. and eds. Richard A. Pierce and Alton S. Donnelly. Seattle and London: University of Washington Press. Originally published in St. Petersburg, Russia, 1861-63.

[97] Trelease, Alan W. 1962. "The Iroquois and the Western Fur Trade: A Problem of Interpretation." *The Mississippi Valley Historical Review* 49:32-51.

[98] Trennert, Robert A. 1981. *Indian Traders of the Middle Border: The House of Ewing, 1827-1854*. Lincoln: University of Nebraska Press.

[99] Trigger, Bruce G. 1976. *The Children of Aataentsic*. 2 vols. Montreal: McGill-Queens University Press.

[100] Turner, Frederick Jackson. 1891. *The Character and Influence of the Indian Trade in Wisconsin: A Study of the Trading Post as an Institution*. Johns Hopkins University Studies in Historical and Political Science, 9th Series, 11-12. Baltimore: Johns Hopkins Press. Reprinted, eds. David Harry Miller and William W. Savage, Jr. Norman: University of Oklahoma Press, 1977.

[101] Van Kirk, Sylvia. 1980. "Fur Trade Social History: Some Recent Trends." In *Old Trails and New Directions: Papers of the Third North American Fur Trade Conference*, eds. Carol M. Judd and Arthur J. Ray, pp. 160-73. See [50].

[102] ———. 1980. *"Many Tender Ties": Women in Fur-Trade Society in Western Canada, 1670-1870*. Winnipeg, Manitoba: Watson & Dwyer Publishing Ltd. American ed., Norman: University of Oklahoma Press.

[103] ———. 1983. "'What if Mama is an Indian?': The Cultural Ambivalence of the Alexander Ross Family." In *The Developing West: Essays on Canadian History in Honor of Lewis H. Thomas*, ed. John Elgin Foster, pp. 123-36. Edmonton: University of Alberta Press.

[104] VanStone, James W. 1976. "The Yukon River Ingalik: Subsistence, the Fur Trade, and a Changing Resource Base." *Ethnohistory* 23:199-212.

[105] Vaughan, Thomas, and Bill Holm, eds. 1982. *Soft Gold: The Fur Trade and Cultural Exchange on the Northwest Coast of America*. Salem, Oregon: Oregon Historical Society.

[106] Weber, David J. 1971. *The Taos Trappers: The Fur Trade in the Far Southwest, 1540-1846*. Norman: University of Oklahoma Press.

[107] Wheeler, Robert C., Walter A. Kenyon, Alan R. Woolworth and Douglas A. Birk. 1975. *Voices From the Rapids: An Underwater Search for Fur Trade Artifacts, 1960-73*. Minnesota Historical Archaeology Series, No. 3. St. Paul: Minnesota Historical Society.

[108] White, Bruce M. 1983. "'Give Us a Little Milk': The Social and Cultural Significance of Gift Giving in the Lake Superior Fur Trade." In *Rendezvous: Selected Papers of the Fourth North American Fur Trade Conference, 1981*, ed. Thomas C. Buckley, pp. 185-98. See [9].

[109] Whitner, Robert L. 1983. "Makah Commercial Sealing, 1860-1897." In *Rendezvous: Selected Papers of the Fourth North American Fur Trade Conference, 1981*, ed. Thomas C. Buckley, pp. 121-30. See [9].

[110] Williams, Glyndwr. 1970. "Highlights of the First 200 Years of the Hudson's Bay Company." *The Beaver* 301 (Autumn):4-59.

[111] Wishart, David J. 1979. *The Fur Trade of the American West 1807-1840: A Geographical Synthesis*. Lincoln/London: University of Nebraska Press.

[112] Woods, Patricia Dillon. 1980. *French-Indian Relations on the Southern Frontier, 1699-1762*. Studies in American History and Culture, No. 18. Ann Arbor, Michigan: UMI Research Press.

Index

Note: References in regular type are to the alphabetical listings that follow each essay, those in italics to discussion in the text. Co-authors are listed individually; the abbreviations "ed.," "trans.," "comp.," etc. preceding page references indicate editors, translators, or compilers of the works mentioned.